Fluid Borders

Fluid Borders

LATINO POWER, IDENTITY,
AND POLITICS IN LOS ANGELES

LISA GARCÍA BEDOLLA

UNIVERSITY OF CALIFORNIA PRESS
Berkeley   Los Angeles   London

Portions of chapter 3 appeared previously in Lisa García Bedolla, "The Identity Paradox: Latino Language, Politics, and Selective Dissociation," *Latino Studies* 1 (2003): 264–83.

University of California Press
Berkeley and Los Angeles, California
University of California Press, Ltd.
London, England

Library of Congress Cataloging-in-Publication Data
García Bedolla, Lisa, 1969–
    Fluid borders : Latino power, identity, and politics in Los Angeles /
Lisa García Bedolla.
       p.   cm.
    Includes bibliographical references and index.
    ISBN 0-520-24368-4 (alk. paper) — ISBN 0-520-24369-2 (pbk. : alk.
paper)
       1. Hispanic Americans—California—Los Angeles—Interviews.
2. Working class—California—Los Angeles—Interviews. 3. Hispanic
Americans—California—Los Angeles—Politics and government.
4. Hispanic Americans—California—Los Angeles—Ethnic identity.
5. Hispanic Americans—California—Los Angeles—Social conditions.
6. Los Angeles (Calif.)—Politics and government. 7. Los Angeles
(Calif.)—Social conditions. 8. Social classes—California—Los Angeles.
9. Power (Social sciences)—California—Los Angeles. I. Title.

F869.L89S753   2005
979.4'9400468—dc22   2004065937

Manufactured in the United States of America
14   13   12   11   10   09   08   07   06   05
10   9   8   7   6   5   4   3   2   1

This book is printed on New Leaf EcoBook 60, containing 60% post-consumer waste, processed chlorine free; 30% de-inked recycled fiber, elemental chlorine free; and 10% FSC-certified virgin fiber, totally chlorine free. EcoBook 60 is acid-free and meets the minimum requirements of ANSI/ASTM D5634–01 (*Permanence of Paper*).

To my family
Past, present, and future

Contents

List of Illustrations		ix
Acknowledgments		xi
1.	Latino Political Engagement: The Intersection of Power, Identity(ies), and Place	1
2.	Legacies of Conquest: Latinos in California and Los Angeles	26
3.	A Thin Line between Love and Hate: Language, Social Stigma, and Intragroup Relations	61
4.	Why Vote? Race, Identity(ies), and Politics	100
5.	Community Problems, Collective Solutions: Latinos and Nonelectoral Participation	137
	Conclusion. Fluid Borders: Latinos, Race, and American Politics	175
	Appendix A: Study Respondents	193
	Appendix B: Interview Questionnaire	199
	Notes	203
	Bibliography	251
	Index	271

Illustrations

TABLE

1. Total white and nonwhite populations in Los Angeles County,
   1860–1930   41

FIGURES

1. Percent voting for Propositions 187, 209, and 227   98
2. Electoral turnout in Montebello and East Los Angeles,
   1990–1998   134

Acknowledgments

This book is a major revision of my dissertation, which I completed at the Yale University Department of Political Science under the supervision of Rogers Smith and Cathy Cohen. Both Rogers and Cathy supported my ideas and the work from start to finish. They read various drafts of the dissertation and encouraged me to improve the design and the analysis. Since I completed my Ph.D., they also have provided very helpful advice regarding my research and career trajectories. I would like to thank them for their time and efforts on my behalf. Also at Yale, Don Green provided critical and constructive comments that have been invaluable to the final work. I especially appreciate his contributions as he was not an official member of my committee.

The Chicano/Latino Studies program at the University of California, Irvine (UCI), and the Department of Political Science at California State University, Long Beach, allowed me time off from teaching that was critical to the completion of this project. My thanks also to Katherine Tate,

Vicki Ruiz, and David Meyer for their willingness to read drafts of the introduction and for their constructive comments. Vicki's help in particular made it clear to me why historians write so much better than political scientists. The feedback from talks I have given at the University of Maryland; Georgetown University; the University of California, San Diego; the University of California, Los Angeles; the University of California, Santa Barbara; the University of California Center for Latino Research; and UCI led me to rethink many of my key concepts. In particular, I would like to thank Michael Alvarez, Edwina Barvosa-Carter, Cristina Beltrán, John Bretting, Amy Bridges, David Easton, Heather Elliott, Henry Flores, Luis Fraga, Bernard Grofman, Elise Jaffe, Kent Jennings, James Jennings, Andrés Jiménez, Alethia Jones, Tamara Jones, Valerie Martínez-Ebers, Lorraine McDonald, Melissa Michelson, Ricardo Ramírez, Doug Reed, Andy Rich, Ray Rocco, Rudy Rosales, Shawn Rosenberg, Mark Sawyer, Ron Schmidt Sr., Dorie Solinger, Janelle Wong, and Stephen Weatherford for their helpful comments on various parts of this book. I would also like to thank Susan Manness and Patricia Rosas for their editorial assistance. Becki Scola and Susana Marín provided invaluable research assistance. At the University of California Press, Naomi Schneider has been very supportive and responsive throughout the process. Sheila Berg did an excellent job of copyediting. Jacqueline Volin and Chalon Emmons, along with the anonymous reviewers, have ensured that the finished product is much better than the original manuscript. Any errors that remain are entirely my own.

The interviews from which this work is drawn would not have been possible without the generous help of Garfield High School Principal Antonio García; former Assistant Vice Principal Cheryl Barkovich at Garfield High School; Principal Dolores Díaz-Carrey at the City Terrace Campus of Garfield Community Adult School; former Montebello Adult School Principal and current Montebello High School Principal Jeffrey Schwartz; and Montebello High School Counselor Denzil Walker. They all went above and beyond what was expected; they not only allowed me to talk to their students but also provided me with quiet space to conduct the interviews and made the entire process incredibly easy. But, most of all, I would like to thank all the respondents who so generously shared their life stories and their feelings with me. My only regret is that I could not include all of the information they shared. My hope is that I have been able to do justice to their eloquence and experience.

On a personal note, this book is dedicated to my family. I would like to thank my grandmothers, Catalina María de la Magdalena Costa Ascoli de Ruiz and María de los Dolores López Muñiz de García, for sharing their strong spirits with me, for their unconditional love and feeding, and for giving me the foundation to be proud of myself and my history. My hope is to someday have half their strength of character. I thank my father, Manuel Pedro García, and my stepmother, María de la Caridad García, for their support, which has made my life infinitely easier in so many ways, and for resisting the urge to ask why I was taking so long to finish this book. Thanks to my husband, José Luis Bedolla Rosiles, for editing the entire manuscript on many occasions and for always pushing me to do and be better. I hope the final product lives up to his expectations. And, finally, these stories are for my son, Lucas Joaquín Bedolla García. May he always be proud of who he is and where he came from.

ONE Latino Political Engagement

THE INTERSECTION OF POWER, IDENTITY(IES), AND PLACE

Power concedes nothing without a demand. It never did and it never will.

Frederick Douglass

Studies of political engagement rarely mention crossing borders.[1] Yet an examination of the experiences of immigrants in the United States highlights the many boundaries, both physical and psychological, that immigrants must cross before they become engaged politically. This is a different way of thinking about borders. It moves away from merely considering boundaries between nation-states and toward seeing the many barriers that exist within the U.S. polity itself. To recognize these boundaries, we need to look at what Vicki Ruiz calls "internal migration," immigrants' process of "creating, accommodating, resisting, and transforming the physical and psychological environs of their 'new' lives in the United States."[2] Internal migration is an ongoing process of psychological, social, and cultural accommodation undertaken by immigrants and their children, and it must precede political engagement. This book focuses on the process of internal migration among Latino immigrants and their children and the way in which having to cross multiple borders affects their relationship with the U.S. political system.[3]

The notion of border crossing has both geographic and psychological significance. In terms of geography, migrants clearly have chosen to cross a line dividing nation-states. After arriving in the United States, they encounter additional physical boundaries as they settle in places that provide differential access to transportation, jobs, services, and housing. These boundaries affect their everyday lives and chances for socioeconomic mobility.[4] In terms of psychological borders, immigrants leave their home countries with a certain understanding of self and nation, but this will evolve with time as they experience life in the United States.[5] I do not attempt to analyze migratory adjustments as a whole; instead, I focus on one aspect of immigrant accommodation: the political engagement of immigrants and their children. To do so, I compare the political attitudes and behavior of Latinos in two areas of Los Angeles County, California: East Los Angeles and Montebello.

Understanding the accommodation process is important because the migration story does not end with the immigrant generation. Like their parents, U.S.-born Latinos often remain geographically and socially separated from the Anglo majority.[6] Latino children quickly learn that they belong to a smaller, bounded circle within the larger circle of the United States. Thus, "racism and xenophobia shape both the meaning and social value attributed to [their] ethnic identities and to their lived experience of national belonging in contemporary U.S. society."[7] For Latinos, the adaptation process is complicated by the country's long history of discrimination against and exclusion of their community.[8] Because they are members of a marginal group in the United States, Latino immigrants and their children confront multiple boundaries that affect their socialization into the U.S. political system—boundaries that they are not always empowered to cross.[9]

This is not to suggest that Latino immigrants have no personal agency, defined as "the capacity, condition, or state of acting or of exerting power."[10] They influence and are influenced by the larger social, economic, and political environment. An analysis of the immigrant experience must engage the tension between structure and agency.[11] Most political studies assume near-absolute agency on the part of political actors, making participation a question of personal choice, rather than of legal or structural constraint. I instead use what Yen Espiritu calls "an agency-oriented theoretical perspective," which considers how immigrants "are transformed by the experience of . . . migration and how they in turn transform and remake the social world around them."[12] Individuals make personal choices. Their choices are constrained by the institutional environment, but their actions can alter that environment in some ways, which in turn affects the nature of their subsequent personal choices. For Latino political engagement in particular, what is key is the interaction between collective identity and structural position. Again, each influences and is constitutive of the other. For Latinos to perceive that they are full members of the U.S. political community and that they are empowered to act within that community, they must develop a positive attachment to their group and a belief that, however stigmatized it may be, that group is worthy of their political effort. This process entails shifts in Latinos' internal and external boundaries. For both immigrants and their children, this process changes according to time, place, and circumstance. Major parts of the process are not completely under their control. The varied political outcomes of the process are the focus of this book.

LATINO POLITICAL ENGAGEMENT: IDENTITY MEETS SOCIAL CONTEXT

What exactly is meant here by the terms *Latino, group,* and *identity*? Many analysts are uncomfortable with the word *Latino* because it refers to an artificially constructed category that masks important cultural, social, economic, and political differences that exist among different groups of Latin American origin.[13] I use *Latino* to describe a particular social group in the United States, one composed of immigrants of Latin American origin and their descendants. My concept of *group* rests on Iris Young's definition of a social group as "a collective of persons differentiated from others by cultural forms, practices, special needs or capacities, structure of power, or privilege."[14] According to Young, what makes a collection of people into a group is "less some set of attributes its members share than the relation in which they stand to others."[15] Thus, all members of the "Latino" group do not have to have the same interests or concerns but rather must be similarly situated within U.S. society. This structural aspect of identity is often overlooked, yet it affects strongly how Latinos interact with the political system on the individual level.

How group members identify themselves affects the ways in which they relate to larger collectivities, such as their racial group and the U.S. nation-state, in general. I define *identity* as an individual's self-conceptualization that places the individual either within or in opposition to a social grouping. This definition accepts that "a group is constituted not only when all members share the same characteristics with one another, but also when the members stand in a particular relationship to nonmembers."[16] This relational understanding of identity attempts to bridge the individual-level and contextual aspects of identity formation.[17] It acknowledges the cognitive aspects of identity while also situating identity processes in their social context in order to see people as "whole." As Judith Howard explains, that means "recognizing that both our everyday lives and the larger cultures in which we operate shape our senses of who we are and what we could become."[18]

For immigrants and their children, the sense of "who we are" and "what we could become" is profoundly influenced by the experiences of crossing, and not being able to cross, multiple borders. As a result, an analysis of the Latino experience in the United States must be situated at the intersection of power, collective identity(ies), and place. All affect where Latinos are positioned and where they end up positioning themselves vis-à-vis the larger political community. We must remember that this interaction between agency and structure does not occur in a value-neutral environment. Because accommodation occurs in a stigmatized context, and includes processes not always under Latinos' control, "power" must be kept at the forefront of the analysis.[19]

The exercise of power is a key aspect of the experience of stigma. I emphasize the effects of stigma because stigma is somewhat different from discrimination. The latter infers a concrete negative experience or denial of some benefit (a standard often used by the courts to determine the presence of discrimination). Stigma is imposed on individuals who "possess (or are believed to possess) some attribute, or characteristic, that conveys a social identity that is devalued in a particular social context."[20] Power is an important part of the equation, in that "stigmatization is entirely contingent on access to social, economic and political power that allows the identification of differentness, the construction of stereotypes, the separation of labeled persons into distinct categories, and the full execution of disapproval, rejection, exclusion and discrimination."[21] This less tangible aspect of racial hierarchy is very powerful, and it affects the life experiences and social interactions of all people of color in the United States. Studies have shown that members of stigmatized groups internalize societal stereotypes early in life, which negatively affects their future socioeconomic status and psychological health.[22] The process is also mutually reinforcing, in that when a stigmatized group accepts its lower status, its members are less likely to challenge the structural barriers they face.

Latinos' experiences of stigma, and the resulting perceptions of relative individual and group power, influence both the internal and external aspects of the adjustment process. Internally, feelings of stigma make it difficult for Latinos to feel positive about themselves and their larger group. Externally, their opportunities and choices are limited by a structural context that is often also the source of information regarding negative group attributions. Thus, analyses of marginal groups must consider how feelings of stigma affect attachment to their social group(s), as well as to the political system as a whole. To ignore this is to ignore an important part of the incorporation story.

Therefore, how a group member responds to feelings of stigma, along with the political resources and opportunities available in his or her political context, affects the group member's political engagement. Since publication of *The American Voter,* studies of political behavior have emphasized the role that resources play.[23] Socioeconomic status has been found to be especially important.[24] This is intuitively logical: Those with more income and education are more likely to have the time and cognitive ability to engage in politics. They are also more likely to be employed in occupations that provide them with civic skills.[25] For subordinate groups in U.S. politics, other factors may fall under the rubric of political "resources": the level of affective attachment individuals feel toward the larger social group, that is, psychological capital; and the politicization and political opportunities available in the group's social context, that is, contextual capital. I find that the presence of these resources enhances group members' feelings of agency and their political engagement, regardless of their socioeconomic status.

Mobilizing Identity(ies) as Psychological Capital

For those who study political participation and social movements, a vexing question is why certain individuals are motivated to act while others are not. The key is not simply whether or not an individual was invited to get involved, but rather why the invitation was accepted. Although rational-actor theories, such as those developed by Mancur Olson, would lead us to expect collective action to be rare, in fact, people act collectively all the time.[26] Why? Social movement scholars argue that the existence of mobilizing identities, in addition to the availability of political resources, is key.[27] However, these scholars say little about where these kinds of mobilizing identities come from, why they exist for some group members and not others, or how to foster engagement by encouraging the creation of these kinds of identities.

This book examines the concept of a mobilizing identity and considers this kind of collective identification a form of "psychological capital"— social capital that exists within the individual psyche and gives a person the motivation to act on behalf of the collective. I define a mobilizing identity as an identity that includes a particular ideology *plus* a sense of personal agency. Ideology here is "a world view readily found in the population, including sets of ideas and values that cohere, that are used publicly to justify political stances, and that shape and are shaped by society."[28] A mobilizing identity is different from an ideology in that it includes not only a particular outlook on the world but also a sense of having the ability to have an impact on that world.[29] Of course, it is likely that an individual's feelings of agency are closely related to that worldview. For example, if an individual believes power is controlled by the few at the expense of the many, it is unlikely that he or she will possess a mobilizing identity as I define it. But in this study I find that individuals with very similar worldviews had very different responses to those views. That difference, which I call personal agency, was the product of their affective attachment to their social group—their ability to have a positive collective identification with that group in a stigmatized social context—combined with a positive view of the group.

Using the term *collective identity*, singular, does not imply that individuals possess only one identity.[30] As intersection theorists, such as Kimberlé Crenshaw and Patricia Hill Collins, have aptly pointed out, different identifications, such as race, class, and gender, combine to form one identity— what Howard describes as "the whole person."[31] My understanding of collective identification does not require that individuals choose one group identification over another. Rather, I am focusing on the relational aspects of identity formation.[32] In other words, collective identity is less about how one sees oneself, that is, one's personal identity, and more about the values and attributions one feels are attributed to his or her group(s) because of how the group(s) is seen by others. Thus, particular group identifications are the result of particular understandings of self and group in relation to other (hierarchically ordered) selves and groups.[33] A sense of group attachment and "place" within the social hierarchy in the United States affects how an individual understands political information and how he or she chooses to act on that information. My respondents' strongest attachment was to a particular racial group, Latinos. In another context, gender or sexuality might have been more prominent. The importance of context to identification underscores the situational aspects of identity and the fact that race identity, as I show, is informed by experiences of gender and class as well. This discussion of collective identity should not be seen as reifying a particular understanding of community or as using a static definition. Rather, I conceptualize collective identity(ies) as shifting, situational, contextually driven understandings of self and place in particular historical moments.[34]

Instead of defining a positive collective identification as psychological capital, sociologists consider it a form of social capital. As such, it has been found to have important effects on immigrant adaptation, self-esteem, and academic success. In their study of the adaptation of second-generation Vietnamese youth in New Orleans, Min Zhou and Carl L. Bankston found that "strong positive immigrant cultural orientations can serve as a form of social capital that promotes value conformity and constructive forms of behavior, which provide otherwise disadvantaged children with an adaptive advantage."[35] They argue that this kind of psychological capital is more important than human capital for the successful adaptation of younger-generation immigrants.[36] Similarly, Rubén Rumbaut observed that how immigrant youth "think and feel about themselves is critically affected by the parents' modes of ethnic socialization and by the strength of the attachment that the child feels to the parents and the parents' national origins."[37] Finally, María Eugenia Matute-Bianchi found that Mexican American youth with strong ethnic identification are more likely to be successful in school.[38] These studies suggest that when immigrants feel positive attachments to their group, despite any negative attributions they may perceive, it helps them to adapt better in the United States.

This is also true in this study. The Latinos with whom I spoke tended to situate their discussion of political issues in the context of their feelings about being Latino. Their identities as members of a Latino community, however defined, framed their understanding of political events. Their interpretation of those political events, or their ideology, was similar across the sample. However, the degree to which they felt empowered to act on that worldview varied. All respondents felt that negative government policies targeted Latinos. All but three saw themselves as part of a stigmatized group. Those whose answers indicated a positive affective group attachment and a positive view of their group also believed they had the ability to act on behalf of their group. This sense of agency is related to group attachment and group self-image, and it is what makes an identity mobilizing. That identity, or psychological capital, serves as an important individual resource. Ideology provides only a particular interpretation of the world. The degree to which the respondents were able to see their group in a positive light is what gave them the sense that they could act. The issue is not simply racial identification but also the content of that identification and the resulting psychological resources it provides the individual, and by extension, his or her social group.

Put simply, for individuals to choose to act, they must feel that they are a part of something and that that "something" is worthy of political effort. That feeling of attachment and group worthiness is what motivates them to act on behalf of the collective. This affects their engagement in the full range of political activities, from protest to community politics to voting in presidential elections. It affects their propensity to participate as well as the nature and content of that participation. In the American political context, race enters the picture here. In racial terms, the American political community has long been defined as white Anglo-Saxon Protestant.[39] Only recently have other racial groups been allowed to participate formally in the system. It is reasonable to expect that members of nonwhite racial groups may have difficulty identifying with, or feeling a part of, a system that historically has not included people who look like them.[40] This also may explain why white racial identification may not have a significant impact on whites' participation. It is less about whether whites have a racial identification than that their identification is in congruence with the larger political system. There is no conflict, or contradiction, between whites' racial identification and their larger political attachments.

For members of marginalized groups, there is a contradiction. The respondents in this study consistently defined "politics" as being separate and distant from them. Therefore, their ability to feel part of the U.S. political system is more complicated, and potentially contradictory, than it is for whites. The experience of stigma acts as an important boundary between how they see themselves and how they see the larger political community. In this context, how members see their marginalized social group and the feelings of worthiness they attach to it is what gives them a sense of efficacy and the motivation to act politically. This is where we see the mobilizing potential of collective identity(ies). Whereas almost all respondents said they felt their social group was being attacked during the 1990s, those who felt the need, obligation, and ability to act on behalf of their group were those who felt an affective attachment to it. As a result, when their group was threatened, they felt it was worthy of their protection. More important, they felt enough personal agency to believe that their actions *could* protect it. Therein lies the major difference among the respondents: A sense of personal agency is critical. It is the key to political engagement, and it increases as affective attachment to the social group increases.

This idea of affective group attachment is similar to but not the same as what Michael Dawson calls "linked fate." Dawson sees linked fate as the extent to which the individual sees his or her fate (social, economic, or political) as related to the fate of the larger group.[41] Feelings of linked fate have been found to influence African American political behavior.[42] However, it is possible to feel that one's fate is closely tied to that of the group, yet feel very negative about the group itself or pessimistic about one's ability to effect change on behalf of the group.[43] In this case, feelings of group consciousness without a sense that the group is worthy could move group members toward less participation, rather than more. Individuals' affective group attachment may say more about their sense of personal efficacy, and how efficacy relates to group membership, than feelings of group consciousness alone. The findings from this study suggest scholars need to look more deeply at the nature of racial identification and how it varies within and among racial groups, as well as how group consciousness, group attachment, and perceptions of stigma affect levels of political efficacy and activity within racial groups.[44]

To that end, it is important to locate the source of affective group attachment. Among the respondents, family, school, and community were especially crucial. Political socialization studies have found that the family strongly influences the development of political attitudes, and I find similar effects in this sample.[45] The degree to which parents discussed their family and cultural history with their children seemed most important. Respondents who knew their families' migration histories were much more likely to express positive feelings about their racial background. Of course, this might reflect better general communication with the parents, which translates into higher self-esteem. However, for those who actually engaged in political activity, historical information and a sense of cultural pride were more important motivators than was self-esteem. In any case, for members of marginalized groups, self-esteem and group identity are interrelated, so it is likely that high self-esteem affects group identity and vice versa, blurring the distinction between the two.

With regard to school, students who had taken Chicano Studies or Multicultural History courses were much more likely to report having a positive attachment to their social group, whether or not they discussed their cultural history at home.[46] On the community level, the East Los Angeles respondents in particular mentioned that cultural events, such as the 16th of September parade and celebrations marking Mexico's Independence Day, instilled in them a positive sense of community.[47] The importance of this kind of historical information makes sense in a stigmatized context. The respondents were very aware of the negative images associated with their group, and historical and cultural knowledge may serve as an important counternarrative to that prevailing view.[48] A positive view of the group fosters feelings of agency because, to feel empowered to act, a person must have an alternative vision of how things could be. A counternarrative may be unnecessary for nonstigmatized groups because they automatically perceive that the system is meant to serve their interests. For stigmatized groups, the larger social context is crucial to fostering a positive sense of group identity and group worthiness. Among the East Los Angeles respondents, a favorable social context— family, school, community—fostered the development of mobilizing identities.

Collective identity can have negative consequences as well. A lack of this kind of psychological capital may depress engagement. Zhou and Bankston found that the least adaptationally successful Vietnamese youth were "overadapted," in that they viewed themselves neither as Vietnamese nor as Americans and simply drifted between the two identities.[49] A similar but not identical process was apparent among the Montebello respondents in this study. Zhou and Bankston were looking at socioeconomic adaptation. In this study, the Montebello respondents and their families were middle class and thus socioeconomically well adapted. However, that socioeconomic success did not translate into high levels of political efficacy, as the political behavior literature would lead us to expect.[50] The Montebello respondents also maintained a high level of racial identification. Like the Vietnamese youth, they felt they were not "American" because, for them, being "American" meant being "white," and all but one did not define themselves as white.[51] Yet they also lacked a strong positive sense of what it meant to be "Latino." As a result, they lacked psychological capital and possessed a *de*mobilizing identity, one that depressed their feelings of efficacy and political engagement.

This understanding of the importance of collective identity again highlights the interaction between individual agency and larger structure. Individuals cannot shape how others see their social group (and, by extension, themselves).[52] Members of groups that are constructed around ascriptive characteristics have little choice regarding their inclusion in those definitions.[53] So, if social psychologists are correct in positing that individuals want to have a positive collective identity, members of devalued groups need to find a way to resolve this conflict in order to maintain self-esteem in the face of negative attributions. Regarding politics, a positive group attachment and feelings of group worthiness provide members of marginalized groups with stronger feelings of personal agency. That psychological capital helps them to become more engaged with the larger polity. Political efficacy, then, is not just a product of the individual psyche but of the structural context in which the individual is situated and of the individual's ability to garner the psychological resources needed to overcome the negative images attributed to his or her racial group.

Opportunity Structures: The Role of Contextual Capital

Psychological capital refers to group members' feelings of personal agency. Contextual capital—social capital that arises from the area of settlement and the larger social context—relates to structural constraints. Both interact and affect the process of political engagement. Contextual capital matters for two main reasons: an immigrant's place of settlement affects (1) access to institutional and organizational resources and (2) the development and nature of immigrant social networks. Thus, levels of contextual capital affect Latinos' attitudes toward politics, opportunities for political mobilization, and actual political activity.

Unlike the prominent scholar Robert Putnam, who focuses on social capital at the community level and defines it as the degree of associational involvement and participatory behavior in a community, I believe the *type* of organization matters, particularly whether it is ethnically based.[54] To measure social capital, Putnam looks at, among other things, memberships in voluntary associations, newspaper readership, and expressions of trust in authorities. However, his analysis does not differentiate sufficiently among organizations. For him, membership in a union is the functional equivalent of membership in a bowling league.[55] Yet social capital studies of marginal communities have found that not all organizational activity has the same impact. Certain types of organizations, particularly neighborhood associations, have been found to have a greater positive effect on participants' sense of community and civic engagement than other types.[56] Similarly, an experimental study of the effects of mobilization on Asian American electoral turnout found that get-out-the-vote contact was more effective in areas with a larger presence of Asian American social, political, and cultural institutions, such as ethnic newspapers, social service organizations, and Asian-centered political organizations.[57] Although Putnam is correct in arguing that people's social and political context affects their response to political stimuli, it seems that for marginal groups, specific types of institutional activity and membership are of greater significance. In this study, I also found that ethnic organizing, even if not explicitly political, influences social capital levels within marginal groups and seems to have a beneficial long-term effect on feelings of efficacy.

Formal political institutions—such as local, state, and national governmental bodies, party organizations, electoral rules—also form an important part of the social context by facilitating or impeding political activity.[58] East Los Angeles and Montebello have fairly comparable institutional structures that are typical for California: nonpartisan local office holding, a strong county government, and a weak party system.[59] The main difference is that Montebello has a local municipal government, whereas most of East Los Angeles is unincorporated, which puts it under the jurisdiction of the Los Angeles County Board of Supervisors.[60] This institutional environment affects the political mobilization of individuals, particularly by political parties. In addition, the resources available to institutions in different areas varies, which affects opportunities for engagement and mobilization. Thus, place of residence is important because it affects the levels of ethnically based organizational activity and formal institutional resources that are available.

The final contextual variable is the racial makeup and politicization of a person's social networks. Sociologists have long explored how individuals are incorporated into social networks and the effects those networks have on socioeconomic opportunity.[61] Sociologists see social networks as a source of benefit to individuals because they create feelings of "bounded solidarity" among network members. This bounded solidarity encourages actors to act altruistically on behalf of their group, sect, or community.[62] The motivation is especially powerful because it is located in the larger societal context and enforced by local community norms. However, unlike many sociologists, because local context shapes the opportunities individuals will have to develop different kinds of networks, I view these networks as a contextual variable. Here again, the individual and the context are interacting in important ways, but the distinction between them can be unclear. For the study of marginal communities, an emphasis on the contextual aspect of networks shows the degree to which a person can and cannot control his or her social circle. Structural constraints determine the availability of those networks and the resources they may offer.

One of the greatest of these constraints is the degree to which a person's social networks include people of other races. People's social networks tend to be remarkably homogeneous in terms of race, particularly for blacks and whites.[63] A survey in Detroit found that 73 percent of whites reported having no black friends, and 57 percent of blacks said they had no white friends.[64] Similarly, a national probability sample found that only 8 percent of adults reported having a person of another race with whom they "discuss important matters."[65] Although in part this may be the result of individual choice, it also is likely a product of the high levels of residential segregation in the United States, combined with the effects of social stigma. In her study of Mexican Americans in Santa Paula, California, Martha Menchaca found that Anglos and Latinos engaged in what she calls "social apartness," resulting in two distinct ethnic communities that interact only rarely.[66] This separation was voluntary only on the part of Anglos; the Mexican Americans had little choice regarding the degree to which they were "allowed" to interact with whites. Interracial contact is embedded in a stigmatized context.[67] The racial composition of the larger context and the levels of stigma attached to each group strongly affect who will be included in a given person's social networks.

The racial homogeneity of social networks is important because the levels of politicization within them strongly influence voting attitudes and behavior. David Knoke found that "structural relations are critical to shaping Americans' political behaviors. Being embedded in a strongly partisan political environment and talking about political matters with others are significant factors in national electoral participation."[68] Ronald Lake and Robert Huckfeldt also found that the existence of political discussion and information sharing within social networks has significant positive effects on political activity and engagement.[69] Among Latinos specifically, Melissa Marschall posited that "the real key to understanding political participation lies in the social and institutional context that shapes political engagement."[70] Similarly, Natasha Hritzuk and David Park concluded that "social structural variables"—voting rates among the respondent's social networks, organizational affiliations, frequency of religious service attendance, and mobilization—have important effects on participation and that the politicization of the respondent's social networks has the strongest contextual effect.[71]

Of course, it is difficult to know if politically interested individuals seek out social networks that engage in political discussion, or if they become more interested in politics because of the political discussion to which they are exposed in their networks. At the very least, the social networks literature shows that Americans have fairly homogeneous social networks, both at home and in the workplace, and the degree to which networks are politicized affects members' political engagement and activity. Thus, a member of a racial group that is not politically engaged is less likely to have access to social networks that foster political activity, regardless of his or her personal propensities. This is especially problematic for an immigrant group in which many members are noncitizens or have limited experience with the U.S. political system, as is the case for Latinos. Hritzuk and Park contend that "different means are required to draw Latinos into the political process since, due to their predominantly immigrant status, they tend to be less integrated into American society than are blacks."[72]

However, social networks are important for another reason: they are spaces where group historical memory and collective experience are shared. Latinos in Los Angeles have experienced second-class citizenship since 1848, when the city became part of the United States. They have faced labor-market discrimination, political exclusion, and social and geographic segregation.[73] Families of the third-plus-generation respondents in this study were integrated into U.S. society when segregation and discrimination were at their height, and that experience has affected the socialization of subsequent generations.[74] Because the communities where second- and third-plus-generation respondents live are highly segregated, when new Latino immigrants settle there, most of their interpersonal interactions are with Latinos whose families experienced historical exclusion and discrimination.[75] Thus, immigrant Latinos' social networks are largely composed of other Latinos, immigrant and native born. The native born socialize the immigrants, using historical memory to educate them regarding their place in U.S. society. Though de jure discrimination no longer exists, its residual effects remain within Latino communities and social networks, and this affects the integration of new immigrants.[76]

To understand Latino political attitudes and engagement, we must examine the effects of Latino psychological and contextual capital. As Zhou and Bankston point out, "The effect of ethnicity depends on the microsocial structure on which ethnicity is based, as well as on the macrosocial structures of the larger society. . . . [A]n explanation of differential patterns of adaptation must take into account the normative qualities of immigrant families and the patterns of social relations surrounding those families."[77] Again, individuals are affecting structure and structure is affecting individuals. The interaction between these two spheres is what gives Latinos their sense of place in the political system and influences their ability to engage with it.

This is quite different from the approach political scientists usually employ to study the roles of identity and context in political behavior. Although scholars of history, literature, psychology, and sociology have focused on questions of identity when examining Latino behavior, for the most part, political scientists have not.[78] Perhaps this is because mainstream studies of political participation generally have not emphasized how identity affects political behavior.[79] In contrast, studies of African American political participation have placed great emphasis on how identity affects African American political activity.[80] Scholars of Latino political participation still debate the role that identity plays in that process. Some, like Louis DeSipio, argue that because ethnic identification has not been found to have a statistically significant effect on Latino political behavior, ethnicity "rarely proves the most salient factor in political decision-making," and thus there is no "routine ethnic impact on individual political behavior."[81] Others, like Carol Hardy-Fanta, see changes in personal identity as fundamental to how Latinos choose to incorporate themselves into politics.[82] Most analysts fall somewhere in between, seeing identity as having an impact on political activity but not necessarily as central to Latino political behavior.[83]

Part of the problem may be how political scientists measure identity and the effects of context. Identity is usually measured as a dummy variable showing whether or not the respondent identified with a particular racial group. However, my findings from Montebello and East Los Angeles indicate that not all collective identities have an equal capacity to mobilize. Thus, that variable could be measuring very different kinds of identities simultaneously. Measures of social context generally are not included in surveys, except in questions about membership in organizations and whether a respondent has been contacted by a political campaign. Putnam's work reveals the importance of the relationship between social capital and political behavior and the need to develop better ways to measure the effects of contextual factors, particularly those of social networks.[84] Individual political behavior must be examined in the context of the "whole" person, that is, in a manner that considers both psychological and contextual factors.

These factors are especially important for marginal groups, and the failure of previous studies to include them may help to explain why the findings on Latino political behavior vary so widely. For example, in 1980, Ray Wolfinger and Steven Rosenstone found that Latinos vote at almost the same rate as Anglos.[85] However, in 1989, María Antonia Calvo and Rosenstone found that Latinos voted at significantly lower rates.[86] Studies using the 1991 Latino National Political Survey (LNPS) found that Latinos vote at lower levels than Anglos but that some Latinos participate in nonelectoral politics at higher rates.[87] Using the Citizen Participation Study, Sidney Verba, Kay Lehman Schlozman, Henry E. Brady, and Norman Nie found that Latinos participate in both electoral and nonelectoral activities at significantly lower rates.[88] All these studies use very different sampling techniques and methodologies to identify "Latino" respondents, measure identity in a variety of ways, and incorporate measurements of the effects of stigma and social context to varying degrees.[89] Those differences may partly explain the variation in their findings. Incorporating better measures of Latino identity and context into future studies should provide scholars with a more complete picture of Latino incorporation patterns.

THE STUDY

In November 1994, Proposition 187, which called for denying education, health care, and social services to undocumented immigrants and their children, was approved by more than 60 percent of California voters. The campaign surrounding Proposition 187 garnered national media coverage and fomented the largest mass protests the California Latino community had seen since the 1960s.[90] Schools were the location for much of this political activity. In mid-October 1994, junior high and high school students in Orange, Los Angeles, and Ventura Counties began walking out of school en masse.[91] According to the Los Angeles Times, more than ten thousand students walked out in protest during October and November. Students also organized and participated in rallies, teach-ins, and petition-signing drives. They walked precincts and worked phone banks until election day.[92] Most of these students were Latino.

Many observers believed that this high level of activity would have long-term effects on the political engagement of these youths. Dennis McLellan of the Los Angeles Times noted, "It is hard to recall another issue in recent years that has galvanized so many high school students throughout California, most making their first foray into political activism."[93] Jon Markman, also of the Los Angeles Times, called this activity a "real-life civics lesson," and James Trent, a professor of education at the University of California, Los Angeles, said the students "won't be the same anymore."[94]

As a graduate student watching events unfold from afar, I also believed that the Proposition 187 campaign marked an important historical moment in Latino politics in the United States, one that needed to be documented and analyzed. How would participation in this kind of political activity affect the development of Latino political attitudes and activity? Would youth involved in these actions be more politically engaged later in life? Would feelings of identity and efficacy change as a result? This study is meant to shed light on these questions. I began my investigation with what is known about political behavior. Studies of political participation using both Anglo and Latino samples have consistently found that socioeconomic status is the best predictor of political behavior.[95] Thus, it was reasonable to assume that class issues would affect Latino behavior in the post–Proposition 187 context as well.

With that in mind, I compared students from two Latino-majority areas in Los Angeles that were involved in the protests against Proposition 187 but that varied in terms of class. I focused on East Los Angeles, a working-class Latino area, and Montebello, one of the few middle-class, Latino-majority cities in the United States.[96] Montebello residents are more likely to speak English and less likely to be foreign born than are the residents of East Los Angeles. Because geographic and psychological boundaries can significantly influence the political socialization process for immigrants and their families, a comparison of Montebello and East Los Angeles allows us to see how two very different environments affect Latino political attitudes and activity.[97]

I conducted one hundred in-depth, semistructured interviews during summer 1996 and winter 1996–1997.[98] Because much of the organizing against Proposition 187 occurred in schools, I concentrated on four schools, Garfield High School and Garfield Adult School in East Los Angeles and Montebello High School and Montebello Adult School in Montebello.[99] Half of my respondents were high school seniors at the time of the interviews, which meant that they had been sophomores during the walkouts protesting Proposition 187. That experience gave them the opportunity to be politically engaged in a way that was rare for their age group. The rest of my respondents were adult school students in both areas, almost all of whom had been living in California during the Proposition 187 campaign.[100] They too had experienced the heightened political activity during the summer and fall of 1994.

The sample respondents were as diverse as the Latino community itself. Most (83 percent) were of Mexican origin, but individuals of mixed Mexican/other Latin American origin were also represented. The respondents were between sixteen and sixty-eight years of age; two-thirds were first or second generation, and the remaining respondents were third-generation or more. Forty-nine were female, and fifty-one were male. Some respondents had been in the United States for more than twenty years; others had arrived less than a year before. Most of the respondents were full-time students. Those who were employed had occupations ranging from tattoo artist to executive assistant. (For a complete list of the interview respondents, with their generational and citizenship status, see Appendix A.)

The interviews were voluntary, and depending on the preference of the respondent, they were conducted in English, Spanish, or both (for the interview questions, see Appendix B). They averaged one and a half hours in length, but some went on for as long as six hours, and all were audiotaped. In transcribing the interviews, my goal was to be faithful to the respondents' words, including any grammatical errors.[101] I used the interview transcripts to create a database, sorted the responses by area, gender, and generation, and employed content analysis to find recurring themes. I organized the book's chapters based on the main findings of that analysis.[102]

With qualitative work, generalizability is always a question. This methodological approach makes "a basic assumption . . . that the meaning people make of their experience affects the way they carry out that experience."[103] I used what Anselm Strauss and Juliet Corbin call "grounded theory," meaning "theory . . . derived from data, systematically gathered and analyzed through the research process."[104] With such a method, the researcher does not begin with a preconceived notion but rather "allows the theory to emerge from the data" so as to offer insight and enhance understanding of the phenomenon in question.[105]

Yet some may question the validity of those insights. Because this study was conducted in the aftermath of an important historical moment in California politics, one could argue against its applicability to other contexts. There are at least three reasons why I believe my findings provide insights into the wider Latino political incorporation process. First, the Proposition 187 campaign brought to the foreground anti-immigrant tendencies that have always been present in California and U.S. politics.[106] Second, the findings on the political detachment of English monolingual third-plus-generation respondents are consistent with quantitative studies of Latinos, particularly the LNPS.[107] Finally, the findings on the increased Latino mobilization that occurred after Proposition 187 coincide with other qualitative and quantitative studies of Latino political participation in California during the mid- to late 1990s.[108] In this book, through Latinos' own voices, I show how members of marginalized groups engage in the complex process of negotiating their relationship with the U.S. political system and the role of collective identity and social context in that process.

PLAN OF THE BOOK

This book examines how the overall political and social context in California during the 1990s affected Latino political attitudes, activity, and identity. The 1990s were a difficult period for Californians, especially Latino Californians. Economic recession, natural disasters, riots, and several ballot initiatives perceived to be directed at limiting the opportunities for Latinos in the state made this period historically important. These events echoed the negative experiences that Latinos have faced throughout California history, but during the 1990s, expressions of power were much more overt than previously. Because Latinos were being described openly in the media as "undesirables" and "outsiders," they were better able to see how power was operating in relation to themselves and their communities.[109] Thus, unlike in most periods, political issues and the state of the Latino community were in the forefront of their minds.

Chapter 2 describes the racialized environment that characterized

California politics during the 1990s and shows how that environment was a reflection of Latinos' historical experiences in California. The chapter begins with a look at the economic and political factors that drove the Proposition 187 campaign and connects that proposition to two other anti-Latino initiatives on the California ballot during the 1990s: Proposition 209 to end affirmative action in the state and Proposition 227 to end bilingual education. The analysis then turns to an overview of how Latinos have been incorporated into Los Angeles politics and society since annexation. That discussion is followed by brief political histories of Latinos in East Los Angeles and Montebello. These histories serve as the foundation for subsequent political mobilization.

Chapter 3 describes the relations between immigrant and native-born Latinos in a stigmatized context. Perceptions of stigma had important negative effects on the respondents' social identities and feelings of group worthiness. Consistent with the findings of other studies on the effects of stigma, these Latino respondents were very aware of how other groups negatively stereotype their group. Though they had little contact with Anglos, they perceived that these stereotypes affect all aspects of their lives, from shopping in a non-Latino neighborhood to finding a job. I find that, in response, many of the U.S.-born Latinos are selectively dissociating themselves from immigrant Latinos.[110] They are often hostile to immigrants and refuse to speak Spanish in an attempt to force them to assimilate more rapidly. They hope that if immigrants assimilate more quickly, it will weaken negative stereotypes. New Latino immigrants, in turn, get the message that group cohesion is limited and that speaking Spanish only is an impediment to social and economic mobility.[111] This has a number of negative effects: it lowers the self-esteem of new immigrants, decreases language maintenance in the second generation, and diminishes group cohesion and feelings of shared collectivity, which has implications for policy proposals that target immigrants.

Chapter 4 examines electoral participation. Women in the sample were the most likely to participate in voting. In general, the respondents from both areas said they felt that Latinos were under attack. However, responses varied according to the respondents' levels of psychological and contextual capital, particularly their affective attachment to their social group, their feelings of group worthiness, and the levels of politicization that existed within their social networks. The positive group identity among Latinos in East Los Angeles motivates them to become more involved in electoral politics. Conversely, the Montebello respondents' lack of an affective group attachment has the opposite effect, making them feel more pessimistic about politics in general. These differences in racial identification result in different responses to the same political environment.

Unfortunately, the presence of Latino elected officials does not seem to be having an effect on these responses. At the time of the study, both areas had Latino representatives at the national, state, and local levels.[112] Yet the respondents, like many Americans, knew little about their representatives, and they were largely unaware that their representatives were Latino. This may be due to an absence of political discussions and access to political information within those Latinos' social networks. At the very least, it shows that descriptive representation cannot have a positive effect on Latino political attitudes if the constituents are not aware their representatives are Latino. This suggests that the effect of the presence of Latino representatives may also vary by context and merits future research.[113]

Chapter 5 looks at nonelectoral participation in both areas. Again, women were much more likely than men to participate in marches and protests. In terms of community work in general, respondents of both genders from East Los Angeles were much more positive than were those from Montebello about their ability to solve their area's problems. Hardy-Fanta argues that political consciousness begins at the point at which an individual understands that individual problems are a collective issue and thus need to be resolved on a collective level.[114] It seems that the presence of mobilizing identities among the East Los Angeles respondents, regardless of gender, motivate them to act on behalf of their neighborhoods. The long organizational history in the area also seems to be facilitating this process. In contrast, because they lack this psychological and contextual capital, the Montebello respondents have very low feelings of efficacy regarding nonelectoral participation and think that problems should be left to government. At the same time, they do not trust the government to solve problems, leaving them pessimistic about Latinos' ability to find effective collective solutions to problems.

CONCLUSION

My findings are important for a number of reasons. First, they highlight how the interaction between identity and context can affect political attitudes and behaviors. As Jimy Sanders points out, social capital is "useful in explicating how ethnic-based forms of social organization and collective action are embedded in interpersonal networks and how these forms of organization and action generate and distribute resources."[115] However, the key is to grasp the role of interaction in this process. Social context can construct identity, but identity can also transform the social context.[116] Both aspects are continually influencing and transforming the other. It is important, therefore, to focus on the relational aspects of these processes and how they affect individuals' relationships with their social group and the political system in general.[117]

Second, my findings show the important roles of power and stigma in shaping how members of subordinate groups understand their political "place" in the United States. That sense of place is affected by the interaction of psychological and contextual capital. As a result, group identification, feelings of efficacy, and political motivation can vary significantly among racial-group members and across contexts. This means that the issues or movements that mobilize particular Latinos will vary depending on where they live and the extent to which those things appeal to their group identity(ies). However, my findings also raise a cautionary note: The absence of affective group attachment and politicized social networks can have the opposite effect, depressing mobilization. Thus, effective mobilization strategies must be politically meaningful from the standpoint of a person's group identity, and they must be context-specific. Our current Latino political leadership could use this important information to make more meaningful connections with their constituents and to mobilize Latinos more effectively.

Finally, my findings suggest that low participation rates among Latinos are not due simply to issues of culture and poverty. Some scholars have argued that Latino political disinterest is the result of inherent cultural traits.[118] Peter Skerry calls it the Mexican tendency to *aguantar*, that is, the willingness to tolerate negative experiences without combating them. Likewise, scholars who argue that socioeconomic status is the key factor driving Latinos' low participation rates assume that those rates will not change significantly until Latino incomes and educational levels increase. Both positions presuppose that a change in Latino participation patterns cannot be expected in the short term and that even long-term change would require a fundamental structural shift. This study suggests that this may not be the case.

Many Latinos are aware of policy issues and politics, but some do not feel that they, or their group, will benefit from being involved in the formal political process. This highlights the importance of identity and social context to political participation among stigmatized groups. In the case of East Los Angeles Latinos, affective attachment to their social group and feelings of group worth serve as sources of psychological capital, counterbalancing their sense of group stigma to motivate area residents to act politically. The result of this process is exemplified by the creation and success of the Mothers of East Los Angeles, a group of Latino housewives who successfully organized against the construction of a prison and a toxic incinerator in their area.[119] If that kind of collective orientation could be fostered in other Latino areas, either through mobilization or organizational efforts, it would promote increased participation by serving as a counterbalance to residential segregation and low socioeconomic status. This study shows that examining the nature and effects of the interaction between identity and context can help us to better understand the political integration of subordinate groups in the United States. That examination may also help us to find alternative methods for fostering their civic engagement and political empowerment.

TWO

Legacies of Conquest

L.A. is the most populous Mexican city outside Mexico, and as
such it has a dual nature. It is the great southwest—frontier of
our "Anglo" culture, but also the *north*west—frontier center
of the Mexican. It is the focus of an undigested minority in
U.S. life that goes largely unnoticed by the majority.

Christopher Rand, 1967

Although the 1990s were an especially turbulent time in California politics, the moves to restrict immigration and immigrant rights form part of
a long tradition in California history. Since California became part of the
United States, Latinos have been subjected to social and geographic segregation, economic discrimination, and political exclusion, and they have
continually resisted this subordinate status.[1] Since the turn of the twentieth century, East Los Angeles in particular has been a center of Latino
organizational and cultural life. This has served as an important source of
contextual capital for Latino residents. Montebello, for particular historical reasons, lacks this organizational tradition, leaving its residents with
less available contextual capital, despite their higher socioeconomic status. In the following chapters we will see the ways in which these differences in historical and social context have affected Latino attitudes
toward politics and political engagement, especially in the nonelectoral
arena.

THE 1990S: RECESSION, DIRECT DEMOCRACY, AND RACIAL THREAT

During the 1990s, California experienced riots, floods, fires, an earthquake, and the worst economic downturn since the Great Depression. California voters passed three initiatives—Propositions 187, 209, and 227—all of which "were designed to impose fundamental restrictions on 31 percent of the state's population, its Latino community."[2] An analysis of the politics behind these initiatives shows the degree to which they reflected an overall environment of racial threat toward Latinos, an environment that echoed previous periods of racial and ethnic hostility. Because the fieldwork interviews took place soon after the Proposition 187 campaign, I begin with a discussion of the politics leading to Proposition 187, which laid the groundwork for the subsequent campaigns.

When former U.S. Senator Pete Wilson was elected governor of California in 1990, he inherited a state on the brink of fiscal crisis. Although the period from 1987 to 1991 had seen an economic boom, the state budget was in deficit during three of those years.[3] The budget woes were exacerbated by military cutbacks and an economic downturn. California lost 830,000 jobs between 1990 and 1993.[4] In 1992 per capita income in California declined for the first time in a century.[5] From 1990 to 1994 manufacturing jobs dropped by 15.7 percent in the state overall and by 23.8 percent in Los Angeles County.[6] During that same period, the state's overall unemployment rate almost doubled, from 4.9 percent in 1990 to 9 percent in 1994.[7] In Los Angeles County, the unemployment rate jumped from 5.5 to 9.7 percent.[8]

In his first state budget cycle, Wilson faced a $14.3 billion budgetary shortfall, which he tried to offset with "a combination of tax increases, budget cuts, and onetime bookkeeping shifts."[9] He increased income and sales taxes, taxes on automobiles and alcohol, and fees at state colleges and universities, cut welfare grants, and suspended automatic cost-of-living increases for welfare recipients. Although these measures helped the situation, the state continued to operate in a deficit. By the 1993–1994 fiscal year, the deficit was so large that the state had to take out a two-year "swing" loan of $7 billion in order to "balance" the budget.[10]

Governor Wilson, an ambitious politician with his eye on a possible run for the White House, found himself on the eve of his campaign for reelection in a situation in which state revenues were not keeping up with spending. Yet, as a Republican, he had already faced strong criticism after his 1991 tax increases. Increasing taxes again to cover the shortfall would threaten his chances for reelection and his future political ambitions.[11]

In addition to the economic crisis, California had undergone a significant demographic shift. More immigrants arrived in California during the 1980s than during the previous three decades combined.[12] Nearly one quarter of all legal immigrants to the United States at this time settled in California.[13] As a result, from 1960 to 1990, the foreign-born proportion of the California population rose from 9 percent to 22 percent. In Los Angeles County in 1990, over a third of the population was foreign born.[14] Most of the immigrants arrived from Asia and Latin America, with the largest proportion from one country—Mexico.

For many Californians, these demographic changes were a source of concern. A 1992 Roper poll found that 63 percent of Californians (compared to 54 percent nationwide) thought that current immigration laws let in too many immigrants.[15] In the same poll, 78 percent of Californians said they felt immigration was a financial burden on their state.[16] A February 1993 Los Angeles Times poll found that 63 percent of Los Angeles residents felt that there were too many immigrants in the city. Polling also showed that Californians, especially southern Californians, were concerned not only about immigration generally but also about its effects on their neighborhoods. For example, a 1993 Los Angeles Times poll of Orange County residents found that 40 percent of whites felt that the ethnic makeup of their communities was changing, 21 percent felt that Latinos were the primary group "moving in," and 43 percent felt that that demographic change was negatively affecting their neighborhoods.[17]

Local and state politicians were quick to try to capitalize on this growing anti-immigrant sentiment. In June 1993 the Orange County grand jury called for a three-year ban on immigration in order to ease the burden on government services.[18] During the 1993 state legislative session, more than thirty immigration-related bills were introduced, compared to only two in the previous session.[19] Most aimed to restrict undocumented immigrants from receiving state services, such as health and welfare benefits, educational opportunities, and driver's licenses.[20] Governor Wilson backed one of these bills, which demanded that the federal government pay California $1.5 billion to cover the state and local costs of providing welfare, Medi-Cal, and other services to undocumented and recently legalized immigrants.[21] Many politicians made direct links between their anti-immigrant proposals and the state's economic concerns. A sponsor of two anti-immigrant bills introduced in the legislature, State Assemblyman Gil Ferguson (R–Newport Beach), asserted, "This is the hottest button going. As people hear about job losses and the state deficit, the backlash against illegal aliens grows."[22] State Assemblyman Mickey Conroy (R–Orange), a sponsor of three bills, including one proposing the construction of a prison in Baja California to house illegal immigrants who commit crimes in California, went even further: "We're to the point now where we're making our own citizens suffer to pay for the illegals."[23]

As these anti-immigrant measures were being debated in Sacramento, conservative groups began tapping into anti-immigrant sentiments among the populace at large. In May 1993, the Virginia-based American Immigration Control Foundation sent direct-mail solicitations to California residents that characterized illegal immigration as a "national security threat" and demanded that the military be called in to protect the border.[24] The foundation also claimed that illegal immigrants were voting in presidential elections. By mid-1993, many national anti-immigration organizations, such as the Federation for American Immigration Reform (FAIR), saw California as the place "where a good deal of the action is on immigration and illegal immigration."[25] Other groups, such as the Citizen's Committee on Immigration Policy, formed in response to the lack of movement in the legislature on these issues. Frustrated with Sacramento's failure to act, the Citizen's Committee and other anti-immigrant groups organized to take these issues directly to the people through the ballot-initiative process. These legislative proposals in Sacramento, and the political coalitions that grew out of them, formed the basis for the movement to pass Proposition 187 in 1994.

Proposition 187 was a state ballot initiative sponsored by an organization called Save Our State, a loose coalition of anti-immigrant forces chaired by Ron S. Prince, an accountant from Orange County. In addition to denying state services, such as education and health care, to undocumented immigrants, the measure required that providers of those services—teachers, doctors, nurses—report individuals to the Immigration and Naturalization Service (INS) if they suspected them of having undocumented status.[26] The measure was coauthored by Alan Nelson, a former INS commissioner, and Harold Ezell, Nelson's former West Coast director. As its name suggests, Save Our State used imagery that pictured a California "sinking" under the "flood" of immigration.[27] Governor Wilson made his support of Proposition 187 a mainstay of his reelection campaign, thereby moving the focus away from the state's economic problems. The initiative resonated so strongly with voters that it passed overwhelmingly even though the official campaign was "ill-financed, loosely organized, and at times seemingly adrift."[28] It also managed to get Wilson reelected to a second term despite California's economic and budgetary crises.

Although the proposition's provisions targeted all undocumented migrants, many of the statements by the pro-187 forces, including the campaign advertising, made it clear that the target was not just migration but especially Latino migration. One of the most controversial television advertisements run by Governor Wilson's campaign began with the words, "They keep coming." It showed grainy black-and-white footage of people running between cars at the San Ysidro–Tijuana border crossing. Clearly, the image was intended to invoke Mexican-origin migrants. The proposition's proponents were reported as saying that they "are clearly troubled by population shifts that . . . have rapidly transformed their once-familiar communities into strange and dangerous places where English is heard less and less."[29] Robert Lacey said California was becoming a "Third World state" and blamed immigration for the plummeting value of his house. He even claimed that his wife could not find work because she could not speak Spanish.[30] Ruth Coffey, an activist who ran the group Stop Immigration Now, wrote in her campaign materials, "I have no intention of being the object of 'conquest,' peaceful or otherwise, by Latinos, Asians, Blacks, Arabs, or any other group of individuals who have claimed my country."[31] Similarly, another Proposition 187 supporter, Glenn Spencer, head of the Sherman Oaks–based Voice of Citizens Together, characterized illegal immigration as "part of a reconquest of the American Southwest by foreign Hispanics," and he said, "Someone is going to be leaving the state. It will either be them or us."[32]

Latinos in California heard these overt and covert messages and recognized that their group was being targeted. Unfortunately, the attacks were not limited only to rhetoric. Even before the passage of Proposition 187, there were reports of police and INS agents harassing Latinos because of their citizenship status. On April 21, 1993, two white men attacked Irma Muñoz, a twenty-year-old engineering student at the University of California, Davis. They beat her and wrote anti-immigrant statements such as "Go home illegal wetback" on her arms and legs.[33] On May 20, 1993, border patrol officials stopped Heriberto Camargo, a sixteen-year-old resident of San Diego, as he was walking out of a corner store. When he failed to produce his birth certificate, they handcuffed him and placed him in a van. He was released when his mother produced the certificate.[34] In August 1993, Eddie Cortez, the owner of a car repair shop and at the time the mayor of Pomona, California, was pulled over by INS agents while driving home from work. They questioned him at length regarding his migration status and threatened to put him in a van "with the rest of them."[35] Cortez, who, ironically, is a conservative Republican, said he was shocked and embarrassed by the treatment he received. That same month, the U.S.-Mexico Border Project of the American Friends Service Committee reported a sharp rise in beatings of undocumented immigrants near the border, evidenced by increasing numbers of migrants found with head injuries and broken jaws.[36]

The passage of Proposition 187 and the slow economic recovery in California after 1994 did not significantly decrease the racial threat for Latinos in the state. A good example is the story of the "tagger shooting."[37] In 1995, William Masters II was a thirty-five-year-old, Anglo, part-time actor from the San Fernando Valley. On January 31, Masters came upon eighteen-year-old Rene Arce and twenty-year-old David Hillo as they were spraying graffiti on a Hollywood Freeway overpass. He shot both young men, killing Arce and wounding Hillo. Both were unarmed and shot from behind. The coroner's report estimated that Masters was about thirty feet away when he shot Hillo. Later, Masters claimed he shot Arce and Hillo in self-defense because one of them was brandishing a screwdriver. However, in press statements after the incident, Masters referred to the two youths as "skinhead Mexicans," and in his initial statement to police, he said he shot them "because they were spray painting."[38] Hillo was prosecuted for felony tagging, but District Attorney Gil Garcetti declined to file felony charges against Masters, "ruling that Masters reasonably felt threatened when Hillo brandished a screwdriver."[39] Masters was convicted on misdemeanor gun charges and sentenced to three years' probation and thirty days picking up trash. He served no jail time.

It seems that Masters's act struck a chord with many in the Los Angeles area. After his initial arrest, the Los Angeles Times reported that the police were "overwhelmed" with calls supporting Masters.[40] One visitor to the jail offered to take Masters to dinner for performing a "profound service to the community."[41] Masters himself expressed confidence that he would go free; he believed it was unlikely that prosecutors could find twelve people to convict him.[42] Gary Henderson, recipient of the 1995 North Hollywood Good Neighbor Award, was so impressed that he rededicated his award to Masters. In response to an editorial by the Four Winds Student Movement that asked what kind of message Masters's sentence of probation sent to Rene Arce's family, Ryan Erickson, a resident of Santa Clarita, wrote to the Los Angeles Times that Arce "made choices . . . that contributed to his own demise" and that he should "take responsibility" for his actions. It seems that the only person who ended up taking responsibility was the deceased, and certainly not the man who shot him.

These events reflect a system hostile to Latinos on a number of levels. First, Masters shot the youths because of racial assumptions he made about them, yet this crime was not conceptualized nor was it prosecuted as a hate crime. Second, the criminal justice system treated Hillo and Masters very differently. Though Hillo was wounded, police interrogated him for six hours and told him, falsely, that a security guard had witnessed the shooting.[43] Masters's story was never questioned in depth, and when he gave his statement, the police rarely interrupted him.[44] The police never investigated Masters's claim that he shot Hillo and Arce because they were "spray painting" and that he did not know Hillo had a screwdriver until he approached the body. The District Attorney's Office concluded its investigation in three days, before they received the coroner's final autopsy report, which determined how far Masters stood from his victims when he shot them.[45] The only person ever in real jeopardy of spending time in jail was Hillo.

Although Wilson and many of the proponents of Proposition 187 argued that they were motivated by economic concerns, the campaign in favor of the measure had strong racial overtones. Not surprisingly, the next proposition on the statewide ballot, Proposition 209 in 1996, was an explicitly racially oriented measure that ended all affirmative action programs in California. There were important overlaps among the participants in both campaigns. For example, Mickey Conroy, the Republican assemblyman, was honorary co-chairman of the California Civil Rights Initiative, the group sponsoring Proposition 209. Californians against Discrimination and Preferences, the primary support group for the proposition, explained that the initiative was needed "to end the regime of race and sex-based quotas and preferences and set-asides now governing state employment, contracting, and education." Clearly, this proposition was racially targeted. During that campaign, there was no real debate about affirmative action as a policy program or discussion about its strengths and weaknesses. Exit polling showed that Anglos were much more supportive of the proposition than were other racial groups.[46] Multivariate analysis of the polling data has shown that racial concerns, rather than economic ones, are what drove Anglo voting on Proposition 209.[47]

The final anti-Latino initiative, Proposition 227, was on the ballot in California in 1998. It proposed to end bilingual education in the state and was funded and promoted almost entirely by the Silicon Valley millionaire Ron Unz. Unz has gone on to sponsor similar initiatives in Arizona, Colorado, and Massachusetts. Like the Proposition 209 campaign, there was little debate about the actual merits of the initiative. Unz himself repeatedly stated that he had never been a teacher or spent time in a bilingual classroom.[48] He often said his initiative was based on "common sense" rather than research.[49] Despite attempts by the educational community to make voters understand that many of Unz's assumptions flew in the face of established research in the field of education, "the non-Latino electorate of California voted with their gut to enact the referendum."[50] In his detailed analysis of the metaphors used to describe bilingual education and the Latino students in those classrooms, Otto Santa Ana shows that the same kind of language used during the Proposition 187 campaign was used in 1998 to describe students with limited English proficiency. In the public discourse surrounding the initiative, Spanish-speaking Americans were repeatedly constructed as foreigners.[51] Santa Ana argues that Proposition 227 was not about education but rather "reaffirm[ing] an increasingly antiquated view of America," one that is Anglo and English-only.[52]

The political environment for Latinos in California during the 1990s echoed previous periods of nativist backlash in the state. Not all of these targeted Latinos. For example, in the 1880s, California was the source of the anti-Chinese sentiment that led to the 1882 Chinese Exclusion Act. In 1913, targeting Japanese immigrants, California passed the Alien Land Law, which prohibited noncitizens from owning land. During World War II, only those Japanese living in California were interned, though the Japanese population in Hawaii was much larger and more proximate to the enemy.[53] As I discuss in more detail below, the 1930s and 1950s in California saw mass deportations of Mexicans, some immigrants, some native born. Thus, what happened in California during the 1990s was not a new phenomenon. A look at the history of Latinos in Los Angeles shows the degree to which events during this decade were a continuation of the conflict and hostility that Latinos have faced in California since the American conquest of the Southwest.

LATINOS IN CALIFORNIA
AND LOS ANGELES POLITICS

Understanding the political context of the 1990s is important because that was the historical moment the respondents in this study were living when they were interviewed. Yet the current political status of Latinos in southern California forms part of a long history that predates Americans' arrival in the Southwest. The Latino community's social, political, and economic experiences during the first few decades after annexation laid the foundation for their subsequent inclusion in Los Angeles politics and society. Because Latino immigrants arriving in the present day are socialized into politics by the U.S.-born Latinos in their neighborhoods, this historical memory remains and affects how Latinos see the U.S. political system.

Los Angeles became part of the United States during the annexation of the northern territories of Mexico in 1848 at the end of the Mexican-American War. In 1848, Los Angeles was the largest city in southern California. Organized around a hacienda system, its economy was based on cattle ranching. This semifeudal economic system was one of the justifications Americans used for the Mexican-American War and subsequent appropriation of the Southwest.[54] Americans in favor of the war argued that Mexicans had no right to the land because they were not using it to its full capacity.[55] Americans described themselves as having a providential right to the land; it was "manifest destiny" to control it and use it for the sake of the Anglo-Saxon race.[56] The war was seen as a "test" of sorts between the Anglo-Saxons and the "mongrel" Mexicans. Anglo success in the war was interpreted as proof of Anglo economic and military superiority.

This tension between Anglos and Mexicans remains throughout Los Angeles history. As the historian William Deverell emphasizes, the "myth" that was created for American Los Angeles relegated all that was "Mexican" to a romanticized past that was not part of the "modernizing" present. He goes on to say, "Understanding Los Angeles requires grappling with the complex and disturbing relationships between whites, especially those able to command various forms of power, and Mexican people, a Mexican past, and a Mexican landscape. . . . [N]arratives about Mexico and Mexicans are integral to the city's cultural and economic rise during the period between the Mexican American War and World War II."[57] American Los Angeles was built on top of a city and a society that were already there. The city's leaders and promoters dealt with this tension by defining "Mexicans" as "of the past" and Anglo-Saxons as "of the future."[58] The result was that the extant Mexican-origin population in southern California at the time of annexation was slowly removed from the centers of social, economic, and political power.

The word *Californio* connotes the Mexican-origin population living in California at the time of annexation. Southern California Californios did not give up their power without a fight. Unlike in northern California, the first two decades of American rule in southern California were conflict ridden.[59] Between 1850 and 1890 Los Angeles earned the reputation of being one of the most violent cities in the West.[60] From 1850 to 1870, there were thirty-five vigilante hangings, more than in the much larger city of San Francisco.[61] According to Albert Camarillo, during the 1850s in Los Angeles, "race-related lynchings, murders, social banditry and dramatic court trials approximated a race war. . . . Racial conflict, both collective and individual, between the newly arrived Americans and the Mexican population shaped the tenor of the times."[62] As late as 1860 commentators remarked that everyone in southern California was armed.[63] This may be an indication that annexation was strongly contested and resisted by the Mexican population in the area.[64] Deverell contends that the war did not end in 1848 and that documents from the period show contemporaries describing Los Angeles during the 1850s as a place wracked by "race war."[65] He believes that Los Angeles has never recovered from the blood and ethnic hatred of the 1850s.[66]

Despite this resistance, eventually the Anglo population took control of the city through manipulation of the legal, economic, and political systems.[67] Annexation changed the legal system in the Southwest from the civil-law tradition governing Mexican jurisprudence to the American common-law system. Lack of familiarity with the legal system and the English language placed the Mexican population at a great disadvantage. In that context, the Anglo community also used the legal system to control, both socially and economically, the Mexican and other nonwhite populations. As Leonard Pitt points out, "Naturally, the introduction of the Anglo-American legal system in 1850 and the accompanying repeal of all Spanish and Mexican statutes and institutions (except the *juezes del campo*) caused the native-born some discomfort and insecurity. But, whereas the initial transformation represented the inevitable change of systems, later enactments sometimes seemed intent on mischief-making alone."[68]

This was especially true of the state legislature of 1855, which "passed six laws—sumptuary, labor, and immigration—which bluntly or obliquely injured the Spanish-speaking."[69] One was a Sunday law prohibiting "barbarous or noisy" traditional Mexican Sunday pastimes, such as attending bull, bear, or prize fights, horse races, circuses, theaters, bowling alleys, gambling houses, or saloons.[70] Another was a new foreign miners' tax, which included all Spanish speakers, foreign or native born.[71] They also passed an antivagrancy act, called at the time the "Greaser law," which made it illegal for Mexicans to be caught not working.[72] Socially, the Sunday and Greaser laws served to control the visibility of Mexicans on the streets and also to limit the public practice of traditional Mexican culture.

If the Mexicans were arrested under these new laws, their use in chain gangs and as convict labor assured that they served an economic purpose: "The first work of the town council of 1850 was to reenact many of the old ordinances and add new ones. . . . [S]ome of the more interesting articles of legislation, especially the first three, [are the ones] that established chain gangs. The gangs were usually composed of Indians arrested for drunkenness. They were employed in public works, and . . . could be leased to private citizens. When their sentence was over, the Indians were usually given a bottle of liquor along with their freedom."[73] It is important to remember that the "Indian" population included Native Americans in the area and also lower-class, darker-skinned Mexicans.[74] After annexation, legal instruments like these were used to keep these sectors of the population under social control and available as a source of virtually free labor.[75]

Economic control was exerted through the transition to a capitalist economic system and the dispossession of upper-class Mexican *hacendados* (owners of large landholdings). This was the result of a number of factors, including illegal actions on the part of some Anglos, differences between Anglo and Spanish land and tax law, and bad weather.[76] Although there were some hacendados whose lands were taken illegally, about 75 percent of the land claims brought to court during this period were found in favor of the original landholder.[77] Unfortunately, the average time it took to settle a claim was seventeen years.[78] Many Mexicans had to mortgage their lands to pay their legal fees. Also, under the Spanish tax system landholders were taxed on a percentage of what the land produced in a given year. If there was a loss, there were no taxes. Under the U.S. system the land was assessed and taxed, regardless of what it produced. Unfortunately for the Californios, the 1860s brought extreme drought and flooding to the area, which decimated the cattle industry. Despite these losses, the hacendados still owed taxes on the land and often owed mortgages as well. Many had to sell their land just to pay the legal fees and taxes. As a result, by 1890 the vast majority of former hacendados had lost their lands.[79] It is estimated that by the turn of the twentieth century, 70 percent of Mexicans in California had to work as laborers.[80]

As Anglos began to attain more control over southern California's economic system, they also slowly took control of the political system. During the first few decades after annexation, Mexicans and Anglos shared political power in California. Californios were actually overrepresented at California's 1849 constitutional convention.[81] But the exercise of full citizenship rights was possible only so long as Californios were defined as white. The 1849 Constitution gave voting rights to U.S. citizens and white male citizens of Mexico. Initially, the definition of who constituted a "white male citizen of Mexico" was rather flexible. For example, one of the Californio delegates to the constitutional convention, Manuel Domínguez, was a dark-skinned mestizo.[82] But the rules regarding white blood became more restrictive over time. In 1849, having one-half or more of "Indian" blood would lead one to be considered not "white," and one-half or more of black blood made a person "mulatto." In 1851, the law was changed so that one-fourth Indian blood meant a person was not "white." That many Mexicans were mestizo and that the law was made more stringent only in terms of "Indian" blood suggest that the 1851 change was meant to restrict the citizenship rights of the California Mexican population. One example is Pablo de la Guerra, a prominent landholding Californio from Santa Barbara, who was prosecuted in 1870 for trying to exercise the rights of a white person.[83] That standard remained in effect in California until the twentieth century.[84]

The Democratic Party controlled southern California politics through-out the nineteenth century and lured upper-class Mexicans into the party with the promise of political offices as rewards.[85] This led to heavy turnout among the overall Mexican population, and the Californios were rewarded with political offices. From 1850 to 1859 Californios were elected or appointed to eighty-three local or state offices.[86] But this shar-ing of power began to deteriorate fairly quickly as hostilities toward the Californio population began to grow more heated in the state. By 1855, these conflicts became evident when Know-Nothing J. Neely Johnson was elected governor and other Know-Nothings held the offices of lieu-tenant governor, superior court judge, comptroller, treasurer, attorney general, land surveyor, state printer, and state senators and assembly-men. During this election, the Know-Nothings pledged to fight against free immigration, "Romanism" in government, and "foreign influence" in the schools and state militia.[87] In Los Angeles, Californios saw this platform as a potential threat to their political life, social life, and religion and organized against it. They called the Know-Nothings *Ignorantes*, and during the 1855 election, "*Californios* who never before had voted took the trouble to do so . . . , in recognition of the seriousness of the issues."[88] As a result, Los Angeles County was one of only two counties in Cal-ifornia where the Know-Nothings were soundly defeated.[89]

Despite the local defeat of the Know-Nothings in southern California, the statewide success of the party's anti-immigrant platform reflected the declining power of the Californios and the increasing hostility toward them across California by the mid-1850s. The public humiliation of three prominent Californios in the late 1850s is indicative of this trend. The first instance occurred during the 1856 presidential election when Antonio Coronel, a former mayor of Los Angeles and prominent Democratic Cali-fornio politician, was running again for mayor. Fellow Democrats publicly referred to him as "*el negro* Coronel," the Black Coronel. On election day, Anglo Democrats assembled near the polls shouting, "Here comes another Greaser vote! Here comes another vote for the Negro! If Coronel, the Negro, comes out to vote, stop him!"[90] During this same election, the local Democrats tried to split Los Angeles County into two districts in order to increase Anglo control of city elections and weaken the Californio vote.[91]

The second event took place in April 1857, when Manuel Domínguez, one of the signers of the California Constitution of 1849, a county supervisor of Los Angeles, and a highly respected Californio, was not allowed to testify on behalf of a defendant in a San Francisco court because the Anglo lawyer for the plaintiff argued that his Indian blood legally barred him from doing so. The judge agreed and dismissed Domínguez from the stand.[92] The third event was in 1858, when a constable seized former California Governor Pío Pico to testify in a minor legal matter and literally dragged him to appear before the San Francisco court.[93]

These experiences in the 1850s marked the first steps toward the complete erosion of Californio political power. In 1859 Californios attempted to capitalize on the weakening of the Democratic Party statewide by creating a "People's Slate" of former Whigs, Republicans, and independents. They ran Californios for a number of key offices but were soundly defeated.[94] Local politics in Los Angeles remained under the control of the conservative Democratic Party, and the revolt weakened Californio power by diluting the Mexican vote and raising doubts among Anglo Democrats about Californio party loyalty. As a result, the number of Californios holding office decreased after 1860; by the turn of the new century, no Californios held office in California.[95]

This internal Democratic Party conflict between Californios and Anglos coincided with a dramatic increase in the Anglo population and a concomitant decrease in the importance of the Mexican vote. The late nineteenth century saw large numbers of Anglo in-migration to California. As Table 1 shows, this in-migration resulted in a significant decrease in the proportion of the state's Mexican population. One clear indication of the decline of Californio power is the fact that by 1875 the minutes of government bodies were no longer printed in Spanish.[96] Through the 1870s Californios still periodically held the position of mayor of Los Angeles and a few were in the state legislature. But, largely because of gerrymandering and the population changes outlined in Table 1, there has been no Latino mayor of Los Angeles since 1872, and there were no state legislators until the 1960s.[97] As Gutiérrez argues, "By the 1870s, and certainly by the 1880s, unfavorable population ratios, combined with Americans' use of gerrymandering and other forms of ethnic exclusion,

Table 1   Total White and Nonwhite Populations in Los Angeles County, 1860–1930

	Total Population	Spanish-Speaking	Indian	Chinese	Negro
1860	4,385	2,565	2,014	11	87
1870	8,504	2,131	219	234	134
1880	11,183	2,231	316	1,169	188
1890	50,395	n/a	144	4,424	1,817
1900	102,479	3,000–5,000	5	2,111	2,131
1910	319,198	9,678–29,738	81	1,954	7,599
1920	576,673	29,757–50,000	189	2,062	15,579
1930	1,238,048	97,116–190,000	616	3,009	38,894

SOURCE: Albert Camarillo, *Chicanos in a Changing Society,* 6th ed. (Cambridge, Mass.: Harvard University Press, 1996), 116, 200.

gradually forced Mexican Americans out of the political arena. Consequently, by the turn of the century, Mexican Americans had lost virtually all direct voice in local and state political affairs."[98]

Thus Mexican Americans were effectively shut out of both California and Los Angeles politics and were socially and economically subordinate to the Anglo population. According to Deverell, "Within a few short decades, drought, legal entanglements, intermarriage, the imposition of a new political economy, outright thievery, and the removal of *Californios* from positions of political power had turned the world upside down. California, the spoils of both place and name, belonged now to the victors."[99]

This social, economic, and political subordination was followed by the social and geographic segregation of the Mexican population in Los Angeles. Over time, two distinct societies developed in Los Angeles— one white, one Mexican. According to James P. Allen and Eugene Turner, "For the vast number of Angelenos the residential areas of whites and Mexicans were coalescing into two very large communities, socially and geographically separate and unequal."[100] By 1872, "half of the town retained its Spanish character, while the other half was becoming American."[101] Mexicans remained concentrated mainly in the central plaza, an area called Sonora Town, which was separate from Anglo settlements. As a result, southern California society was "fundamentally structured along 'white' and 'Mexican' lines, determining where one lived and worked as well as one's social status."[102] Robert M. Fogelson paints a vivid picture of what Mexican life was like in Los Angeles between 1850 and 1885:

> They . . . lived in dreadful accommodations. They had no money to erect houses in fashionable neighborhoods, and in any case would not have been welcome there. They congregated in the vicinity of the old business district, where they rented crowded quarters in dilapidated dwellings. They took little interest in politics, regarding authority as a threat and avoiding it as a precaution, and politicians showed little concern for them. They did not join fraternal societies or worship in Protestant churches; nor did they cooperate with civic committees or contribute to commercial organizations. Instead, the Mexicans retained . . . their own institutions. . . . Unassimilated, unwelcome, and unprotected, these people were so thoroughly isolated that the American majority was able to maintain its untainted vision of an integrated community.[103]

Thus, the social segregation of Anglos and Mexicans that had existed in Los Angeles since annexation eventually also became geographic segregation. Before 1860, Mexicans made up 75 percent of the city's total population.[104] During this period, community segregation was not geographic but social. After 1860, as Mexican economic and political power decreased, the community began to become more geographically concentrated. By the 1880s, 70 percent of the Mexican population lived in either the central plaza or the southern section of the city. The arrival of the railroads to the city in the 1870s had led to industrial development around the central plaza. This made housing expansion impossible.[105] To flee this concentration and shortage of housing, around 1887 some Mexicans began moving into East Los Angeles.

From 1887 on, the trend has been the increased geographic segregation of the Mexican American community into one barrio on the east side of the city of Los Angeles. It is unclear to what extent this concentration and segregation was forced by the Anglos or self-imposed by the Mexican population. There is no question that the use of racially restrictive real estate covenants limited the areas where Mexicans were allowed to purchase or rent housing. As a Los Angeles realtor from the 1920s said, segregation is "not a problem" because "our realtors do not sell [to] Mexicans and Japanese outside certain sections where it is agreed by community custom they shall reside."[106] A Glendale realtor concurred, stating that through enforcement of "suitable race restrictions, we can maintain our high standard of American citizenship," which was critical in "an American town like Glendale."[107] According to Deverell, after 1880 "the dominant Anglo society set about creating certain cultural and physical boundaries by which to contain this expanding [Mexican] population, the sheer size of which troubled whites."[108]

Yet Richard Griswold del Castillo argues that Mexican residential concentration was the product of poverty and ethnic pride.[109] Until this time, the core of the Mexican barrio had been located in the poorest section of downtown, the area with the oldest construction. Yet this area had a high population density, and the cost of housing was high. The new area of East Los Angeles thus had more available space and was more affordable than the plaza area. In addition, as the Mexican "barrio" grew in East Los Angeles, it had positive effects on group support and cohesion, which in turn encouraged others to move to the area. From a group standpoint, the "creation of the barrio insured ethnic survival. Proximity of residence reinforced the language, religion, and social habits of the Mexican Americans and thus insured the continuation of their distinctive culture."[110]

One result of this geographic and social segregation is that throughout much of the twentieth century and into the twenty-first, there has been limited contact between formal U.S. government institutions and the Mexican population of East Los Angeles, and the two societies have remained largely separate. Those interactions that have occurred generally have not been positive. For example, during the 1930s, the Los Angeles Police Department (LAPD) took it upon themselves to undertake the widespread deportation of Mexicans in Los Angeles.[111] The Great Depression hit Los Angeles hard. In order to take "aliens" off the relief roles and to keep them from taking jobs from "Americans," large numbers of Mexicans were deported or were asked to leave "voluntarily."[112] It is estimated that from 1929 to 1939, nearly half a million Mexicans were deported from Los Angeles, many of whom were U.S. citizens.[113] This deportation experience was repeated during the 1950s when, because of the economic recession that followed the Korean War, the INS reported removing approximately 1.3 million Mexicans from the United States.[114] These deportations once again were carried out with the assistance of the LAPD.

There were other negative interactions between the Mexican American community and the Los Angeles Police Department. In 1942 the so-called Sleepy Lagoon incident occurred: twenty-two "pachuco" gang members were arrested for the alleged murder of a rival gang member in East Los Angeles.[115] The victim was murdered after a party. There was little evidence as to what had actually happened, no wounds on the body, and no witnesses. The police picked up the twenty-two suspects at their homes, long after the murder had taken place. The most compelling piece of evidence was that they were pachucos and had attended the party where the victim was murdered. After a highly irregular trial, an all-white jury found the twenty-two guilty of charges ranging from assault and battery to first-degree murder.[116] This led to the creation of the Sleepy Lagoon Defense Committee, which worked for their release. The decision was reversed two years later when a higher court ruled that the defendants' constitutional rights had been violated and that there was no evidence linking them to the crime.[117]

While the Sleepy Lagoon defendants were in jail, in spring and summer 1943, the Zoot Suit Riots occurred.[118] Hundreds of U.S. Navy sailors on shore leave attacked Mexican pachucos in East Los Angeles. One of their battle cries was "Let's get 'em! Let's get the chili-eating bastards!"[119] Many Mexican youths were stripped, had their hair shorn and their clothes torn off, were beaten by the mobs, and then were arrested by Los Angeles police officers for disturbing the peace. Despite the fact that the sailors had instigated the riots, none was arrested. The police did arrest more than six hundred Mexican Americans during the violence, many as a "preventive" measure to keep them from inciting violence on the streets.[120]

As is the case with instances of segregation, the line between coercion and individual choice is blurred. On the one hand, there is no question that incidents such as those described above made it clear to Mexican

Americans that Anglo society was hostile toward them and that leaving their immediate area may result in negative outcomes.[121] On the other hand, many of the members of the community remained in their barrio by choice. The key is that the segregation experience created a negative relationship between formal Anglo institutions and the community, one that remains today. This is despite the fact that formal legal structures supporting segregation are no longer in force.

A more positive result of this segregation was the development of a distinct Mexican American identity in Los Angeles and the maintenance of Mexican language and cultural life. Before annexation, class divisions were quite salient in Californio society. Most upper-class Mexicans did not necessarily see themselves as having anything in common with their lower-class neighbors.[122] Many of the rancher class supported annexation because they felt they would prosper economically under American rule and because they were generally disenchanted with the central government in Mexico City.[123] During the first few years after annexation, there was a great deal of intermarriage between the Anglo and Mexican upper classes, and a clear class distinction was made between the hacendados and their families and the rest of the Mexican population. This distinction is one of the reasons that some Mexicans were legally categorized as "white" after annexation.[124] To a large extent this classification was applied only to upper-class Mexicans; the rest were included in the "Indian" category.[125]

As a result of the loss of Californio political and economic power, class distinctions eventually became less important within the Mexican American community, and a broader "Mexican American" identity began to develop. Gutiérrez argues that "the combination of military conquest and the subsequent racial prejudice and social subordination helped pull Mexican Americans together by providing the political and social context in which a new sense of community and common purpose would develop. . . . [T]his rising level of ethnic awareness provided the basis on which Mexican Americans would later contest their political and socioeconomic subordination in American society."[126]

Griswold del Castillo agrees with the assessment that the hostility and discrimination experienced by Mexicans during this period led to the creation of a broad multiclass Mexican American identity. He argues that this process was facilitated by the development of a Spanish-language press, which had not existed during the Spanish and Mexican periods. The Spanish-language press "increased Mexican Americans' solidarity by reporting common experiences of persecution and discrimination."[127] Among these "common experiences" were lynchings, employment discrimination, problems with land claims, and prejudice.[128] The press also created a sense of community by reporting on cultural celebrations in the community. It used *la raza* as a generic term to describe people of Mexican origin. This term was a reflection of a new self-definition within the Spanish-speaking community, one based on race instead of class or culture. Because Anglos viewed them as a separate race, "the Spanish-speaking were forced to redefine their loyalties in racial terms."[129]

As a result of these changes, solidarity among Mexican Americans increased. Social organizations and political clubs were organized that drew the community together by defining the boundaries of cultural and ethnic life.[130] The Mexican American experience after annexation, then, was both negative and positive. The Mexican-origin population was forced into a position where they were socially, economically and politically subordinate to the Anglo population. They were socially and geographically segregated from the core institutional structures of Los Angeles but were able to create their own internal institutions. As a result, that very segregation allowed the community to retain its distinctive character, including its language and cultural traditions. The segregation experience also led to the development of a more inclusive Mexican American identity and more solidarity in the community as a whole. Yet Mexican Americans were highly aware of their subordinate position, and of their lack of power within city and state political institutions. This history, both positive and negative, has affected Mexican American attitudes toward the political system and political participation.

EAST LOS ANGELES

East Los Angeles, which currently has a population of about 126,000, is located just east of downtown Los Angeles. One segment of it falls within the boundaries of the City of Los Angeles and the other, fifteen square miles, is unincorporated Los Angeles County land.[131] In the nineteenth century, Jewish developers established Boyle Heights in the area that is now city land, and City Terrace, Maravilla, and Belvedere on what is now county land. Initially intended to be Jewish residential neighborhoods, they later became home to large Russian and European immigrant communities.[132]

Mexican-origin people have always lived in the area but first began moving to East Los Angeles in large numbers in 1887. This migration expanded along with the rapid growth in Mexican immigration early in the twentieth century. Most of these immigrants were fleeing the violence and displacement caused by the Mexican Revolution. Between 1910 and 1920, the Mexican population in Los Angeles grew from five thousand to more than thirty thousand, and tripled from 1920 to 1930.[133] The resulting crowded living conditions along with the industrial development that had begun with the arrival of the railroads left plaza residents with little choice. They began moving to the east side of the city. Most settled Maravilla and Belvedere, where they lived alongside settlements of Jews, Armenians, and Russians. After the 1910s, many of the European immigrants began to move to the west side of the city, and East Los Angeles slowly became a majority Mexican area.

From 1910 until the late 1970s, East Los Angeles served as the center of Mexican American life in Los Angeles. Politically, the movement of the Mexican American community from the central plaza to the east side resulted in the literal removal of the area from Los Angeles politics. While Boyle Heights is part of the City of Los Angeles, the rest is unincorporated Los Angeles County land. Practically, the unincorporated area has to depend on the county government for services and does not have its own local government, fire, or police force. Institutionally, the area is governed by the Los Angeles County Board of Supervisors, which was made up of five members throughout much of the twentieth century. Each supervisor represents millions of constituents, ensuring that the area's vote is so diluted that there is little chance of its having any direct political influence. For example, there was no Latino representation on the County Board of Supervisors until the 1990 Garza ruling, in which the Ninth Circuit Court of Appeals ordered the creation of a Latino-majority

Los Angeles County Supervisorial District.[134] That district became the First District, and it is currently represented by Gloria Molina, the first Latino to serve on the board in the twentieth century. The court based its ruling on proof of historic gerrymandering and exclusion of the Los Angeles Mexican American population. Similarly, the portion of East Los Angeles that is within the Los Angeles city limits constitutes only a small percentage of the city as a whole, and thus the Latinos in that area have less ability to elect their own representatives or to influence city politics. The segregation of the Mexican American population into East Los Angeles, then, also resulted in their political separation and exclusion from Los Angeles city and county politics.

Nevertheless, this geographic concentration of population did allow the Mexican American community to retain its cultural life. Throughout the twentieth century, Belvedere Park was a center of community life. The community held annual celebrations for Cinco de Mayo and the 16th of September, which recognize Mexican independence from the French and the Spanish respectively. Immigrants tended to settle in the barrio because it was a source of social and economic networks and facilitated their transition into American society.[135] But it is also important to keep in mind that while many Mexicans chose to remain in the area because of social and kinship ties, those that desired to leave could not move to Anglo neighborhoods because of restrictive real estate covenants and general prejudice.[136] Here again we see the two sides of residential segregation: the creation of the barrio allowed for the maintenance of Mexican cultural life and the development of group solidarity, but the concentration of the population was not by choice and limited Mexican Americans' social, economic, and political opportunities.[137]

Mexican Americans in Los Angeles counteracted the negative effects of this lack of opportunity through the development of racial solidarity. The development of a Mexican American identity after annexation also led to the creation of *mutualistas,* or mutual aid societies. These organizations developed in the nineteenth century in Mexico and were present throughout the Southwest by the 1870s. They served social welfare functions; many of them explicitly banned discussions of religion or politics at their meetings. Interestingly, they defined "politics" as being the political situation in Mexico and not the civil rights problems being faced by Mexican Americans in the United States.[138] These organizations served the needs of both citizen and noncitizen Mexicans and were essentially working class in character. They provided an important safety net for people in a vulnerable socioeconomic position. They also facilitated the incorporation of new immigrants into the community. The mutualista "acted as a crucial institutional buffer that eased new immigrants' adjustment to the United States. . . . In addition, the intimate contact that occurred between Mexican Americans and Mexican immigrants in the culturally familiar *mutualistas* helped to break down barriers between the two groups, improved communication, and promoted a spirit of cooperation among them."[139] Mexican Americans in East Los Angeles, then, responded to their subordinate status by developing group solidarity and important support systems for the most vulnerable members of their group.

Though this kind of community organizing was present throughout the early twentieth century, in most cases Mexican American organizations went out of their way to emphasize that they were not overtly "political." Mexican American organizations such as the League of United Latin American Citizens (LULAC) that organized during the 1920s and 1930s were operating in a very hostile and nativist environment. As a result, they took great pains not to be seen as making political demands but as simply fighting for the "American" way of life.[140]

World War II served as a watershed. After the war, for the first time, large-scale political organizing on the part of Mexican Americans took place in Los Angeles. The first explicitly political Mexican American organization in California was the Community Service Organization (CSO). It was created by working-class Mexican World War II veterans upset about their treatment on returning from service. Many had difficulty getting access to their GI Bill benefits and generally felt disillusioned about returning from the war to a segregated society. Like many African American veterans during this period, Mexican American veterans used their veterans' status to demand full inclusion and civil rights.[141]

The CSO began as the Community Political Organization (CPO) and evolved into the CSO in 1947 when the group organized support for

Edward Roybal's unsuccessful bid for a Los Angeles City Council seat. Fred Ross, a disciple of Saul Alinsky and the Industrial Areas Foundation, originally organized the CPO. Much of the organization's legwork was done by Mexican American steelworkers and volunteers, who later formed the backbone of the CSO. Their effective confrontational style is largely credited with Roybal's subsequent election to the Los Angeles City Council in 1949.[142] He was the first Mexican American to serve on the Los Angeles City Council in the twentieth century. He left the city council in 1962 to run for a congressional seat, which he won. Another Mexican American did not sit on the city council until Richard Alatorre's election in 1985, twenty-three years later.

The CSO also helped to train organizers such as César Chávez and began pushing for political rights for Mexican Americans. Many of the veterans involved in the CSO were able to attend college under the GI Bill and continued to organize for more political power. Their influence was limited by the fact that during this period, the Latino vote was diluted by gerrymandering, making the election of Mexican American officials difficult.[143]

The next political organization that came out of the Mexican American community in Los Angeles was the Mexican American Political Association (MAPA), which was established in 1959. The organization was created by Edward Roybal to protest what he saw as racist attitudes within the California Democratic Party. Two Mexican Americans had been nominated for California statewide office in the 1950s—Edward Roybal for lieutenant governor in 1954 and Henry López for secretary of state in 1958.[144] The party encouraged both men not to run and subsequently gave no support to either campaign.[145] During the López campaign, some Democratic officials even refused to join López on campaign platforms during public appearances.[146] López ended up being the only statewide Democratic candidate to lose that year. MAPA, whose members were middle-class Mexican Americans, became very active in Los Angeles politics and was instrumental in the successful organization of the Viva Kennedy campaign of 1960. During this get-out-the-vote effort, MAPA worked to register record numbers of East Los Angeles residents. The organization's leaders were later disillusioned when they were ignored by the Democratic Party and the Kennedy administration and not given the political appointments they had been led to expect.[147] Despite this disillusionment, the establishment of MAPA was an important first step in the development of Mexican American political activity in the 1960s and 1970s.

During this period, Mexican American community activity also took the form of grassroots organizing in favor of community development. The first such organizing led to the creation of the East Los Angeles Community Union (TELACU) in 1968.[148] This organization arose as a grassroots barrio movement demanding economic empowerment for the Mexican American community after the Watts riots. Their main goal was to find the venture capital needed to stimulate and develop the eastside economy. The organization's success was facilitated by funds from the Johnson administration's War on Poverty. They also received grants from the United Auto Workers, the Ford Foundation, federal poverty agencies, the Model Cities program, and the Department of Labor. TELACU created a bank, an industrial park, commercial shopping malls, and low-income housing in East Los Angeles, and remains active and influential today.

The 1970s saw other forms of community organizing in East Los Angeles. Early in the decade Mexican Americans in East Los Angeles were deeply involved in the Chicano Movement. In 1970 the Chicano Moratorium March was held in Belvedere Park. The park was renamed Salazar Park in honor of the journalist Rubén Salazar who was "accidentally" shot by Los Angeles Police in an East Los Angeles bar shortly after the march.[149] The 1970s also saw the growth of grassroots organizing in the area. The United Neighborhood Organization (UNO) was established in 1975 to improve living conditions in East Los Angeles. It was based on the Industrial Areas Foundation model and was instrumental in forcing insurance companies to stop redlining the area in the 1970s.[150]

An example of grassroots organizing among women in East Los Angeles is Mothers of East Los Angeles, "a loosely knit group of over 400 women."[151] This organization grew out of opposition to a state plan to build a prison in East Los Angeles. Many of the women who began the organization had been adversely affected by the freeway construction that had divided East Los Angeles communities during the 1960s. Some of the women had been forced to move more than once during that period and transformed that experience into "a springboard for resistance to the state prison, which [to them] represented an additional encroachment."[152] These women used their "traditional" roles and networks to defeat the prison construction, and later to prevent construction of a toxic incinerator in Vernon, a small industrial city adjacent to East Los Angeles. This organization still exists in the area and works with other environmental organizations to address quality of life issues in the community. Mary Pardo argues that "[t]hese women have defied stereotypes of apathy and used ethnic, gender and class identity as an impetus, a strength, a vehicle for political activism. They have expanded their— and our—understanding of the complexities of a political system, and they have reaffirmed the possibility of 'doing something.'"[153]

Over the course of the twentieth century, then, East Los Angeles became home to numerous effective and politically significant Mexican American organizations. After World War II, these organizations, while still serving important social and integrative functions, became explicitly political. Although gerrymandering and the area's location in an unincorporated part of Los Angeles County limited Mexican Americans' ability to hold office at the state and local levels, these organizations served important functions on the local level by fostering group cohesion and empowerment. Though there were still many socioeconomic problems in East Los Angeles after the creation of TELACU and UNO, these organizations have achieved important successes and have shown organizers that collective action can make a difference on the local level. As we will see in subsequent chapters, this history of collective group organization has had a beneficial effect on the development of mobilizing identities among Latinos in East Los Angeles.

MONTEBELLO

Montebello is a suburb east of the city of Los Angeles, with a population of about sixty thousand. Montebello is, like East Los Angeles, a majority Latino area, but this has not always been the case. Although Montebello was a Mexican-majority area at the turn of the twentieth century, from the 1920s until the 1970s it was a middle-class Anglo city and was home to many southern and midwestern immigrants. Documents from early-twentieth-century Montebello show the degree to which those who settled there shared a particular racial vision. One example is the annual Pioneer Day celebration, which remembered and honored the settlers who arrived in southern California by covered wagon. During the first Pioneer Day celebration in 1936, the mayor of Montebello said, "We owe much to these pioneers. Let us strive to be what they visioned of the future generations. In those who strive for race perfection the personal and petty individual things are forgotten. This thing which the modern psychologists call 'race vision' must have burned ardently in the hearts of these people who traveled in the covered wagons."[154] This belief in "race perfection" and Anglo superiority, along with the highly segregated status of Mexican Americans, limited the amount of local organization that occurred among Mexican Americans in Montebello, thus decreasing their access to contextual capital.

Montebello was the first Spanish settlement in Los Angeles County. In 1771 the first mission, San Gabriel Archangel, Misión Vieja, was built on the site.[155] It was abandoned in 1776 because of floods, and the Spanish built the San Gabriel Mission nearby. The city also has the dubious distinction of being the location of the decisive battle of the Mexican American War, the Battle of the Río San Gabriel. On August 17, 1847, General Kearney and Commodore Stockton defeated the Mexican garrison defending the southern portion of the state. According to the Montebello Chamber of Commerce, "This struggle annihilated the remaining resistance, and led to the independence of California, a step preceding its admission to the Union."[156]

In addition to being where the Mexican forces were defeated in California, Montebello was home to the famed Californio "bandit" Tiburcio Vásquez, known as the "Robin Hood of California." Vásquez was one of the more famous Californios who maintained resistance to American rule after annexation. That resistance led to the importation of the "El Monte Boys," a group of Texans who moved to El Monte (an area just east of Montebello) during the 1850s. They were involved in numerous lynchings of Mexicans in the area to "establish order."[157] They were also called in periodically to help in other areas of Los Angeles when whites felt threatened by Mexican violence.[158] In 1857, a group of them were seen bowling with the head of a murdered Mexican.[159] Vásquez was finally killed in 1874 in the hills of Montebello while attempting to rob Allessandro Repetto, an Italian immigrant who owned a 5,000-acre ranch in the area.

Repetto died in 1885, and his brother sold the estate to a group of Los Angeles developers: Harris Newmark, Kaspar Cohn, John Bicknell, and Stephen White. Newmark and Cohn took 1,200 of the 5,000 acres and founded Montebello in 1899. At the suggestion of William Mulholland, a town site of 40 acres was called Newmark and the remainder was called Montebello. Mulholland divided the area into five- and ten-acre lots and laid out the water system. At this point, the town was made up primarily of small farms and nurseries and was advertised as an ideal agricultural community.

Two things happened in Montebello in 1905. First, a Benedictine monk moved to Montebello from Oklahoma to build a monastery. It turned out that the site he chose sat on a large reserve of oil, which was important to the future development of the city. Second, the Simons brothers, Joseph, Elmer, and Walter, decided to expand their brick-making business by building a plant in Montebello.[160] They located the plant on a hundred-acre tract located next to the Atchison, Topeka and Santa Fe railroad tracks. They chose Montebello because it had "plentiful clay deposits, cheap land and an available labor force of cheap unskilled Mexican workers."[161] Montebello at the time was described as "beautiful" and "all Mexican."[162] The plant was called the Simons Brick Company Yard No. 3 and included housing for a labor force of one hundred fifty Mexicans and their families.[163] By late spring 1907, the Mexican "Village of Simons" had become a "fully engaged brick-making company town" turning out 160,000 bricks a day.[164] By the 1920s, the brickyard spread out over 350 acres and was the world's largest common brick manufacturing plant. Over its history, the plant "became a microcosm of the divisive social order that dominated southern California during the formative years of the early 20th century."[165]

At the time, the Simons plant was considered a model "industrial town." The plant included "housing, a restaurant, general merchandise store, post-office, school house, amusement hall, water works, electrical plant, etc."[166] By 1907 it even included a company cafeteria to cook for the seventy-five bachelors in residence. The houses rented for $3 to $4 a month and had no foundations (the moisture from the clay would seep upward during the wet winter months). They were single-wall construction, so most families used newspaper to cover the interior walls. There was no electricity and no plumbing. The outhouses were in back, and water could be drawn from spigots outside that were connected to the company well. The houses had woodstoves that were used for both cooking and heating. The roads were unpaved, and some workers were able to purchase livestock that roamed the streets outside the houses. Workers were allowed to have vegetable gardens, which many turned into second incomes by selling the produce, particularly during the wet winter months when the plant was closed.[167]

Since brick making is impossible when it rains, the workers had to make as many bricks as possible during the dry "season." Shifts were nine to twelve hours per day, starting at 3:00 A.M. Work stopped when the sun got hot in the afternoons. Early in the century wages were about 20 cents an hour, and the cost of a subsistence standard of living was $5 to $7 a week. Many of the workers' children worked as well. They were paid a penny a brick to turn them while they dried. The company controlled all aspects of the workers' lives. Workers paid for groceries, shoes, dry goods, and rent on company script or with company credit.[168] The plant had its own Catholic church, and the company had a "marital relations court" to adjudicate domestic disputes. Drinking was forbidden in town, even inside a private home. Violators of company rules were fired immediately. Anyone who even talked about union organizing lost his job.[169] The company provided a dance hall, organized an official band and a semiprofessional baseball team, held boxing matches, and showed films on site.[170]

These efforts to provide entertainment were necessary because the plant's gates were locked at night in order to keep the Mexican workers from leaving the grounds. As a result, the rest of Montebello developed as a highly segregated, Anglo-majority city. In 1916, when oil was discovered on the Benedictine monk's land, the wells were bought by Standard Oil. By 1918 Montebello was producing twenty thousand barrels of oil daily, and by 1920 the city was producing one-eighth of California's crude oil. As a result of the oil boom, between 1920 and 1930 the population increased from 2,582 to 7,564. The boom in development was orchestrated by the Ransom real estate development company, which advertised that Mexican labor was readily available in Montebello and used pictures of the Simons plant as a promotional tool in its advertising.[171] According to Deverell, Montebello grew so quickly as a city because the success of the Simons plant could be presented as proof of the area's industrial promise.[172] Montebello incorporated itself as a city in 1920 with a population of about 2,500.

Montebello realtors advertised the area as a "city of flowers." But from the beginning their vision of Montebello was a segregated one, and "racially restrictive policies and practices occupied center stage in Montebello's city planning through the prewar era."[173] In the 1920s, a prominent Montebello realtor said, "It is the practice of the [Realty] Board to watch carefully to see that undesirable races are kept out of the older sections of town."[174] The same board listed "controlling race conditions and enforcing race restrictions" as one of its top goals.[175] In a 1927 survey conducted by the California Real Estate Association, of the forty-seven cities that replied, thirty-two maintained some kind of segregated "Mexican" district. These districts were enforced through deed restrictions and collusion among realtors and property owners to enforce restrictive covenants.[176] Montebello is listed in the survey as one of twenty-four cities with explicitly racially defined segregated areas. Segregation remained a problem into the 1950s, when Mexican American World War II veterans led demonstrations in Montebello against segregated housing developments.[177]

Segregation in Montebello went beyond housing. The city's pool and playground were off limits to Simons residents.[178] The schools also were segregated. The school located on the Simons grounds, called the "Mexican school" by locals, had only Mexican students. Ostensibly, the Mexican students were integrated once they got to junior high, but they were all placed in the same home room, and most did not go on to high school. Many of the eighth-graders were seventeen or eighteen years old.[179] The education they received was clearly substandard; many of the children of Simons workers did not learn to read and write in English or Spanish until they served in the military in World War II.[180] So, although Montebello had a significant Mexican-origin population throughout its history, during most of that time, the population was literally locked behind closed gates. It is not surprising that a former Simons resident reported rarely venturing out of the Simons plant area because of concerns about how he would be treated.[181]

The Simons plant constituted a "town within a town." For nearly half a century, it appeared on area maps as "Simons."[182] At its height in the 1920s, the plant housed three thousand Mexican workers and their families, a population that was roughly equivalent to the size of the rest of the city of Montebello. The bottom fell out of the brick-making industry in the 1930s as a result of the Great Depression and changes in southern California building codes following the 1933 Long Beach earthquake. The plant remained, however, producing brick at much lower levels. By 1940 the plant housed only eight hundred residents. Of the 182 homes on site, only four had flush toilets. None had bathtubs. The homes had not been improved since they were built almost fifty years before.[183] In 1952, a Los Angeles County health inspector found 90 percent of the houses unfit for human habitation, and the plant was shut down. When the plant closed, the families were displaced. Many ended up moving to South Montebello because restrictive covenants kept them from buying land elsewhere in the city. The area is now called Barrio Simons.[184] During the 1980s, the Montebello City Council considered condemning their homes to make way for new housing projects but was unsuccessful.[185]

The Simons plant is important for two main reasons. First, the bricks produced at this plant literally built Los Angeles, including important city landmarks such as Royce Hall at the University of California, Los Angeles; the University of Southern California; Walt Disney Studios; and many of the mansions in Hancock Park.[186] Deverell contends:

The Simons Brick Company Yard No. 3 was a place of great importance to the growth of Los Angeles in the first half of the century. The company literally helped build the city: its hotels, its universities, its homes, its businesses. Yet ninety years after the construction of the brickyard company housing, Ismael "Mayo" Vargas recalls Simons as a place where human potential was never allowed to flower. Workers at the brickyard worked their entire lives trying to get hold of something approximating the California Dream. But the odds were against them in the hole.[187]

This raises the second important aspect of the plant, the "benevolent paternalism" toward the Mexican population that the plant represented.[188] Why did the Simons brothers need to create a "company town"? Why not simply have their workers live nearby? The *Los Angeles Times* routinely praised the Simons plant as a model of modern industry, a modern "mission," and compared Walter Simons to Father Junípero Serra.[189] The paternalism inherent in this mission theme shows the degree to which this form of industrial organization was meant to control the behavior of Mexican workers and their labor. Deverell contends that the Simons plant was part of larger attempts to "Americanize" and "civilize" the Mexican population in California. He writes, "There is no doubt that self-contained Simons . . . existed as a place where Mexican laborers could be closely attended to, gradually brought forward toward 'civilization.'"[190]

The closing of the Simons plant led to full racial integration in the city of Montebello. Since the 1950s the city has experienced significant demographic change. For example, from 1965 to 1975 the student population of Montebello schools went from being 35 percent to more than 65 percent Mexican origin. Latinos were attracted to Montebello because it was considered the Beverly Hills of East Los Angeles. The perception among many was that "the move from urban settings, especially East Los Angeles, to suburban Montebello was the capstone of Latino upward mobility."[191] As a result, by 1990, 67 percent of Montebello residents were Latino and only 17 percent were Anglo. Thus, it was not until quite recently that the Anglo population of Montebello had to incorporate its Mexican-origin neighbors, and this seems to have remained a source of group conflict. For example, in 1995 one of the two Catholic churches in Montebello attempted to add a Spanish Mass to its services and as a result lost a number of parishioners.[192] This is very different from

Catholic churches in East Los Angeles, all of which hold at least one Spanish-language Mass.

Mexican Americans in Montebello have had a very different historical experience than those in East Los Angeles. They have experienced a much more paternalistic attitude on the part of the dominant group and, likely as a result, much less community-based activity and organization. A 1999 study of social organizations in Montebello supports this position.[193] Similar to my findings, respondents in that study reported low levels of community-based political activity in the city and a general lack of knowledge about what was happening politically.[194] They complained of a lack of good sources of information, such as community newspapers, and reported high levels of political apathy among community members, especially young people.[195] Few said they felt "national and statewide events of political significance had any real impact on their lives."[196] As of that study, Montebello had thirty-seven community-based organizations. But these organizations tended not to be Latino-focused. Instead, they are groups such as Friends of the Library, Kiwanis, Rotary, and the Montebello Historical Society. This lack of specifically Latino organizations might explain why the Latino respondents in Montebello report such high feelings of political alienation and low levels of political efficacy, particularly at the local level.

Thus, though Montebello has had a significant Mexican-origin population since before it became a city, that population has been segregated from the Anglo community until fairly recently. Although segregation led to community organization and identity-based political organizing in East Los Angeles, the same was not the case in Montebello, largely because their activities were controlled by the Simons Brick Company. As a result, though Montebello Latinos are relatively well off socioeconomically, their neighborhoods possess a limited amount of contextual capital.

CONCLUSION

Given the historical experiences of Latinos in California and Los Angeles, the anti-Latino attitudes present in California during the 1990s are not all that surprising. The ballot initiatives of this period echo previous political movements and deportation campaigns against Latino presence in the state. But despite the fact that Latinos in Los Angeles have been in a subordinate social, economic, and political position in southern California society, they have been able to maintain a vibrant cultural and community life. Over the course of the twentieth century, Mexican Americans in East Los Angeles have used local organization to counteract the negative impact of their stigmatized position. Although their political victories have been limited, this organizing experience has left a legacy of group organization and solidarity. In Montebello, for the first half of the twentieth century, the Mexican population was literally fenced off from the rest of the city. Their political, social, and economic life was controlled and proscribed by the Simons Brick Company. The eventual integration of Mexicans into the city of Montebello was not welcome and remains a source of conflict. The result has been little group organization and political activity. In the following chapters, we will see how the historical differences in these communities have affected the psychological and contextual capital available not only to the Latinos who have been living there but also to the new immigrants who recently have settled in these areas.

THREE

A Thin Line between Love and Hate

LANGUAGE, SOCIAL STIGMA,
AND INTRAGROUP RELATIONS

We will have to repent in this generation not merely for
the hateful words and actions of the bad people but for
the appalling silence of the good people.

Martin Luther King Jr.

Scholars studying Chicanos, Puerto Ricans, Cubans, and other Latinos
in the United States have long emphasized the important role of language and culture.[1] Spanish-language use and maintenance (or not) has
been seen as an important aspect of how Latinos define their culture
and identity.[2] Language use affects the integration of Latino immigrants, Latinos' understanding of their own social identity, and intragroup relations. These processes are structured by the negative stereotypes Latinos feel that Anglos have of the Latino social group and by
the way in which those stereotypes are seen as applying, by extension,
to Spanish-language use. I explore here how Latinos' attempts to develop a positive collective identity despite negative attributions affect
their feelings about themselves and the relations between immigrant
and native-born Latinos.

LANGUAGE, IDENTITY, AND SOCIAL STIGMA

The development of Latino group identity is problematic because of Latinos' status as a stigmatized group in the United States. The experience of stigma is at the heart of the question of Latino identity. Jennifer Crocker and colleagues define stigmatized individuals as ones who "possess (or are believed to possess) some attribute, or characteristic, that conveys a social identity that is devalued in a particular social context."[3] The existence of stigma in relation to an individual's group identity(ies) leads him or her to find ways to have a positive attachment to the social group.[4] To do this, social identity theorists contend, individuals may either dissociate themselves from the stigmatized group or, if that is impossible, embrace the group identity and work collectively to improve the status of the group.[5] Similarly, studies of the effects of stigma have found that members of a stigmatized group are usually acutely aware of the negative characterizations of their group, and they will engage in a number of strategies to enhance their self-esteem.[6] These strategies include using only in-group members as points of reference and disengagement and disidentification with certain societal domains.

When examining racialized groups, then, it is important to consider how stigma affects individual and group attitudes. This is different from simply looking at the effects of discrimination. Discrimination infers a concrete negative experience or denial of some benefit. In fact, this is often the standard used by the courts to determine whether they believe that discrimination has occurred. However, in the post–civil rights era this kind of blatant discrimination is not as common. In fact, the "shift in expressions of prejudice away from blatant, unambiguous prejudice, and toward subtle, indirect and modern forms, may paradoxically result in more, rather than less, threat to the self-esteem of stigmatized individuals."[7] This is because stigmatized individuals know prejudice exists but cannot be certain when it is occurring. Individuals prefer to blame failure on themselves, rather than accept that they are the victims of prejudice, because in that way they can maintain some sense of control over the situation.[8] Stigma can also lead groups to believe they should not enjoy "full and equal participation in social and economic life."[9] Members of stigmatized groups often accept the "legitimating myths" of society that justify their stigmatization.[10] So experiences of stigma can have varied, and important, effects on the perceptions, attitudes, and actions of members of stigmatized groups.

The Latinos I interviewed were well aware of the stigma attached to their social group. Javier, a first-generation Mexican from East Los Angeles, put it this way: "They [the United States] always give preference to the immigrant with white skin over the immigrant with dark skin, or that comes from South America, Mexico, or Central America. There's a very big difference." Verónica, a twenty-four-year-old woman from East Los Angeles who is also a first-generation Mexican, expressed a similar opinion about why Proposition 187 was put on the ballot:

> I have an idea that, maybe it was because of racism, no? Because, you know, they always blame us, the Hispanics. There is a great deal of racism, and I feel that that is why they did it. They [Americans] are against the Hispanic race because that is what they see the most. Perhaps this also applies to other nationalities, this racism, but not as strongly as it does for Hispanics.

Juan, a second-generation Mexican-Salvadoran from Montebello, agreed. He said that whites are prejudiced against Mexicans especially because the government wants to "make the perfect United States of America." He went on to say, "They just want to make a perfect country. They don't want us here anymore. They want people to stay where they came from." The Latinos in this sample repeatedly said that they believe prejudice exists against their group and that that prejudice affects how they are treated in this country.

But what is the relationship between stigma and language? As sociolinguists recognize, language is important in the maintenance and expression of ethnic identities. Language use, the representation of shared meanings, and culture have been found to be closely related.[11] Studies of sociolinguistic groups around the world reveal that language is key to how ethnicity is "recognized, interpreted and experienced."[12] Ethnic groups communicate, develop feelings of solidarity, and preserve group histories through language. However, that relationship to language can become problematic when a group's language exists in a subordinate position within a system of sociolinguistic stratification.[13] A paradox arises, as the language is a source of pride and group solidarity, on the one hand, and of stigma, on the other. As a result, "persons who speak the socially disfavored varieties [of language] frequently appear to become alienated from their own variety of language and to judge it as, for example, inferior, sloppy, ugly, illogical or incomprehensible."[14]

Sociolinguistic studies in the Latino community have also shown the important ways in which language use relates to group identity, racial stigma, and social power relations.[15] Ana Celia Zentella finds that for Latino groups of various national origins, the propensity of a group to adopt the Spanish lexicon of another group depends in part on the relative racial and class status of the two.[16] In a more recent analysis of language shift among Puerto Ricans in New York City, Zentella finds that feelings of racial, ethnolinguistic, and economic subordination play a key role in parental language behavior.[17] Similarly, Bonnie Urciuoli argues that Puerto Rican linguistic behavior must be understood in the context of what she calls "racialization"—how the value attributed to particular languages is intimately tied to larger understandings of race and racial hierarchy in U.S. society.[18] So a lack of power and status is an important part of the stigmatization process and affects Latino attitudes toward both Spanish and English. Although these studies have examined primarily the experiences of Puerto Ricans in the United States, their findings lead us to expect that issues of linguistic and racial stigma affect the development of collective identities for other national-origin Latinos.

STIGMA, SPANISH, AND U.S. LANGUAGE POLICY

The history of Latino racial subordination in California is intimately related to the use of the Spanish language.[19] The social stigma attached to Spanish is largely related to the role of the English language in the development and maintenance of U.S. national identity.[20] As the historian Arthur Schlesinger puts it, "A common language is a necessary bond of national cohesion in so heterogeneous a nation as America. . . . [I]nstitutionalized bilingualism remains another source of the fragmentation of

America, another threat to the dream of 'one people.'"[21] From that point of view, in order for American national identity to be cohesive, immigrants must not simply speak English, they must speak *only* English: "The remarkable rapidity and completeness of language transition in America is no mere happenstance, for it reflects the operation of strong social forces. In a country lacking centuries-old traditions and culture and receiving simultaneously millions of foreigners from the most diverse lands, language homogeneity came to be seen as the bedrock of nationhood and collective identity. Immigrants were not only compelled to speak English, but to speak English *only* as the prerequisite of social acceptance and integration."[22] American national identity requires English monolingualism because speaking another language has often been seen as a sign of allegiance to another nation or culture and thus antithetical to being a "true" American: "[L]anguage in America has a meaning that transcends its purely instrumental value as a means of communication. Unlike in several European nations, which are tolerant of linguistic diversity, in the United States the acquisition of nonaccented English and the dropping of foreign languages represent the litmus test of Americanization. Other aspects of immigrant culture (religion, cuisine, and community celebrations) often last for several generations, but the home language seldom survives."[23] This explains why Americanization programs for Mexican Americans and Native Americans forbade the use of native languages, and, for Native Americans, required physical removal from the family in order to remove any un-American influences.[24] Thus becoming a "true" American requires not only the mastery of English but the concomitant loss of the native language as well.[25]

In addition to viewing English monolingualism as the foundation for American national identity, throughout U.S. history individuals promoting a particular racial composition in America have proposed the use of literacy tests and language requirements to achieve their exclusionary goals. For example, during the immigration debates around the turn of the twentieth century, literacy tests were proposed to keep out "undesirable" immigrants from southern Europe. In an 1896 speech to the U.S. Senate, one of the main proponents of these tests, Henry Cabot Lodge, acknowledged that this racially restrictive goal was their main purpose:

"It is found, in the first place, that the illiteracy test will bear most heavily upon the Italians, Russians, Poles, Hungarians, Greeks and Asiatics, and very lightly or not at all, upon English-speaking immigrants or Germans, Scandinavians, and French. In other words, the races most affected by the illiteracy test are those . . . races with which the English-speaking people have never hitherto assimilated, and who are most alien to the great body of the people of the United States."[26] Lodge's argument is strikingly similar to that made by Peter Brimelow one hundred years later. In 1996, Brimelow, an English immigrant, argued that an English-language proficiency requirement for immigration to the United States would be a positive step because it would decrease immigration from Latin America and increase immigration from Europe:

> That [the adoption of an English proficiency test] would make a *big* difference (seriously). The Census Bureau reported a remarkable 47 percent of the U.S. foreign-born population do not speak English "very well" or "at all." So emphasizing English proficiency would inevitably cut down immigration a lot. Particularly of Hispanics. Some 71 percent of foreign-born Mexicans report not speaking English "very well." Essentially all of them—96 percent—speak Spanish at home. In addition, an English-language requirement would probably increase immigration from the developed countries of Europe.[27]

Language skills and English language use, then, historically have been an important basis for American national identity, and this emphasis on language often has had ascriptive, racial undertones. These undertones are heard loud and clear by immigrants who speak "less desirable" languages. As a result, the immigrant language becomes stigmatized, and the adoption of English plays an important role in the development of collective identity and group cohesion within Latino immigrant groups.

SPANISH, STIGMA, AND THE FIRST GENERATION

Immigration studies have long shown that immigrants tend to settle in areas where they already have established familial ties or social networks.[28] Often, social networks are present in communities with large concentrations of immigrants from the same country of origin and even from the same town or village. These settlement patterns provide immigrants with an environment in which they can function using their native language and in which many of the norms and customs are familiar, which eases their transition in the host country.

East Los Angeles and, to a lesser extent, Montebello, are communities of this type. Both have high concentrations of Latinos who are available to provide resources and assistance to new arrivals. East Los Angeles especially has been an entry community for Latino (mostly Mexican) immigrants since the 1910s.[29] Montebello has been less so, because of its historic racial and socioeconomic makeup. But it has a number of businesses and services that cater to the Spanish-speaking population and is located near other immigrant communities, such as East Los Angeles, City of Commerce, and Pico Rivera, where resources are also available to them. In both communities, immigrants can take care of most of the necessities of daily life—paying bills, shopping, going to the doctor—without speaking English or by doing so only in a limited way.

The existence of ethnic enclave communities is often cited as a key reason why new immigrants are not assimilating into U.S. society as rapidly as did European immigrants in the early twentieth century.[30] Proponents of this view have argued that the provision of services accessible to someone who speaks only Spanish makes life easy for immigrants by making it unnecessary for them to learn English or adapt to the mores of the United States. I found exactly the opposite. The first-generation respondents were acutely aware of their linguistic isolation from the dominant culture. These feelings of isolation adversely affected their sense of self-worth, even though they live in Spanish-dominant areas. Some negative feelings arose from their understanding that there is an English-speaking world "out there," from which they are segregated. However, negative feelings also arose from the unpleasant interactions they had in their own neighborhoods with native-born, English-speaking Latinos.

In general, language was an important issue for the first-generation respondents. All but one of them said that language is important for job opportunities, supervising their children's education, or simply negotiating the demands of everyday life. One of the most common phrases they used to describe this feeling was not being able to *defenderse*—literally, "to defend themselves"—socially, economically, or politically. Verónica described the problem as *vergüenzitas,* or little embarrassments, that she felt in situations when people asked her questions in English and she was not able to respond. She said the question, "Oh, you don't speak English?" embarrassed her and left her "feeling bad," even when the other person's intentions were benign.

Marta, a thirty-six-year-old Mexican woman from Montebello, went further, saying that not speaking English is a problem wherever she goes and that people give her "bad looks." She said, "[This makes me feel] very bad, as if I were something that had no value, as a human being, that is, as if we had no rights, and that is not right." A little later in the conversation, her voice very heavy and sad, she said, "I feel like, I feel as if I am not in my place—as if I were in a strange place, because I cannot defend myself as I would like, because I cannot express myself as I would like."

Not "having" English, as they put it, limited where they could go, what they could do, and their ability to protest or even question authority when they felt they were being taken advantage of. Two women, one from East Los Angeles and one from Montebello, talked about their feelings of fear and confusion when they were pulled over for traffic violations. They were both quick to point out that the policemen did not behave badly but that the experience was very unpleasant because all they could do was accept the ticket without understanding fully what it was for and without the ability to speak on their own behalf. These experiences, repeated in many areas of their lives, left them feeling frustrated and powerless.

María, a sixty-three-year-old Guatemalan woman from Montebello, discussed how language affects access to good health care. When I interviewed her, she had just recently spent a long time in the hospital recuperating from a serious gastrointestinal illness that left her on a strict dietary regimen. None of the nurses on the floor spoke Spanish, and she said she felt they resented having to deal with her because of the communication problem. Out of resentment or simply neglect, they often brought her meals that she could not eat. When she complained, the nurses would act as if they did not understand, so she usually went hungry. She talked about how frustrated and angry this made her. However, for her, the worst aspect was the degree to which she felt disrespected and disregarded as a human being. Her frustration stemmed from the knowledge that she was powerless to do anything about it.

Some of the women mentioned similar feelings of frustration and powerlessness when it came to monitoring the progress of their children's education. All of the first-generation women with school-age children said they were very concerned about staying abreast of their children's progress in school. When asked if they went to parent-teacher conferences and other school events, most said yes but complained that it was difficult to communicate with their children's teachers, most of whom did not speak Spanish. The schools generally provided translators for these events, but in most cases there was only one, who, of course, was in great demand. As a result, in many cases parents went to the events but did not have the opportunity to have substantive conversations about their children.

An example of language issues as a source of discrimination in the job market is the story told by Marta. She had been taking English classes for a number of years and felt fairly confident about her progress. Until then, all of her jobs had been house cleaning or factory work. But because she had improved her language skills, she felt confident enough to inquire about a position in an office in downtown Los Angeles. She would be doing mostly clerical work, with little interaction with outside clients, and she felt she had all the qualifications listed in the job description. When she arrived at the office, she said, the boss took one look at her and said to the receptionist in English, "Tell her we don't need anyone anymore." Marta asked why they would not consider her, and the receptionist replied, "We need someone with more English." Marta answered, "How do you know about my English [skills] if you haven't asked me any questions?" But the receptionist would not allow her to apply, so Marta left. She ended up taking a job caring for an elderly Anglo man, which does not pay very well and has long hours, but she needed employment, and that was her only option.

When she told this story, Marta was near tears and very upset. When asked how the experience made her feel, she said:

> Well, I felt, I felt as if they were turning me into something that had no value. I felt sad because I think if I am a person that is looking for work, I am looking for an honorable way to survive, because of the necessity a person has—you have to work to survive. And where there is discrimination, well one feels sad, you feel as if they think that you as a person are not worth very much. And I think that if you are look- ing for a decent job, you are worth something, no? If you look for a decent job, no one is worth less than anyone else, because everyone that looks for an honorable way to make their living deserves their respect, at a minimum.

Rosa, a first-generation Mexican, summed up a number of respondents' feelings about how language limitations lead to discrimination in their lives:

> Yes, when we got to the schools, when we go to our jobs, when we go—whatever service we are trying to obtain, if it is a person that does not speak Spanish. And, the people who speak Spanish, many times they [know how to] speak Spanish but they don't want to speak Spanish [to us]. That is discrimination.

These women's descriptions show that experiences of stigma affect more than their access to services; they have powerful psychological effects as well, decreasing their self-esteem and making them question their role and value in this country.

The general feelings of insecurity, frustration, and powerlessness that these first-generation women expressed are not surprising considering the fact that they are living in an English-speaking society. What is sur- prising is the frequency with which these negative experiences were the result of their interaction with other Latinos, not Anglos. Roberto, a sec- ond-generation Salvadoran, reported that this happens in Montebello:

> I see problems with immigrants. I remember when I was in inter- mediate [middle school]. I would see kids that have Mexican parents, they were Mexican American. There was one who had just come from

Mexico, and they would look at him like, oh, they'd look down on him. And why? You're both Mexican. Either way you both have Mexican blood. I don't see why you should do that.

Forty-year-old-Mercedes, a first-generation Mexican, told a similar story regarding how she was treated in an East Los Angeles junior high school after she first arrived in this country:

> And, I go to junior high and it was the worst experience of my life, everybody called me, because I didn't speak English, everybody called me, us, well, at that time I had two friends, we were together because we couldn't speak English, and people born from here, or speak English, they called us Mexicans, TJs, and other things.

> *Were they Americans or Mexicans who called you that?*

> No, no white people because there's no white people here then, same as now. Same people, if they're not Mexican, their parents are Mexican.

> *How did that make you feel?*

> Um, I don't know, I felt terrible because I wanted to learn English, but I couldn't, I couldn't because people laughed at me and the other girls. One time I had to fight with one of the girls because the things they said just made me explode, so I had to, I fight with one of them. I don't know. I dropped out, I couldn't go to school. I finished ninth grade, but I couldn't go to school here, it was too much.

> *Did that surprise you?*

> Yes, I didn't expect that, because they are your own race, what makes them say those things? I don't know, because they feel superior because they know English, I don't know.

Both Roberto and Mercedes described schools in which Latino students are divided according to whether they are foreign or native born. Mercedes's experience was so extreme that she dropped out of school and did not return until more than twenty years later, after she had had her children. She said the experience had a very negative effect on her self-esteem and that as a result for years she was afraid to express herself verbally in public. Had she had a positive experience in that school, her life and subsequent socioeconomic status may have been very different.

A number of studies have examined the historically conflictual relationship between immigrant and native-born Mexicans in the United States.[31] David Gutiérrez argues that historically relations between Mexican immigrants and Mexican Americans have been a reflection of a deeper debate about the evolution of Mexican Americans' sense of cultural and ethnic identity.[32] Martha Menchaca sees this intragroup conflict as the result of Anglo discrimination and a movement toward greater acculturation among the native born.[33] Gilda Ochoa finds similar conflict between native-born and immigrant Mexicans in La Puente, California, a community near both areas in this study.[34] So the identification of intergenerational conflict among Latinos is not new. What is new is the understanding of the role that language issues play in this process. Because laguage is integral to Latino collective identity, that that language is stigmatized means it negatively affects how group members see that language and those who use that language exclusively. As a result, whether or not a person spoke English, or spoke English with an accent, was very important to these respondents, and was the reason why many of the first-generation felt they were treated badly at work and in the community.

For example, in his description of his experiences at work, Carlos, a first-generation Mexican, talked about the effect speaking accented English has on how he is treated and how it relates to broader problems of self-esteem and self-hatred among native-born Latinos:

Yeah, for example, I have my work here, I have the accent of a Spanish person. I know I can change that with the time, with my work, but right now I really don't know if I want to, because I love my country. If I have the accent of Hispanic people, I know the people talking about me, the Anglo-Saxon when they hear the accent they think that we're stupid, because, for example, I worked in a cleaning room, at first I only knew about grammar; I didn't know how to talk, how to improve my language. There I was trying to make *animo* [be industrious], only cleaning, only like a bus boy. [What] I don't want is that the people think about me like I was less, you know what I mean? Right now I'm working in a market. When I start to talk to customers in Spanish, I can feel the people thinking about me, because they think that I am taking something from them, maybe their work, I don't know. But I think I'm working hard. I have the right to do it. If I am intelligent, I have the right to study.

Do you think Anglos feel that way?

Basically, Spanish people treat me that way. The Anglo-Saxon, most of them are very sympathetic with me. They like me. But Hispanic people, my brother, it's like, most of the time they don't have culture [education]; they see [in me] what they don't like inside of them. They don't like Hispanic people because they're Hispanic people. I am sad about that because I never felt that in my country, but [when] I come here was the first time I felt that.

Here we see the process of shifting boundaries in the first generation. Before Carlos arrived in the United States, he expected to feel connection and solidarity with people of Mexican origin living here. Instead, he feels he is singled out as an immigrant and looked down on by other Latinos because of his inability to speak unaccented English. He feels that other Latinos treat him badly because they have a negative view of their own racial group. The end result is that he feels defensive about and saddened by his position and treatment in the United States. His definition of his own group identity has been changed by this experience.

As we saw earlier in Marta's story about being turned away from a job, immigrants' negative experiences have psychological as well as economic costs. Their feeling of not being able to "defend" themselves stemmed from problems with language and a general lack of understanding of the laws and norms of U.S. society. Many respondents talked about how the lack of knowledge engendered fear. As Marta put it, "We are easily frightened by any little thing, because we are not familiar with many laws." This fear affects their confidence in their ability to make informed and accurate political choices. The first-generation respondents were more likely than those from the other generations to express uncertainty about their ability to "know" anything about politics. This was especially true among the first-generation women. They would repeatedly preface their comments with statements such as "I'm not certain

how things work here, but . . ." or "I know I don't know much, but . . ."
These feelings of insecurity were augmented by their lack of faith in the
Spanish-language media. Many said they felt that Spanish-language television did not provide as much information as English-language television. When asked about political issues, many said that to be well informed, they had to listen to the English-language news.

These feelings of isolation and uncertainty in the first generation affect
not only them but also their family structure and the socialization of the
second generation. Studies have shown that in many immigrant families,
because the parents do not speak English, often it is up to the eldest child
to act as the family's interpreter. It is the child who interacts with public
institutions. This alters family power dynamics: the child ends up being
the authority and the party responsible for taking care of family concerns,
and this decreases the parents' control over the child.[35]

These parent-child dynamics were present in this sample. Bernie is a
good example. He is a nineteen-year-old second-generation Mexican from
East Los Angeles and the eldest child in his family. Although he attended
high school for four years, he did not graduate with his peers because of
his frequent truancy. His mother did not find out about his truancy until
he did not graduate with his class. In his interview, he explained how this
happened. Because his mother cannot read English, it has always been his
responsibility to read the mail and tell her what it says. When letters from
his school about his absences arrived, he either did not show them to her
or lied about the contents. To prevent her from speaking directly with his
teachers, he did not inform her about parent-teacher conferences but told
her that they were no longer held at the high school level in the United
States. Because he was the first of her children to attend high school in the
United States, his mother believed him. She said that her other children
will not fool her, and Bernie feels guilty about lying to her. His role as family interpreter gave him the power to act as a mediator between his
mother and his school and to control what information each had about the
other. In cases like these, language limits first-generation parents' ability
to maintain their authority over and to keep track of their children.

The second generation is also aware of the negative stigma attached to
speaking only Spanish. Ana, whose family came from Mexico, describes

the difficulties her mother has had finding jobs and the bad treatment she receives because of language issues:

> When they see her they assume that she's illegal or something, you know, and that she just speaks Spanish and stuff, you know. And the thing is, my mom, she understands, but she won't say anything, because that's the kind of person she is. It makes me angry when they make her feel bad, *esa gente desgraciada* [those nasty people]. . . .
> That's why she wants to take English classes and stuff. She wants to prove, not only to herself but also to other people, you know, like she may be from Mexico and stuff, but she has a brain.

Araceli, a 1.5-generation Mexican, spoke of similar experiences of people calling immigrant Latinos "wetback" and saying "they're stupid." "And they would laugh, you know, [at] people that don't know how to talk English right." Clearly, speaking English is associated with intelligence, and speaking only Spanish with a lack of intelligence. Those messages are understood very clearly by the second generation.

Because of the overall feelings of powerlessness that the first-generation respondents associated with not being proficient in English, they all felt very strongly that their children should learn English well and as quickly as possible.[36] Many of them saw it as a way to protect their children and keep them from having to experience the discrimination and hostility that they faced. But many also pointed out the contradictory behavior that they believe is the result of this emphasis on English. A number of the first-generation respondents said they felt that first-generation parents' insistence that their children speak English was one of the reasons many of the native born are unwilling to assist immigrants by speaking Spanish. They felt the parents' focus on English makes their children embarrassed to speak Spanish and, by extension, embarrassed about having a Latino background. For example, Marta explained:

> [They do not speak Spanish] because it embarrasses them to speak Spanish. They think that Spanish is something that, I don't know what they think. Even the children, my nephews now do not want to speak Spanish. . . . I don't know, I don't know [where it comes from]. Perhaps

from ourselves, from the parents, who begin, who begin to speak English to their children because, I don't know, because it is difficult, and maybe because they had problems here and they do not want their children to have to go through that. And they give their children the idea that they have to know English, English, so that they won't discriminate against them too.

The first-generation respondents generally agreed that refusing to speak Spanish was a negative development because they saw it as a sign of the native born denying their own heritage. Carlos also saw it as a natural outcome of teenage rebellion but felt that among Latinos it has broader consequences:

Their fathers, most of their fathers, their parents are Latinos. So, when a teenager is growing up, their parents, their thing is to fight against them. So, I think so. Their parents talk with accents, so they don't like it. They like to feel like, like they're from here . . . they're embarrassed of their parents. They want to be like Anglo Saxons. . . . They want to feel, they don't want Mexico, El Salvador. They don't want Honduras. They want U.S.A. And I think they need to find themselves. I don't know if you understand me.

The first-generation respondents also saw embarrassment about being Latino as the underlying reason for the native born treating immigrants badly. Rosa reported:

I don't know [why they don't speak Spanish]. It is because of the same thing, because of culture. Because they don't have that ethic, because they are not familiar with their culture. Because they are a Latino person and they are embarrassed to be Latino. Because they are embarrassed of their language then that person cannot [speak it]. They know how to speak perfectly, but they want to be Americans. So, they, our own people are the ones that create obstacles for us. And if we, ourselves, discriminate against ourselves, I don't see why the white people are not going to do it.

The first generation's experiences with Spanish monolingualism and their conflicts with the native born reflect the difficulty that stigmatized groups have developing a positive attachment to their social group.

Linguistic studies have found that language is critical to the construction of "shared meanings."[37] But what happens when group members do not share the same language? How do they construct shared meanings? Studies show that Latinos are likely to become English monolingual by the third generation.[38] Sociolinguists have found that groups can maintain group identification after language shift, but they say little about how that process relates to questions of stigma.[39] In these interactions between the first-generation and native-born respondents, I believe, we are seeing the complex processes that Latinos, as a stigmatized group, must go through in order to develop a positive collective identity. They know that their language is stigmatized, as is their group. At the same time, Spanish language is a strong marker of Latino culture and history. Thus language is both positive and negative. The result is that the native born have conflicted attitudes toward Spanish monolingualism and, by extension, immigrant Latinos.

SPANISH, ENGLISH, AND LATINO GROUP IDENTITY

It is inaccurate to take from this discussion the idea that Spanish-language maintenance has a universally negative connotation in the Latino community. In fact, the opposite is the case. As María put it:

> Yes it is important that they always maintain their language, whether they come from another country or are born here. It is important because we will always have our roots there, and one day we go and the child cannot speak with his grandmother, or with anyone. That is not correct, no? He can carry the two languages, and any other languages he can learn. If he learns all the languages, that is not a sin. That he forget our language, that is a sin.

A number of respondents from East Los Angeles said they thought it was ridiculous when a Latino "has a *nopal* [cactus] on their forehead," in other words, looks very Indian, and yet does not know how to speak Spanish. Here I examine how language relates to Latino racial identification and find that it is an important symbol delineating how these Latinos identify themselves and their racial group.

Racial identification was strong among the respondents, even those of the second and third-plus generations. Only one of the respondents, a third-plus-generation Montebello woman, defined herself simply as "American." The other ninety-nine respondents preferred to use a racial identifier. Among the first generation, the most favored term was *Mexicana/o* for the Mexicans or *Latina/o* for those of other national origins. Interestingly, none of the first-generation Central Americans used their country of origin as an identifier; instead they preferred the pan-ethnic term *Latino*. Among the second and third-plus generation, the most favored term was *Mexican American,* followed in order of preference by *Hispanic, Latino, Mexicana/o,* and *Chicano*. Milton Gordon argues that assimilation requires "the disappearance of the ethnic group as a separate entity and the evaporation of its distinctive values."[40] According to that definition, these respondents are not assimilated, even in the third-plus generation. At the very least, this suggests that ethnic identity retains significant salience in this community across generations, as has been found among second-generation youth in California and Florida.[41]

After being asked how they identify themselves, many of the respondents voiced their thought processes. "Well," they would say, "Mexicans are from Mexico, and even though my parents (or grandparents) were from Mexico, I was born here so I guess that makes me _____." The most common answers filling this blank were "Mexican American" or "Hispanic." The second- and third-plus-generation respondents said they preferred those terms because they felt they described their experience of being of Mexican origin but not actually from Mexico. It is important to point out that their definition of *Hispanic* in most cases was not how it is defined by the Census Bureau and other U.S. institutions—that is, Mexican immigrants generally were not included in their definitions. In these answers, they were struggling to find a term that described the experience of being born in the United States but being from somewhere else culturally. They were very clear about not seeing themselves as purely "American" or "Mexican" but as something else. This is the experience that is supposed to be captured by the word *Chicano,* but only seven of the respondents chose to identify themselves with that term.[42]

When asked what made a person fit into the category that the respondent had used to identify herself or himself, the most common answer was the degree to which the person spoke Spanish. The connection between language use and identification varied across the generations, in a way that reflected their linguistic acculturation. Among all the generations, the most common reasons given for why people could be defined as "Latino" were Mexican or Latin American origin and the use of Spanish.[43] How they talked about Spanish, however, changed as they became more linguistically acculturated. The first generation tended to define "Latinos" as people who speak Spanish. A few also defined "Americans" as those who speak only English. The second generation defined "Latinos" as those who speak Spanish and English. This in part reflects their general desire to find a term that described their bicultural and bilingual experience in the United States. The third-plus generation was more likely to define *Latino* as meaning "of Mexican descent," rarely making direct reference to language ability. This could be due in part to the fact that all except for one of these respondents had a strong racial identity, but the majority of them did not consider themselves fluent in Spanish. This was especially true of the respondents from Montebello. As has been found in other studies, these Latinos' collective identity and language are related, and the respondents adjusted their definitions of their group identity to coincide with their own levels of linguistic acculturation.[44]

The story of Zali, a seventeen- year-old, fourth-generation Mexican, touches on many of the issues relating to Spanish language and its relationship to Latino racial identity. Zali's mother's family was originally from Texas and had lived there since before it became part of the United States. I have categorized Zali's generational status based on her mother, who is third generation, because she was raised by her mother alone and has had almost no contact with her father since she was a toddler. Her mother learned very little Spanish while growing up in East Los Angeles. Zali said this was because when her grandmother was younger "they would hit them and stuff when they spoke Spanish in schools, so she didn't teach her kids how to speak Spanish." When her mother went to college in the late 1960s, she got involved in the Chicano Movement. This led her to want to get in touch with her culture, so she moved to Mexico City to teach English and improve her Spanish. While in Mexico, she met

Zali's father, got married, and had two children. Shortly thereafter, she decided to leave her husband. Afraid of how she would be treated under Mexican law, she returned to East Los Angeles to become a schoolteacher and raise her children on her own. Zali spoke Spanish until she was three and since then has spoken only English, "because," she said, "my mom's natural language is English. She wanted us to have a good vocabulary. She wanted us to speak correctly instead of having what they call Spanglish. She didn't want that."

Zali said that not speaking Spanish was a problem for her because it meant that she could not communicate with her father when he called. But by far the larger issue for her was how it embarrassed her in her neighborhood:

> I feel somewhat, like, shunned in a way. Yeah, shunned by everyone, you know. Like they call me a "whitesican," and I get so angry! Yeah, they call me a whitesican, and it's horrible sometimes, when I was growing up. Now I understand, you know, that they're just joking and it's more like a pet name, you know, but it hurt when I was growing up. It made me feel like I was missing something—like I didn't fit in because I was born in Mexico and didn't know the culture of Mexico. I felt like kind of, duh, what am I doing, you know? Like, you know how they would say, um, in elementary school, just to like show that people are— well, I don't know why my teacher did this. She said if your name starts with a Z, if your name starts with an L, you go over there. And if you're born in East L.A., and I would be like the only one, or one of the few standing that I wasn't born in East L.A. And then you had to say where were you born, you know, so they could get information about you. And it's like, okay, I was born in Mexico. I couldn't even say Guerrero [the state in Mexico where she was born]. I still can't say it [laughs]. And I couldn't even say where I was from, and it was kind of hard.

Zali felt bad about not speaking Spanish but also, paradoxically, was separated out from her classmates because she was not born in the United States. She was different because she could not speak Spanish and also because she was born in Mexico.

Similarly, a number of the English monolingual third-plus-generation respondents said that not speaking Spanish in their neighborhoods caused problems. Emma, a thirty-eight-year-old, fourth-generation woman from Montebello, enrolled her son in a Spanish class because she thinks it is important to know "what people are saying about you." She recounted a story of a woman calling her names in Spanish and said she was upset because she did not understand the words. Emma heard the woman call her a *pocha,* which she interpreted as meaning "a white person." In Spanish, it actually means a Mexican who does not know Spanish or is removed from Mexican culture. Similarly, Desiré, a twenty-two-year-old woman from Montebello, said:

> I get a lot of criticisms about that, [people say,] "You're Mexican and you don't speak Spanish?" I just tell them, I'm not Mexican, I'm an American. I don't need to speak Spanish. That's always been, kinda my excuse for not speaking Spanish—I was born here, why should I speak Spanish? You should learn English. . . . Why should I learn another language if the main language here is English?

Desiré was the only respondent who defined herself as "American." In this discussion, she clearly felt a need to defend the fact that she did not speak Spanish and to have an "excuse." Her definition of herself as an American seems to be related to her inability to speak Spanish and again shows how language and identity are related among Latinos.

Mary, a fifty-two-year-old, fifth-generation generation woman from Montebello, felt she received bad treatment because she does not speak Spanish. She said, "Some people think I'm snobby because I don't speak Spanish." She also felt it had affected her job prospects:

> People think I'm doing it [not speaking Spanish] because I don't want to, or [that] I understand it, and I read it, and I've lost a lot of jobs because of that. I haven't worked for four years. And, "Oh, you're bilingual," they just look at me [and assume], "Oh, you're bilingual you speak Spanish, you're gonna get this." "And you don't? Your own language and you don't know?" And I never have [spoken Spanish], never. So it has been a problem that way. My own in-laws I can't [communicate with], all I can say is, like hello, because the mother only speaks Spanish and the father does too, but they understand a little bit, but not enough to [really talk]. But if I tell them something they'll understand. I mean, it makes it very difficult.

The above responses reveal the two sides of these Latinos' relationship to the Spanish language. On the one hand, knowing only Spanish causes negative experiences for immigrants; on the other, not knowing Spanish can be a disadvantage for the native born. This is another example of how Latinos struggle to feel positive about themselves and their group. Their collective identification is intimately related to their language, so it becomes problematic for some when they lose their connection to that language. Living in areas where they come into regular contact with immigrants who outsiders define as part of their racial group and yet who, at least from a linguistic standpoint, seem so different from them further complicates how they understand and experience their own group identity.

·

STEREOTYPES, IDENTITY, AND GROUP COHESION

Latinos' relationship to the Spanish language is problematic largely because of the positive value attributed to English-language use, the resulting negative value attributed to Spanish-language use, and the stereotypes associated with both.[45] Bilingualism and monolingualism would be less of an issue in the community if they did not have such important effects on Latino identity, socioeconomic mobility, and life chances. Carlos summed up this relationship when he said, "[Proposition 187] separated us, the Hispanic people. You're Hispanic, I'm Hispanic. If I hear you talking English with an American accent, different from me, I hate you. Why? Because you have things that I don't have." The result is that many of the native-born respondents are attempting to distance themselves from Latino immigrants.

This reaction to social stigma may be a product of the social and political context in California at the time. Studies of stigma have shown that its effects are "powerful, but context-dependent."[46] The political climate in California at the time of the interviews was especially anti-immigrant. Both Proposition 187 and the debates over the 1996 welfare reform explicitly framed immigrants as a "problem" group. It is likely that this context brought to light cleavages that already existed among Latinos but were exacerbated by the rhetoric surrounding these campaigns. This demonstrates that stigmatizing messages can affect cohesion within subordinate groups. The Latinos' negative attitudes toward immigrants reflect expressions of power not only between the dominant culture and Latinos but also within the Latino group itself.[47] The respondents believed Anglos stereotyped Latinos as gang members and "wetbacks." Yet none of the current or former gang members in the sample reported negative experiences with group members, other than their immediate family, for their gang membership. The difference in treatment between gang members and immigrants is logical—fear. A native-born Latino can criticize an immigrant for his or her lack of English skills with few repercussions. But criticizing a gang member could lead to personal harm. Those negatively associated group members with the least power are the most likely to experience negative treatment as a result of their lower status relative to other group members. Similar to Cathy Cohen's finding of multiple marginalities within African American communities, here forces of hierarchy and power operate in important ways within groups as well as between them.[48]

Before discussing the respondents' perceptions of Latino stereotypes, I want to stress that these communities are geographically and socially segregated. Only two of the respondents, whom I discuss at more length in chapter 4, had significant primary-level interactions with non-Mexicans. The remaining ninety-eight respondents lived, worked, and shopped in a Latino-majority world. Though at Montebello High School there were a few Anglo, African American, and Asian American students, the respondents repeatedly emphasized that socially each group remained essentially separate. The members of different races may have been acquaintances, but few people had close friends of another race.[49] Despite their lack of contact with non-Mexicans, the answers the respondents gave regarding the kinds of images they felt Anglos had of Latinos were remarkably consistent. From the first-generation homemaker and mother of six to the fourth-generation gang member, their answers were strikingly similar. This shows the degree to which members of racialized groups are aware of the negative images attributed to their group, even when they have little direct interaction with members of the dominant culture.

When asked if they felt Anglos had a negative image of Latinos, only three respondents said they did not. By far the most commonly reported negative image was that Latinos are seen as gang members. Second was the image of Latinos as wetbacks or illegal aliens. The respondents expressed the general feeling that Anglos saw Latinos as uneducated, dirty, lazy, and stupid. These perceptions were consistent across genders, areas, and generations. The one generational difference regarding perceptions was that the first-generation respondents were more likely than the second and third-plus generation to say that Anglos' negative image was one of Latinos taking advantage of welfare. Again, this is most likely the result of the fact that the 1996 welfare reform bill was being debated at the time of the interviews and that Proposition 187 recently had been passed. Both laws were promoted based on the argument that immigrants, both legal and illegal, were taking advantage of the welfare system and that the abuse had to be controlled. It is understandable that the first-generation respondents would be especially sensitive to these charges.

The second- and third-plus-generation respondents were more likely than first-generation respondents to say that the most common negative image of Latinos was of *cholos,* gang members or criminals. Their focus on the "gangster" image could be due to their relative youth and their perception of how they are portrayed in the mass media. The second- and third-plus-generation respondents were generally younger than those in the first generation. Recent studies have shown that African American and Latino youth see themselves portrayed negatively in the media. A poll by Children Now of 1,200 Euro-American, black, Asian, and Latino youths age ten to seventeen found that children of all races agreed that television news portrayed blacks and Latinos, especially young people, more negatively than other groups.[50] Similarly, in their study of KABC news coverage in Los Angeles, Frank Gilliam and colleagues found that in stories about crime, even when the race of the suspect was not identified, viewers remembered seeing a black suspect. They found that 90 percent of the false recognitions on the part of viewers involved African Americans or Latinos.[51] These perceptions of the representation of Latino youth in the news media were also present in this sample. The second- and third-generation youth were especially concerned with news coverage that portrayed only Latinos as gang members, and they reported feeling that those images negatively affected how they were treated by the larger society.

This is probably why the second- and third-plus-generation respondents were more likely than the first generation to see stereotyping as the most damaging form of discrimination Latinos faced. They felt these negative stereotypes caused Anglos to judge them by sight. Ana's feelings about this were typical:

> [I want people to know j]ust that we're not all bad. But, there's like good in everyone, you know. Even the so-called troublemakers or whatever, they're doing it for a reason. Just, maybe something's not right at home, or something, like, they're really nice inside. People just expect them to be bad, and they think, "Oh well, I'm expected to do this, so I'm just gonna go ahead and do it," you know. Everyone expects them to be a troublemaker, so it's just assumed you go do it. Even like teachers or something, you dress a certain way and they just automatically assume oh, you're bad. And it's like the first impression, I hate that. First impressions are what people think of you. I hate that.

Norma, a second-generation Mexican-Salvadoran, echoed Ana's feelings when expressing concern that people made assumptions about her based on the clothes she was wearing:

> Well, I went to Magic Mountain [an amusement park] with my friend. They were dressed like, you know, all teenagers they dress like gangsters but they're not. Um, we went and then some security, they tell us to take off our jackets and they were like searching us and my friend had Mi Vida Loca [the name of a chola gang] and they told her why did she have that if she's not from there.[52] And she goes she just likes that, she likes tattoos. And they were telling us that they were, like if we did something wrong that they were gonna kick us out of the park, just because we were dressed like, you know . . . I don't know. I think that's wrong, because they, they don't know [anything about us], they did that because of the outside, because of what we were wearing, you know. That's not right.

In addition to reporting having been followed in stores or searched when entering amusement parks, a number of respondents complained about bad experiences they had had with police. Interestingly, none of the respondents mentioned these experiences when asked if they had ever experienced "discrimination." Rather, they came up in other parts of the conversation. The respondents from East Los Angeles in particular tended to discuss these events as a regular part of their day-to-day lives. Here are some examples:

> We were standing around like at my friend's house, and he [the police officer] was like, you look familiar, and I had never seen him before. They stopped and searched us, and they didn't find anything, so they just left. (Abraham, second-generation Mexican)

> Yeah, just walking down the street, they [the police] will ask what are you doing? Outside my house. I was outside with a friend and he's like, the cop was like, well what are you doing out here? And I'm all I'm just here, talking, and he's like why? And I was like do you have a right to be questioning me? Am I doing something wrong? Because, just let me know, and then I'll answer you. And he was like, oh, well, we're just checking and he drove off. But I was like, God, I can't believe it! . . . I was mad! I can't believe that! Outside my house, I was just sitting there with a friend, my friend's bald, so the cop was like, do you know her?[53] Like he was harassing or bothering me. And then he starts questioning me, like, what are you doing? And I was like, you don't have a right to do this, I know you don't. (Araceli, second-generation Mexican)

These respondents' answers were consistent in that they all felt strongly that their outward appearance dictated how persons of authority— whether teachers, security guards, or police— treated them.

The respondents from both Montebello and East Los Angeles agreed that these kinds of experiences were more likely to occur if they left their Latino neighborhoods and ventured into a "white" area. Many of the negative experiences the respondents mentioned had happened in places such as Seal Beach, Thousand Oaks, and Diamond Bar, which are relatively affluent, majority Anglo cities. Richard, a third-generation Mexican, offered a typical experience:

> I have a girlfriend that lives out in Thousand Oaks, and there's nothing there but Americans, there's like no Mexicans at all. So I mean, I'm used to it, so it doesn't bother me anymore. I mean, they just look at me in a bad way, they just stare, you know. But it doesn't bother me at all.

Why do you think they stare?

Because there are no Hispanics there, you know, so it's like shocking to them seeing me. Because it's not like here. Out there there's like a lot of American people, you know, in Thousand Oaks.

Do you think Hispanics in places like that get discriminated against?

I pretty much think so, because it's all like one kind over there.

Arturo, a first-generation Mexican, spoke of a similar experience when he visited Diamond Bar:

Like this weekend I went to Diamond Bar, went to see my friend there. Have you ever been to Diamond Bar? It's pretty white. So we walk into Denny's to use the restroom. We knew people were talking about us. . . . When we walked in, they didn't say nothing. But when we were walking into the restroom, they were just looking at us. We walk in, not a word, they [all] stopped talking. We came out and they were just looking at us. They were talking about us.

Jesús, a second-generation Mexican, had problems during a college visit:

We went to some trip and there were a lot of white people there. It was a trip to college. And, like, they just like, look at you, and they're like, "Oh, what are you doing up here?" You know? Like, it was, you could say a white neighborhood, and they were like looking down at you, like, trash, or whatever. And they told us, you know, there were a couple that said stuff to us. They like, they feel, they don't want to be around you. That's how it is.

Like many respondents, Richard explicitly said that discrimination is not a problem in his area because "most people in here are Mexican, so it's all the same." It is only when you leave that Mexican area that you risk being treated badly.

All respondents were aware of living in an environment of racial threat. In addition to general reports of native-born Latinos being harassed regarding their migration status, one of the more disturbing stories that came out of the interviews was that of a group of white skinheads severely beating a Mexican youth in "old town" Whittier.[54] A few of the respondents, from both areas, mentioned the story. They reported that the skinheads literally had begun to peel the skin from his body before being stopped by police. I have not been able to confirm that this event took place. But for the respondents who shared the story with me, whether or not it actually occurred was less important than the fact that the overall racial environment in Los Angeles at the time was such that they believed it easily could be true. They said that at the very least it would make them think twice before going to old town Whittier.

These kinds of stories help to explain why most of the respondents rarely left the general vicinity in which they grew up. The majority reported only rarely going to the beach, the mountains, or any city outside a ten-mile radius from where they lived. In that context, Linda's frustration makes complete sense:

> Every time I go to places like that, [white neigborhoods] right away like we'd get into trouble. It makes me like, you know how they say we're not supposed to think about color. But they're doing that—they're only looking at the outside, how we look, but they don't even know the inside.
>
> *How do you think they could get to know the inside?*
>
> By not giving into conclusions, you know, right away thinking stuff about us.
>
> *Have you had people say something to you, or is it just a feeling?*
>
> Yeah, it's a feeling like, the look on their face, you know, is bad.

Fear of racial animosity goes a long way toward explaining why Montebello and East Los Angeles remain highly segregated and insular: it is generally understood that you will be treated better if you remain with people like yourself. This is very similar to what Menchaca found in her study of Santa Paula, California. Though segregation is no longer legally enforced, it has been replaced by what she calls "social apartness."[55] Mexican Americans in the "Mexican" area understand that they will not be well received if they venture into the Anglo area, and so they simply choose not to.

It makes sense that this conflict with the "outside" world happens in the second and third-plus generations. In addition to often acting as the bridge between their parents and the larger U.S. society, second-generation children are likely to be the first to leave the ethnic enclave and move into employment with Anglos. In the Los Angeles labor market, socioeconomic mobility generally means moving into industries where the dominant language is English and the dominant racial group is Anglo. Immigrants and less educated racial minorities generally have been relegated to the informal economy or low-skill, low-paying jobs.[56] Thus it is the upwardly mobile second- and third-plus generation that are more likely to feel affected by how Anglos stereotype Mexicans. And they are the ones that feel compelled to counteract these stereotypes. In many cases, it is the need to counteract stereotypes that leads them to treat first-generation Latinos badly.

Social identity theorists contend that group members will either deny or embrace their ethnic identity. Among the respondents, there is a desire to establish a positive social identity for themselves, but they are not employing either of these two options. Instead, they are engaging in a process of what I call selective dissociation; that is, they are maintaining their identification with their racial group, but instead of dissociating with the entire group, they are excluding from their definitions of their identity those who they see as perpetuating a negative image. It is possible that the respondents, because of the racialized environment and their residence in majority-Latino areas, find complete dissociation difficult. Instead, they were maintaining their racial identity but defining that identity in such as way as to exclude those behaviors, especially in terms of language use, that they consider undesirable and detrimental to the group's collective image. Though gang activity was defined as the most common stereotype applied to Latinos, the respondents often were willing to give gang members the benefit of the doubt. Many saw them as "lost" or as victims of circumstance. That was not the attitude expressed about immigrants. The native-born respondents often saw the problems immigrants faced as "their own fault" and felt strongly that they knew how "they," meaning Mexican immigrants, should act.

A good example is Mary, the fifth-generation woman from Montebello who does not know Spanish. She reported feeling embarrassed when she was unable to offer help to Latino immigrants who spoke only Spanish. But then she said, "They're the ones that oughta learn, so they don't let anybody push them around, 'cause I've seen too much of that. And I say here I am, and I can't help them." She continued:

> I don't know, they should learn. I mean, that's all there is to it. For me, I don't think it's as important for me, because I'm here and I speak English, but it's not as important for me to speak Spanish as it is for them to speak English because they're here. I think they should learn, that way, I don't know, so that they don't have to ask people and think maybe they'll be getting wrong answers. 'Cause I've seen it! And it makes me really angry because, I go, "That's not true!" But how am I gonna tell them the truth when I can't tell them myself?

Mary's feelings about immigrants and language reveal the contradictions surrounding Spanish and bilingualism. On the one hand, she feels guilty for not being able to speak Spanish or provide assistance but then says the problem is theirs, not hers. In our conversation she was very hostile about the times she has felt "un-Mexican" for not speaking Spanish. She told the story of going to buy Mexican bread and being ridiculed by the woman behind the counter when she mispronounced the name of the bread in Spanish. In a near-shout, Mary said her response was, "I says don't laugh at me, I go, you're the one who doesn't even know how to speak English, okay? I'm the one that should be laughing at you, because you don't even know how to speak English!"

Cassandra, a third-generation Mexican who was raised in Montebello and now lives in East Los Angeles, also talked about having problems in her neighborhood because she did not know Spanish:

> I just wish some of these people would learn English! 'Cause I know it would be great to learn Spanish too, and it'd be great to learn Japanese and what other languages—to do that would be fun. But, I think, and it is a requirement, it is a requirement to become a United States citizen to learn the language. And there's a lot of people that come here that aren't legal, so they don't learn it, you know, and they go to an area where they know that they don't have to learn it because it's majority Spanish-speaking and that's where I live. And it bothers me, because I think it

would be good for them to learn English. It would be better for every-body to be able to communicate better in that way. So sometimes when I'm at a store and I don't have somebody that's gonna translate for me, I get frustrated. Because I don't know how to speak and they don't know how to speak English and it's just like, "Oh God!" So, it bothers me a little bit.

Cassandra made a number of interesting points. Her definition of U.S. cit-izenship as related to language recalls the connection between the English language and American national identity. She makes the assumption that those immigrants who do not speak English are undocumented, which indicates the internalization of one of the stereotypes the respondents mentioned, that of non-English-speaking Latino immigrants as wetbacks or illegal aliens. Here she is assuming that language skills have a direct relationship to migration status and that most of the immigrants in her neighborhood are therefore illegal and a problem. Ironically, her frustration about needing a translator in a store echoes the problems mentioned ear-lier by the first-generation women when visiting their children's schools.

Both Mary and Cassandra are concerned that immigrants are taken advantage of, but in essence they think the blame rests with the immi-grants for "refusing" to learn English. Because they see that decision as a conscious choice and one that immigrants have control over, they feel that in some ways immigrants are "asking" to be treated badly. This high-lights the difference between "visible" and "controllable" sources of stigma.[57] Visible stigma is caused by characteristics outside the person's control—race, gender, disability, and so on. Controllable stigma is based on something the person's behavior could change. Studies have shown that the tendency is for individuals to treat more harshly, and with sev-erer social penalties, those who have traits defined as "controllable." In this instance, the native-born Latinos may be seeing Spanish monolin-gualism as a "controllable" trait and therefore treating those with this negative trait more harshly.

This is likely part of what is happening, but power and context also come into play. Both the images of undocumented immigrants and of gang members are considered a problem. Yet immigrants are seen as responsible for their own problems, whereas gang members' problems are attributed to societal structures. During the interviews, the concerns about immigrant behavior and prescriptions for how immigrants should "help themselves" often came after the respondents voiced frustration about the assumptions "Americans" made about "Mexicans" and discussed how those assumptions negatively affected their lives. According to their logic, if immigrants would just learn English and acculturate more rapidly, Anglos would not stereotype Latinos in this way, and that form of discrimination would disappear. Similar to what has been found among African Americans during the Great Migration, these Latinos feel they must "police" their own in order to construct a more positive identity for their group.[58]

In some ways, this is a reasonable assumption from the point of view of the respondents who rarely have any substantive contact with immigrants. They only see the result, which is they are regularly confronted with people with whom they cannot communicate, and with negative stereotypes that they cannot control. What they are less cognizant of is the structural constraints that make it difficult for Latino immigrants to learn English. The majority of Latino immigrants arrive in the United States with low levels of formal education.[59] This makes it difficult for them to sit in a classroom and learn in their native language, much less learn a new one. In addition, adult ESL courses have been oversubscribed since the mid-1970s in Los Angeles County, making it difficult for immigrants to get access to the courses they need. And finally, the fact that wages for low-skilled jobs are generally low and the cost of living in Los Angeles high means that many immigrants have to have more than one job to make ends meet. This limits the amount of time available for them to attend school. All these factors combine to keep Latino immigrants from having the time or the opportunity to learn English in a structured educational setting.

The respondents' assumptions about the propensity (or not) of Latino immigrants to learn English also could be the result of media coverage of the community. Victor Valle and Rodolfo Torres find that a common theme in news coverage of Latinos is Latino "foreignness" or Latinos as illegal aliens.[60] They also report that of four thousand news stories that covered women and minorities in 1992, only 1 percent focused on Latinos, and most of those representations were negative ones.[61] Otto Santa Ana also finds that the media coverage of Proposition 187 emphasized Latinos as foreigners "flooding" the United States and overwhelming state institutions and resources.[62] Non-Latinos are not the only ones affected by these images. In their discussions of stereotypes, most of the respondents said they felt that the negative images of Latinos came from how the media covered the community. Because many of the native-born respondents who expressed these concerns did not have regular interactions with the immigrant sectors of the community, the only images they had of Latino immigrants were those portrayed in the popular media. As a result, they are susceptible to believing those very stereotypes and, logically, feel upset when they are included in them. Their only recourse is to selectively dissociate themselves from those sectors of their group that they believe increase their social stigma.

This is an empirical representation of how discrimination can negatively affect a community and in some ways cause it to turn against parts of itself. The second- and third-plus-generation respondents were frustrated when they were judged by the color of their skin and their dress outside their home communities. These were not pleasant experiences, and in many cases the respondents expressed strong feelings of unhappiness about being judged before people got to know them and about being powerless to change how people react to them. In this situation, it is only natural to search for power where you can find it. In their communities, power comes from knowing English and understanding the U.S. system. Thus, native-born Latinos are attempting to use the limited power they have to change the behavior of the first generation, to make them "fit in" in the United States. By doing so, they are attempting to improve the image of the group with whom they identify. By policing those members of the community that are farthest from U.S. culture, they are hoping to improve their own image. But, unfortunately, those images are created by the mass media, outside of the group.[63] Thus, perceptions of stereotypes have created intergenerational hostility and conflict among Latinos, but that internal conflict does nothing to change or to decrease the detrimental effects of the stereotypes themselves.

Most popular discussions of the situation of racial and ethnic minorities in the United States define the effects of discrimination as concrete, measurable negative effects on a particular individual. For example, a person is denied a job, a promotion, or a real estate loan. It is generally assumed that once these overt expressions of discrimination disappear, the United States will have moved to being a free and fully equal society. This is the underlying rationale for maintaining data on affirmative action hiring practices and other empirical information that can "prove" or "disprove" the existence of discrimination in the United States.

Yet this sample shows another side to the discrimination equation, one that is more intangible but that nonetheless has serious psychological effects on individuals and groups—the effect of stigma and stereotypes on people's group identity(ies). This sample shows the ways in which dominant stereotypes of racial-ethnic groups are understood by members of that group even without the physical presence of the dominant group. Despite their geographic and social separation from Anglos, the respondents have a very clear and consistent understanding of the negative images Anglos have of them. Because of the permeation of mass media and other forms of communication, Anglo stereotypes of Mexicans can be present even when Anglos are not. The respondents' perceptions of these stereotypes in turn affect how they see themselves and other members of their racial group. Their desire to feel good about their group identity(ies) leads them to distance themselves from immigrant Latinos and results in a decrease in group solidarity and cohesion.

POLITICS AND INTRAGROUP CONFLICT

Other than affecting the development of collective identity among Latinos, how does the selective dissociation process affect politics? Intergenerational conflict is important not only because it has negative effects on Latino identity but also because of the effects it has on group political cohesion and the kinds of coalitions that develop around specific policy proposals. Three good examples are the degree to which Latinos in Montebello and East Los Angeles supported Proposition 187, the 1994

California ballot initiative to ban social services to illegal immigrants; Proposition 209, the 1996 ballot proposition to end affirmative action in state government hiring, contracting, and institutions of higher education; and Proposition 227, the 1998 ballot proposition to end bilingual education in California public schools.[64] Given the stated goals of these proposals, it is reasonable to argue that Propositions 187 and 227 were directed mainly at the immigrant population and that Proposition 209 could be seen as affecting all Latinos, including the native born. An examination of area voting on these propositions shows the political effects that can arise from the conflict between immigrants and the native born that I have discussed in this chapter.

Because the interviews were conducted before Propositions 209 and 227 were on the ballot, the respondents were asked only about their attitudes toward Proposition 187. I begin by looking at these attitudes and then turn to an analysis of how both areas voted on all three propositions. When asked about Proposition 187, the respondents' attitudes toward immigrants played an important part in how they felt about the proposition and why they supported or opposed it. Though not all of the respondents were voters, the majority in both areas saw the measure as anti-Mexican, and 70 percent of the sample said they opposed it. The difference lay in their reasons. The East Los Angeles respondents tended to say they were against 187 because it was both anti-Mexican and anti-immigrant; the Montebello respondents mostly said they were against 187 because it was anti-Mexican. As a result, those from Montebello showed more ambivalence toward the measure. While 90 percent of the respondents from East Los Angeles reported being against the measure, only 53 percent of those from Montebello did. Twenty percent of the Montebello respondents said they were in favor of the measure, or said they saw it as both good and bad. In contrast, none of the East Los Angeles respondents said they were in favor of the measure, and over 80 percent expressed strong negative opinions about it, saying they felt it was a direct attack on Latinos. Overall, the Montebello respondents were more likely to say positive things about the measure, even if in the end they said they were against it.

The discussion of reasons for opposing or supporting Proposition 187 shows the degree to which respondents' attitudes reflected how they defined their social group. In their discussions of why they were against it, more than 80 percent of East Los Angeles respondents cited their identification with immigrants as a reason, while only 30 percent of the Montebello respondents did.[65] In general, the East Los Angeles respondents tended to express their opposition to 187 in terms of the connection they felt with immigrants. For example:

> Well, a lot of them, like our family, well they have papers. But you have like other families that's around them that are illegal. You never know, that might just be anyone, you know. . . . I mean, just because they don't have papers or whatever, don't mean nothing. It's just like a border line that doesn't mean nothing, really. Other than that, we're all here. (Linda, second-generation Mexican)

> We all have to be working on the same things, you know? My parents came in the same way, and if they had gone through this [187] then we would have been affected. (Norma, second-generation Mexican-Salvadoran)

> Even if you were born here, maybe your parents weren't or your grandparents or someone along the line, along your heritage. So it's like, you're part of it, part of these people coming here. (Vilma, 1.5-generation Salvadoran)

> [Talking about the protests against 187] It was good to see them marching and expressing themselves against something they don't like. Like there was people that are legal, people from Mexico that are legal. They went 'cause that includes them too. (Sandro, second-generation Mexican)

In contrast, because of their emotional distance from immigrants, the Montebello respondents tended to talk about them as "they." Emma, a fourth-generation Mexican, was the most extreme in this view, seeing economics as a zero-sum game in which benefits for immigrants mean fewer opportunities for the native born:

> The main ones that should be cut off [from welfare] is the people that don't belong here in the United States. Because we're [the native born] the ones that are getting hurt, you know, they're not. . . . This is our home, this is where we live. . . . The immigrants, they get more than we do.

Some Montebello respondents said they could understand immigrants' difficult situation, but many did not identify with their plight enough to oppose the measure. The quotation below, from Collette, a fourth-generation Mexican, is representative of the feelings of ambivalence and distance expressed by many of the Montebello respondents:

> Honestly, I'm gonna tell you what I thought about. I thought, if I was
> an immigrant, of course I would think it was being unfair. And I would
> have been against it. But because I'm not, and none of my family mem-
> bers are, it didn't bother me. Because I knew that none of them would be
> leaving me. I mean I felt bad, for other people, but . . . I wasn't for it, and
> I wasn't against it. I was just neutral, I guess. There were a lot of pros and
> cons to that [proposition]. 'Cause being that there were a lot of immi-
> grants taking advantage of the welfare system. . . . Some of the bad things
> was that families, some people, they would have had to, some people
> were born here and their families weren't. So here they would have to
> leave and what were they gonna do? They're gonna be by themselves. I
> think that was part of it. And probably the fact that a lot of people would
> have thought—I don't know about a lot of things. Probably they were
> being discriminated against and stuff like that. . . . I wasn't for it. Like I
> said, I was okay 'cause my family was gonna stay here. Maybe that's a
> pretty selfish reason, whatever, but that's my reason.

In Montebello the 187 issue was defined as being about "illegals," and respondents made a clear distinction between "legals" and "illegals." Angela, a third-generation Mexican, said she felt "if you're not a citizen you shouldn't be here" that the problem is that "when you hear 'illegal immigrant,' right away you think Mexicans." Cassandra, also a third-generation Mexican, pointed out that it is better if immigrants enter the United States legally:

> I think that it's great that they're coming over here because there's oppor-
> tunities here and that's great, you know. But I just think the people should
> do it legally, no matter who they are, from anywhere, they should do it
> legally instead of coming in here illegally, because it's just harder on them.

The importance of "legality" for the Montebello respondents is clear in the opinion of Caroline, a first-generation Colombian who supported 187. When asked if she thought the proposition would affect her as an

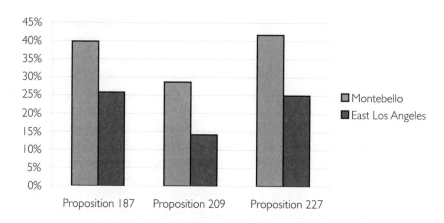

Figure 1.   Percentages of votes in favor of Propositions 187, 209, and 227 in Montebello and East Los Angeles. Source: Election returns recorded by the Los Angeles County Registrar of Voters, 1994, 1996, 1998, compiled by the author.

immigrant, she said, "It doesn't concern me. . . . I'm not a citizen, but I'm legal." This is in contrast to the views of the second- and third-plus-generation respondents from East Los Angeles who were able to imagine themselves and their neighbors being adversely affected by the measure, regardless of their migration status.

These differences might explain how both areas voted not only on Proposition 187 but also on 209 and 227. Figure 1 shows support for all three propositions by voters in East Los Angeles and Montebello, as reported by the Los Angeles County Registrar. As we can see, the support for these propositions was much higher in Montebello than in East Los Angeles. It is possible that the differences between these two areas stem from the larger numbers of Anglos in Montebello. But if that were the case, Montebello's support would be similar across all the measures. In light of what we have seen in this chapter, a more likely explanation is that the salient issue affecting how Latino residents of Montebello voted on these propositions was whom they perceived as being most affected by the measures. Both Propositions 187 and 227 addressed issues of language and the provision of services to immigrants. And in both cases those from East Los Angeles were more likely than those from Montebello to vote against eliminating services for immigrants. In fact, almost exactly the same percentage of respondents from the two areas voted in favor of 187 and 227: 40 percent of voters in Montebello and about 28 percent of voters in East Los Angeles. Proposition 209, which would have adversely affected all Latinos, immigrant and native born, was supported by much smaller margins in both areas. This is just one concrete example of how attitudes toward immigrants and intragroup cohesion could affect Latino voting patterns.

CONCLUSION

Perceptions of stigma cause native-born Latinos to create distance between themselves and immigrant Latinos. In this way, they are hoping to distance themselves from negative stereotypes and develop a positive collective identification for themselves. But the result is that immigrants are excluded from that identity, and that in turn leads to the first generation's ill treatment by other Latinos when they interact with them. Because Montebello has fewer immigrant residents, Latinos growing up there tend to have fewer personal connections to immigrants and thus seem to have developed more negative attitudes toward them. This emphasis on their native-born status, and how that differentiates them from newcomers, is a reasonable response in light of the negative integration history their families have had in Los Angeles. But it is important to understand the impact this intergenerational hostility can have on group cohesion and politics. On the one hand, as we saw in the campaign around Proposition 187, it allows opportunistic politicians to split the Latino vote by exploiting these divisions when writing legislation or referenda. On the other hand, it keeps Latinos from being able to unite and effectively pursue a common agenda. Both these issues will likely affect the shape and development of Latino politics in the future.

FOUR

Why Vote?

RACE, IDENTITY(IES),
AND POLITICS

The Mexican sleeping giant never woke up. It died in its sleep
in the summer of 1993.

Otto Santa Ana

The discussion thus far has focused on the nature and effects of Latino
identity—the identification Latinos have as members of a racialized
group. Yet, like all individuals, these respondents have multiple identities, including gender- and class-based ones. Feminists of color and critical theorists have emphasized the need to look at the intersections of
race, class, and gender in order to fully understand the social, political,
and economic experiences of communities of color in the United States.[1]
However, the attempt to incorporate this kind of analysis into empirical
work raises important theoretical problems. First, we must consider why
exactly we believe that race, class, and gender affect an individual's
worldview, group consciousness, and political ideology. As Michael
Dawson points out, a racially stratified society creates "systematically
different patterns of outcomes . . . [that] shape individual life chances as
well as the perceptions of society, thereby providing the basis for the
huge racial gulf in public opinion."[2] But what exactly do those patterns

look like? How do they vary both within and among racial groups, especially in terms of class and gender? As political scientists, we have just begun to examine and address these questions.[3]

Looking at the effects of race and class in particular, Jan Leighley and Arnold Vedlitz delineate five models of minority political participation: socioeconomic status (SES), psychological resources, social connectedness, group consciousness, and group conflict.[4] The SES model has been the dominant paradigm in studies of political behavior.[5] These studies have found that socioeconomic status—education, income, and occupation—is the best predictor of a person's likelihood to vote. Recent work by Verba, Schlozman, and Brady has moved beyond SES to examine what resources it actually provides people that facilitate their political participation.[6] They found that the factors driving different kinds of participation are different and that "unique configurations of participatory factors—and, therefore, unique participatory publics and sets of issue concerns—are relevant for voting, for forms of participation that require inputs of time, and for forms of participation that require inputs of money."[7]

But, despite the robustness of the SES model in studies of Anglos, the results in studies of the political behavior of other racial groups have been mixed. Katherine Tate found that education and income are only occasionally related to African American participation, and studies of Latinos have found that SES can explain only in part the gap between Latino and Anglo electoral and nonelectoral participation.[8] Also, the SES model cannot seem to explain why, despite the fact that educational and socioeconomic status have increased overall in the United States over the past few decades, political participation levels have decreased.[9] Scholars searching for other explanations have turned to psychological resources— feelings of efficacy, trust in government, and civic duty—as the explanatory factors.[10] Scholars using this approach have found political interest and efficacy have a significant effect on participation.[11] Leighley and Vedlitz treat the emphasis on psychological factors as analytically distinct from social connectedness and group consciousness explanations. But, in fact, all these explanations center on the idea that feelings of "linked fate," "political alienation," "group identity," and "group conflict" have an impact on political attitudes and behavior.[12] In other words, individuals feel connections to particular groups (or not), and their political attitudes and participation are affected by those feelings.

All these models assume that groups will behave in a monolithic fashion, driven by either class or race. Specifically, the SES model presumes that all people of a particular class, regardless of race or gender, will engage in political activity at the same rate, even if they are not necessarily expressing a "class" conscious identity; and group consciousness–identity models also assume that members of a particular racial group, regardless of their gender or class, will behave in similar ways. That these models have not been successfully applied to multiple groups across multiple situations suggests that they are missing important aspects of how participation patterns vary within groups and among different contexts, namely, how the same racial identification can coincide with varied feelings of efficacy and political engagement.

The same may be true in terms of our understanding of the effect gender may have on political participation.[13] Burns, Scholzman, and Verba argue that there are roughly six competing hypotheses that attempt to explain the relationship between gender and political activity.[14] Two hypotheses emphasize how differential demands on women's time, especially in terms of the responsibilities of child rearing and other household duties, keep women from participating in organizations that provide political information and access to political networks. Another focuses on how patriarchal family structures relegate women to the "private" sphere rather than the "public" sphere of politics.[15] Similarly, another argues that male and female socialization patterns in childhood create unique environments for men and women that influence how they make political decisions. The final two emphasize socioeconomic issues, arguing that women's generally lower levels of income, education, and occupational status, in addition to the discrimination they experience in economics and the law, are what decrease their participation.[16] Burns, Schlozman, and Verba test these hypotheses and find that, because of differences in overall political engagement and access to politically relevant resources, men are more interested, informed, and efficacious about politics than are women.

As was the case with theories of group consciousness, this analysis tends to treat women as a monolithic group. An important factor that is missing in the study of race and gender is the way in which marginalization along any of these dimensions affects how individuals see themselves vis-à-vis their community(ies) and the political system in general.[17] The key question is what exactly we believe causes gender, race, or class differences in behavior and attitudes. Is it group identity, marginalization, socialization, or some combination of these? Does one trump the other in certain contexts?[18] For example, the current wisdom among scholars of organizational behavior is that female managers tend to be less hierarchical and to foster more inclusive decision-making environments.[19] Is this just the formal acceptance of a gender stereotype, or are we to assume that female managers really tend to manage this way and that it is because they are women? These female managers are roughly, at least now, of the same class as their male counterparts, so the underlying assumption is that this is a gendered issue. Studies from linguistics have also found that women's linguistic styles tend to be more collectively oriented and less hierarchical than men's.[20] Again, it is not clear *why* this is the case, nor how these tendencies vary by race and class. This highlights the need to better understand the effects of what Diego Vigil calls "multiple marginality," the marginalization of particular populations across multiple dimensions.[21] Intersections scholars argue that racial, gender, and class oppressions are not separate but rather mutually constitutive.[22] Therefore, analyses need to look at the "whole person," rather than attempt to break individuals up into their component parts (i.e., race, separate from gender, separate from class, etc.).

In addition to looking at the whole person, analyses need to pay more attention to the role context plays in making identities mobilizing in particular political moments. A number of recent studies have shown the importance of context for understanding the political mobilization and activity of different racial groups. In their study of the effects of poverty on African American participation patterns in Detroit, Cathy Cohen and Michael Dawson argue that "different neighborhoods produce political environments, which, in turn, structure African American political choice."[23] In addition, they contend that "African American social institutions and networks are critical elements in providing an information nexus through which African American perceptions of racial group interests are framed."[24] They find that poverty affects "perceptions of the effectiveness of political acts, perceptions of community efficacy and perceptions of group influence."[25] In the same vein, Melissa Marschall finds that "attachments to neighborhood and religious institutions most strongly predict the participatory behavior of African Americans and Latinos."[26]

Leighley argues that contextual factors such as elite mobilization, access to relational goods, and the racial-ethnic context are key to explaining the political activity of minority groups.[27] Two recent experimental studies of get-out-the-vote efforts among minority groups also suggest that social context is important. In her study of the effects of mobilization on Asian American turnout in southern California, Janelle Wong finds that get-out-the-vote contact is more effective in areas with a larger presence of Asian American social, political, and cultural institutions, such as ethnic newspapers, social service organizations, and Asian-centered political organizations.[28] Melissa Michelson's results in her experiment among Latino voters in Fresno, California, were similar.[29] She found that Latino canvassers are more effective in mobilizing Latino voters than canvassers of other races and that the mobilization effects were greater in low SES Latino neighborhoods. All these studies suggest that we need to take more seriously how local context frames racial groups' collective identities, especially in terms of whether or not certain kinds of political messages will mobilize them to engage in politics.

Thus, experiences of stigma and marginality, along one or multiple lines, affect the development of an individual's group identity(ies). Those identities, in turn, interact with the social context in which that individual is situated. Again, we are seeing structure interact with agency, and vice versa. In this chapter and the next, I explore how the interaction between identity and context has an important effect on respondents' political attitudes and how they choose to engage the political system, both formally and informally. I begin the analysis by looking at the respondents' attitudes toward "politics" in general. Given that naturalization is the first step in formal political incorporation, I then turn to a discussion with the first-generation respondents regarding their attitudes about naturalization. Finally, I relate that to a larger discussion regarding the respondents' attitudes about formal electoral politics and reported levels of electoral participation.

INTEREST IN POLITICS

I opened the discussion of respondents' attitudes toward politics by asking them, "Are you interested in politics?" This question is important because studies of the effects of social networks on political participation have shown that frequent political discussions within networks are essential to participation.[30] Conversely, having infrequent political contacts or no discussion partners at all has been found to decrease electoral participation. The causality in this case is largely circular. If members of a social network have no interest in politics, they are not likely to discuss politics. That lack of discussion, in turn, depresses political interest, and so on. The propensity of network members to discuss politics also is likely to be related to political mobilization. Those groups with high levels of political contact are more likely to have political discussion within their networks because contact often leads to discussion.[31] So the existence of political interest among individuals and within their social networks is an important first step in their political engagement.

I purposely did not define the word *politics* for the respondents. In her study of Latina community activists in Boston, Carol Hardy-Fanta found that the women did not define their activism as participating in "politics."[32] Therefore, I thought it was important to let the respondents define the word for themselves. None of the respondents interpreted this question to mean area or local politics; all interpreted the question to refer to national politics and elections, which they tended to relate to Anglos and see as distant and separate from them. Because *politics* generally was defined as something outside the community, it is not surprising that few expressed an interest in it. Eighty-three of the one hundred respondents said they were not interested in politics. This lack of interest was consistent across genders, generations, and areas. In general, the question elicited stuttered and incoherent responses such as "I don't know" and "It doesn't catch my eye." Those who explained why they were not interested in politics tended to talk about politics in terms of "us" versus "them."[33] The answers of both the male and female respondents were similar in this regard and showed that they saw political power as located in the realm of "politics," which is outside their local sphere. For example:

> I'm not into politics, any of them. I mean, politics, like the White House, just the whole thing. I don't know about politics, or like the Republicans, or whatever, I heard that they were against us or whatever, I just don't know. (Jay, fifth-generation Mexican)

> I don't know. In a way [I'm interested in politics] because it changes. In a way yes, I'm interested in the changes the government makes, like the propositions, you know, things like that, that hurt our raza, our people. (Araceli, second-generation Mexican)

In the second quotation above, though Araceli expressed some interest, it is based on the fact that "the government" is able to make "changes" that cause harm to her racial group. Jay's and Araceli's responses are similar insofar as both see the political system as one that is acting on them, rather than one in which they can act. Their feelings of disempowerment vis-à-vis politics are a reflection of their overall understanding that there are forces of power at work in the political system, forces over which they have little voice or control.

Though disinterest in politics was present throughout the sample, the underlying reasons varied by gender and generation. The generational differences reflected differences in how the respondents understood the relationship between personal agency and institutional structures. The first-generation respondents emphasized their own agency and tended to say that they were disinterested because of a personal lack of information and ability to "know" what was happening in the United States. The second and third-plus generation, in contrast, emphasized structure and were more explicit about their disinterest stemming from their overall feelings of disempowerment within the political system. This movement across generations from personal to structural explanations could be the result of the respondents' process of socialization into a position as members of a stigmatized group in the United States. This could help to explain why native-born Latinos have been found to have lower levels of political trust than the foreign born.[34] Power is an important part of the stigmatization process. It is reasonable, then, that having experienced stigma would make an individual aware that he or she has less power relative to members of less marginal groups. In terms of gender differences, I found that men were three times more likely than women to express an interest in politics, which may be a reflection of differences in male and female conversational styles, a point I return to later.[35]

The first-generation respondents most often said they were not interested in politics because they felt they did not know enough about it. In discussions of immigration, it is commonly assumed that first-generation immigrants do not get involved with politics in the United States because they are still focused on the politics of the home country.[36] Among these immigrants, disinterest in U.S. politics did not stem from focusing on what was happening in their countries of origin. Instead, home country politics became a problem only to the extent to which they used it as the lens through which they viewed politics in the United States. Those who came from countries with only limited democracy said that immigrants sometimes assume that democracy functions in the same way in the United States. Mercedes, a first-generation Mexican, told me:

> Because, I don't know, because you come from a country where, even if you vote they [the PRI] already know who is going to win. So we think that here things are going to be the same. In fact, perhaps in some areas it is the same, but in others we don't know yet. What we are seeing is that the person you vote for, the one that wins the most votes is the one that is going to win. But, we arrive here, well, accustomed that way, with that mentality that, even if you vote, your vote does not count. Because, in the end, the one that they want is going to win.

Instead, the bigger problem faced by the first-generation respondents was their overall feeling that they were incapable of fully understanding politics in the United States. Both men and women said that while they felt it was important, especially because they believed Latinos were being attacked politically, it was difficult for them to develop an interest in politics.[37] They considered politics too confusing and complicated to have an accurate opinion about what was going on. This lack of confidence in their ability to interpret and understand U.S. society was especially prevalent among the women. Most of the first-generation women expressed a lack of confidence in their own opinions. The women from this group, when asked to be interviewed, tended to say something like "All I have ever done is take care of my husband and children. I do not have anything interesting to say!" After a bit of coaxing, it turned out that they did have a lot to say, and they had very firm opinions about group problems and the education of their children. But their general insecurities regarding their own opinions were magnified when discussing the realm of politics.

Only two of the twenty first-generation women expressed any interest in politics. In general, the women's voices would become lower and more tentative when they answered these questions. When asked if they paid attention to the presidential campaign, most laughed nervously after they said no and quickly gave reasons why they could not, almost as if they felt they were doing something wrong. The women often said that, given everything that was happening politically at the time, they knew they should pay attention but just could not bring themselves to do so. It was too confusing, too complicated for them to understand, and so they were generally just not interested. The following responses are good examples:

> It does not attract my attention, no, politics does not interest me. The thing is that I don't understand much. With regard to politics I don't understand much. They can say this and that and I don't even know what that means. I don't even know what a Democrat is, what that is or what it means. (Marta, first-generation Mexican)

> I would not be able to tell you exactly why [I am a Democrat], like I told you before, I regularly don't understand politics. But it seems like they are more, like they do more for human beings. Not in terms of benefits but that they have more consideration for the necessities of poor people. (Ester, first-generation Mexican)

> I am not sure. Well, I voted in the primary. I'm not certain if I have to vote for the same person. What happens is that here there have been

many changes in the politicians, and so I'm not sure. It's a lot of information [to understand]. (Mercedes, first-generation Mexican)

My findings with regard to the first-generation women's disinterest in politics support David Leal's finding that noncitizen Latinos were more likely to be politically engaged when they were well informed.[38]

The first-generation men were four times more likely than the women to say that they were interested in politics. Interestingly, their descriptions of why they were interested were similar to the women's reasons for their disinterest. The men tended to say they were interested in learning more about the political system because they did not feel they knew enough yet. Like the women, they said that they were trying to pay more attention to the news in order to be up to date about what was happening politically. One male respondent, José Luis, showed a great deal of sophistication in his analysis of the presidential campaign and the obstacles facing Latino legislators because of their minority status. Despite his detailed knowledge about politics in the United States, however, he repeatedly said that he felt he did not know anything and that he wished he understood things better. He then went on to tell me he had had only five years of primary education in Mexico and did not feel quite comfortable in English, so he did not feel he *could* know anything. This man read newspapers and watched television news regularly, in both Spanish and English, but all that information did not give him confidence in his ability to *really know* what was going on. Our discussion about his party identification is a good example:

> I still define myself more as a Democrat because they are more in favor of the poor, yes more on the side of [those in] poverty, more for helping people. And the Republicans are like a party of the rich, of millionaires and multinational corporations. Companies that give a great deal of money for [political] publicity. Although, if a Democrat has a good attitude, good intentions towards Latinos, towards immigrants, they are not going to let him win, because it still depends on the Congress, it depends on the Senators and all that. That's why the welfare law is going to pass very soon. Bill Clinton can be against it. But, if he does not do it, he will have big problems. That's what I think. If he does not sign that bill, he will remain on par or drop below [Robert] Dole [in the polls]. He has to approve [the bill] in order to gain a few votes.

When I said that it seemed to me that he did have a good idea about what was happening in the political system, his response was, "I would like very much to know more, but I have no education. I only received a primary education in Mexico. [That is why] I am studying, but I do like [politics]." He feels his lack of education makes it impossible for him to understand what is happening in the United States, no matter how much he reads and how much he informs himself.

The first generation's reasons for their interest (or not) in politics highlights the interaction of a number of factors. First, the male and female differences in terms of their confidence in their overall capacity to have opinions on political matters reflect the gender hierarchy and the fact that women's issues are often relegated to the private sphere whereas men's issues are considered public.[39] Because politics is public, men seem to feel more comfortable in that sphere. But the first-generation respondents, male and female, were not very confident about their ability to understand the U.S. political system. This may be a product of intergenerational hostility (see chap. 3). The first generation, because they are new to this country, regularly find themselves in unfamiliar situations. Often the native born do little to facilitate those experiences. The result could very well be a lack of confidence overall. Those experiences, in turn, color how they see politics and their ability to understand that sphere.

Second, the first generation's expressed interest in politics seems to be a product of the political environment at the time of the interviews. Of the seventeen respondents in the sample who expressed an interest in politics, nine were first generation and four were 1.5 generation.[40] That means that only five of those expressing political interest were second generation or more. All but one of the politically interested first-generation respondents said that their interest was driven by the political environment at the time and their concern about the changes in the laws affecting them. So their interest is, to a large extent, a product of the environment of racial threat in which they are living. Here we see political interest being driven by the political context and, to some extent, resulting feelings of social stigma.

The native born had a different reaction to the same political environment. They tended to say they were not interested because they felt they had no power to make a difference in the political arena. Female and male respondents from both areas reported feeling that "things are already decided," so that their individual participation cannot really make any difference:

> People in general say, like the people in office say, oh, that the system works for you, we'll help you out or whatever. But I don't know, I don't think it does. Because you see on the news, they don't treat all the people right. They don't treat us fair, you know. They don't want to be equal. (Juan, second-generation Mexican)

> [We] can't do nothing. They always get what they want anyways. (Armando, second-generation Mexican)

> It's not, it [politics] won't change. Because you have to go further out to make things change. You know, like with Clinton, he's not gonna change what's here. Things are gonna be the same. Things are gonna be harder. They're gonna be more harder now than they were before. As the years go by it gets harder and harder. We're all gonna suffer more and more. (Emma, fourth-generation Mexican)

> Not much. I'm just not interested [in politics]. I don't get much involved in it. If there's a war, I'll go [he's planning on joining the military], it doesn't matter. Mostly politics is just bull, most of it is. But, I don't find it [of] much interest [to me]. (Chris, fourth-generation Mexican)

The second and third or fourth generations paint a picture of people feeling uncertain about politics and also disempowered. Because many of these respondents, especially of the second generation, were part of the high school sample and teenagers when they were interviewed, it is possible that their disinterest in politics is no different from that of other Latino adolescents. In a national survey of youth attitudes toward voting, Latino youth were found to have the least trust in government and to be the least likely to believe that their vote counted.[41] Importantly, young Latinos were found to be the least likely racial group to report having discussed politics with their parents.[42] In their national study of youth civic attitudes, Scott Keeter and colleagues found that whether or not parents discuss politics with their children can be an important factor in determining youth civic engagement.[43] It is possible that the uncertainty about politics expressed by the first-generation respondents translates into the absence of political discussions at home. The general lack of family political discussions among Latinos could have an overall depressive effect on the political interest and engagement of the second generation.

The older native-born respondents in this sample tended to be of the third-plus generation. In their responses about politics, they expressed even more pessimism than their younger second-generation counterparts. A few, like Gilbert, said that the government is consciously trying to hurt Latinos instead of help them, and for that reason nothing good can come from politics:

> [T]hat's what I see with the government and all that. They don't really want to see these communities come up, you know. One, because la raza's so big, votes, counting, on the vote side of it, you know, they know that if we consolidate.[44] That's been proof of fact already. The Pomona Freeway, the Long Beach Freeway, they wanted to divide it [the community] because of the strength in numbers, you know.[45] And then, and then you get the politicians that come out of this community, you say, dang, they get there, they make all kinds of promises to the people, and the people get them in and then boom! They stab 'em in the back, you know. They start siding with other politicians, you know. And they pat each other on the back. I've sat on the congressional panels with a bunch of city leaders and I talk with them, and they always ask me, what is it about you? Why is it that you refuse to leave the community? And I tell them, because people like you refuse to stay in the community. You want to try to dictate things. Even now they're saying whether or not it's a democracy, but there is a certain amount of dictatorship in the sense that they, it's like, well, we'll permit so much to go in there, but you're going to have to do this for us. And it's not a thing of saying from the heart that we want to see the community change. What they're doing is we're gonna get something, and then we get ours and we'll let so much go, you know.

Gilbert is referring to the historical experiences of Latinos in southern California—the freeway construction that physically divided East Los Angeles and had a negative effect on Latino neighborhoods in that area. His lack of interest is related to a different part of the social context, community history.

One interesting difference in the third-plus generation is that none of the men in this group expressed an interest in politics. This is true despite the fact that most of them are middle class and one of them, Gilbert, quoted above, was a Brown Beret during the Chicano Movement.[46] Gilbert lived in East Los Angeles and was an evangelical minister who found God while serving eighteen years in prison for assault and armed robbery. Though he felt strongly about the importance of his ministry, he did not believe that any overtly political action can make a difference. In his view, the government hates all Mexicans and will do anything to keep them from succeeding, and there is nothing that anyone can do about it. Needless to say, he has no interest in participating a political system that he sees as determined to destroy him and his racial group. Though Gilbert was pessimistic about electoral politics, however, he was extremely active in his community and interacted regularly with elected officials. Since leaving prison, his life's work has been to help young people get out of gangs. Yet he believed that the potential effectiveness of that work was limited to his immediate neighborhood. Like many of the native born, he believed his ability to exert any influence over politics "out there" was limited at best.

Since the native-born respondents tended to define *politics* as things the government or politicians were involved in, they were unlikely to include their own activism in their definitions of the political. Many did not include the protests they had participated in against Proposition 187 as political activity, because they viewed politics as the exercise of power outside of the community. It is likely that these feelings of distance and separation from the political process are in part reflections of the geographic segregation that exists in both areas. However, it is important to reiterate that all the elected representatives at all levels of government for both these areas were Latino. But this did not seem to make the political institutions in which they operate seem any more accessible to the respondents. I believe this is largely because the respondents see power as located in those institutions and therefore outside their control. This finding is different from that of Adrian D. Pantoja and Gary M. Segura and indicates that the effects of descriptive representation on feelings of political efficacy and alienation may also vary by context.[47]

Here we see different aspects of the social context driving Latinos' levels of political interest. The strong anti-immigrant political climate is pushing the first generation to pay attention to politics, but their lack of knowledge about the U.S. political system generally made them lack confidence in their political opinions. The native born, likely because of the absence of political discussions within their families and social networks, also expressed little political interest. In addition, because of the negative historical experiences Latinos have had in these areas, which many in the third-plus generation actually experienced, these respondents tended to define politics as "out there" and about "them" rather than "us."

How can we explain the seventeen respondents who were interested in politics? What can we learn from their responses? First, gender was a key distinction, with men more than three times more likely than women to have expressed an interest. In contrast, the female respondents were more likely than the males to report actually having participated in electoral politics, as I discuss below. In chapter 5 I demonstrate that the same trend exists with regard to nonelectoral participation. The male respondents tended to express higher feelings of efficacy than the females, yet they were less likely to have actually participated in those activities. This could be a reflection of different linguistic styles on the part of men and women, with men being less willing in a conversational setting, especially with a woman, to admit they lacked these feelings of efficacy because it may put them at a conversational disadvantage.[48] Here perceptions of relative power are gendered; men were more likely to overstate their power, women to understate it. As a result, there is some distance between these Latino men's attitudes and their actual participation in politics, and the opposite is the case among these Latina women.

Second, the generational differences were not as expected. The first generation was by far the most likely to say they were interested in politics. Many analysts assume that for the most part immigrants are not interested in the politics of their adopted country. In this sample, it seems that was the case before the political changes of the 1990s. The 1996 immigration and welfare reform bills were being debated in Congress at the time of these interviews, and many legal immigrants were concerned about possible changes in their status. All but one of the first-generation respondents said this led them to become more aware of what was happening politically. But that political context should also have had a positive effect on the political interest of the second and third-plus generation. Proposition 187 had recently passed, and Proposition 209 was on the ballot that November. The political mobilization in the community around these two propositions was focused on schools and thus on these second- and third-plus-generation respondents. Many of them had participated in protests against these issues. And yet that experience did not lead them to express an interest in politics.

This may be a reflection of differences between immigrants and the native born in terms of attitudes toward U.S. government institutions. Immigrants are a self-selected group. Most Latino immigrants come to the United States for economic reasons, but they also come because of a general belief in the openness and freedom that characterize the U.S. political and economic systems. In addition, immigrants have a point of reference, their home country, with which to compare their political experiences in the United States, which can make the U.S. system look more positive. As a result, it is likely that the first generation simply has more faith in the fairness of U.S. government institutions. The native born, on the other hand, did not choose to be present in this country and have no point of reference. All they know is that they regularly experience social stigma and that their social networks contain limited political discussion. In addition, they live in areas that rarely are targets of political mobilization. So they are less likely to see U.S. political institutions in a favorable light, and they consider politics something that has little relevance in their particular social context.[49]

Third, two of the four women who said politics interested them were members of the third-plus generation. Both were the only respondents who reported having significant primary social interactions with racial groups other than Latinos. An examination of their experiences highlights how racially homogeneous and depoliticized social networks affect group political engagement. Cassandra was an eighteen-year-old woman who grew up in Montebello. At sixteen, she dropped out of high school, and got pregnant shortly thereafter. When her father found out she was pregnant, he threw her out of his house. She went on public assistance and kept the baby. At the time of the interview she was receiving welfare and living in a multiracial family shelter in Boyle Heights. She was at the adult school as part of the GAIN program.[50] She said she had never been interested in politics before but that the family shelter she lives in brought in speakers during the fall election and required all the residents to attend the talks. They also provided campaign information, and the residents talked a great deal about the election because they were concerned about how the proposed welfare reforms would affect them. She said that being surrounded by people who cared about these issues had changed her outlook and that she had learned a great deal about politics just by living in the shelter and attending adult school.

> I really don't think it was because I didn't want to [pay attention to pol-
> itics], it was the type of lifestyle that I lived, what I was exposing, have
> you ever heard that saying, "The circles that you walk in"? You know,
> it's like you're always doing the same thing and you're around people
> that don't really care. So, you put somebody around a bunch of people
> that do care and that do know about what's going on, and you start to
> somehow, you know, pay attention more and to get more involved and
> to get more educated. So, leaving the people that I used to hang around
> with and choosing a different crowd so to speak, or a different type of
> one, and just a whole other lifestyle you're exposed to a whole, you
> know, world of new things. Things that I wouldn't pay attention to
> when I was out there doing nothing, you know, good, but that I pay
> attention to now because of what I do. You know, how could you know?
> You know, if you go to school, and you know, you stay home or you
> turn the TV on you hear about, you know, the elections and the cam-
> paigns, you know, all that's going on. And you go to school and people
> talk about this stuff, so you become interested in it, you know. And
> that's why, I guess.

Cassandra is a good example of the importance of social networks to political socialization. As David Knoke points out, "People constantly compare themselves to those with whom they have close ties and seek to emulate the attitudes and actions of these intimates."[51] Of course, that the political reforms occurring during that period were directly affecting her livelihood also played a role in increasing Cassandra's interest in politics. But the key issue for her was that her environment changed and that she was exposed to different kinds of people. Those people helped her to feel more confident about herself and her abilities. This new consciousness and identity changed her outlook on politics.

The other politically interested third-plus-generation woman was Collette, a forty-two-year-old, fourth-generation Mexican American woman who worked as an executive secretary and lived in Montebello. She recently had been laid off from her job with Bank of America and was at the adult school to improve her typing and computer skills. She expressed strong interest in the 1996 presidential campaign and said she was interested in politics because she thinks the president has a strong influence on the state of the economy. She said she became interested in politics because of her family: her grandfather, father, uncles, and brothers were in the military.[52] They served in World War II, Korea, and Vietnam. She said that because they had risked their lives as a result of other people's political choices, her whole family became much more interested in political issues, and now they discuss politics whenever they get together. She also talked a great deal about how she felt about working in a majority Anglo environment. She felt that Anglos generally assume all Mexicans are "ignorant and unsophisticated." To contradict their stereotypes, she took great pains to express herself well in English and to stay informed about current events. Her interest in politics and her need to be informed are related to her family, her work environment, and her desire to not be included in negative stereotypes of Mexicans. Again, we see the power of social networks and family political discussion in fomenting political interest and the role stigma can play in that process.

In an interesting way, like the first-generation respondents, both women had become interested in politics as a form of self-protection. Cassandra was concerned about keeping her welfare benefits. Collette was concerned about maintaining a good self-image in the face of perceived discrimination and about the safety and well-being of her family members in the military. Both were acquiring knowledge in order to counteract their insecurity. Yet neither saw politics as a way to have an impact on the world. Both were gathering information in order to maintain their status quo. Even though they are native born and speak primarily English, the reasons for their interest in politics are similar to those of the first generation—self-protection rather than real empowerment.

ATTITUDES TOWARD NATURALIZATION

For immigrants, the first step toward exercising the right to vote is naturalization. Immigration scholars see naturalization as a significant step in the integration of immigrants and in determining their future political power. Alejandro Portes and Rubén Rumbaut argue that the rate, rapidity, and level of citizenship acquisition within different immigrant groups determine their ability to affect and influence politics in the United States.[53] Louis DeSipio argues that low levels of Latino citizenship are a key factor that needs to be addressed before this situation can improve.[54] But there are many factors, geographic, sociodemographic, and institutional, that influence rates of naturalization and, in turn, immigrants' formal attachment to U.S. political institutions.

Among immigrant groups, those from countries contiguous to the United States, Mexico and Canada, historically have had the lowest rates of naturalization.[55] In the case of Mexico, scholars have argued, these low rates are not only due to the country's physical proximity to the United States but also to the low levels of educational attainment and socioeconomic status of Mexican immigrants. No study has determined conclusively why physical proximity would have such a negative effect on naturalization. Some argue that it makes it easier for the immigrant to maintain the hope of eventually returning to the home country, even if that never actually occurs. It also makes it easier to maintain ties to family and the home country in general, which makes it more difficult for immigrants to let go of the home country nationality and become citizens.

Another set of reasons given for low naturalization rates among Mexican and other immigrants is bureaucratic or institutional problems with the U.S. Citizenship and Immigration Services (USCIS), formerly called the Immigration and Naturalization Service. A quantitative study of Latino political attitudes, the Latino National Political Survey, found that while Latinos had a strong psychological attachment to the United States, many still had not become citizens.[56] DeSipio argues that this is in part because of fear of the (former) INS and putting oneself through the formal citizenship process.[57] That studies have found that the INS rejected the applications of immigrants from some countries at higher rates than others indicates that these fears are not unfounded.[58] Many immigrants also fear that if they fail the citizenship exam, they will be deported or their permanent resident status will be revoked, making maintaining the status quo more attractive than subjecting themselves to the perceived whims of U.S. immigration officers.

An analysis of my respondents' attitudes toward U.S. citizenship provides a glimpse of the factors influencing their decisions about naturalization and how that decision-making process relates to their attitudes toward voting. There were thirty-five foreign-born respondents in this sample. I classified twenty-seven as first generation and eight as 1.5 generation because they had lived in the United States since they were young children and had gone to school in the United States. I include them in this discussion because, though they have spent most their lives in the United States, they still must make a conscious decision about whether or not to become naturalized citizens.[59] This is something the native born do not have to do. Nine foreign-born respondents were from the high school samples, twenty-six from the two adult schools. Because most of these respondents were from the adult school, my sample is biased toward those who want to become naturalized. This is due to the fact that most of the first-generation respondents came from ESL or citizenship classes and thus probably would not have been at the adult school had they not already decided to initiate the citizenship process. Despite this limitation, the sample provides insight into the reasons underlying the growing rates of naturalization among Latinos and how that process relates to their political incorporation.[60]

Of this group of respondents, twenty were women and fifteen were men. On average, they had been in the United States for 15.8 years. When I remove the three respondents who had been in the United States for less than two years, average time in the United States increases to 17.2 years. On average, the women had been in the United States longer than the men, with averages of 19.1 and 11.4 years, respectively. This may explain why there were more women than men in this group. Time in the United States has been found to be one of the strongest determinants of naturalization, with Latinos being in the United States an average of 13 years before naturalizing.[61]

Eighteen of the foreign-born respondents were from Montebello and seventeen from East Los Angeles. Seven were already citizens, and twenty-eight were noncitizens. Of those twenty-eight noncitizens, only four said they did not definitely plan to become citizens. Two of those said they were uncertain because they had been in the United States for less than two years and had not yet decided to remain here permanently. The other two were high school seniors from the 1.5 generation. One said she felt she could not become a citizen until she could choose between being a Democrat or a Republican. The other said he felt that naturalization would mean that he would have to give up his identity as a "Mexican" and that he was not yet comfortable with the idea of doing that. This is a common reason given by scholars for why Mexicans do not naturalize.[62] Those concerns were voiced by a few of these respondents, but most said they felt naturalization was simply a bureaucratic act that would not affect their identity or their "Mexicanness." This suggests that in an era of transnationalism the relationship between citizenship and national identity is not as strong as it once was.[63]

The foreign-born respondents gave similar reasons for wanting to become citizens. The vast majority of the first-generation respondents—thirty-one of thirty-five—said they felt citizenship was important because of the changes in immigration law and because they felt they were being attacked by politicians such as Pete Wilson.[64]

> Because if they are going to have so much anti-immigrant sentiment, well, then the best, the best option is to be a citizen. Because once you become a citizen a person has their, there is no insecurity of any kind. In order to have those benefits in this country, one has to be a citizen. Within a few years who knows what will happen? Perhaps that will change and not even the citizens will have the right to so many things. So in my opinion the best way to integrate myself totally into this society is to make myself a citizen. Independent of the benefits that I would have. Yes, it's more the anti-immigrant sentiment. In addition, they say that people as citizens have the right to vote, and by means of the vote you can make many changes in all kinds of things. So, all these people, instead of going around complaining about this and about that, it's better to make yourself a citizen so you will have a voice by means of the vote. It's possibly the only way for one to better his situation here as a Latino in this country. (Javier)

[I did it] [b]ecause of the same, the politicians, the laws that they're passing. So that possibly as citizens we'll have a bit more of a defense. [It's because of] Proposition 187, what happened around that proposition. If the politicians decide to do things, pass laws or what have you, if they passed that proposition, they can pass many more. So one is risking themselves a lot [not being a citizen]. (Rosa)

The first-generation respondents talked about no longer feeling secure as permanent residents and said they feared that their immigration status could be changed at any time. A number of people said they were watching the news every night to ensure that they would not break a law they had not heard about before. These feelings of insecurity were so great that two respondents said they felt it was only a matter of time until even naturalization could not protect the foreign born from being denied benefits or rights.

These feelings of attack and uncertainty led the respondents to talk about naturalization as a way to "fight back" and "count" in this country. Many saw naturalization and voting as linked; they were first steps toward protecting themselves and their families. But there were gender differences among the first-generation respondents in terms of how they conceptualized this need for protection. As has been found in other studies of gender differences in language and politics, the men talked about the need to fight back in more individual terms, saying that they needed to respond strongly and assert their rights.[65] Rafael's feelings of anger and frustration were typical of the male respondents:

Well, I know, I took it [the citizenship class] because of so many attacks some government officials have made on the Latino community, some laws that they have passed against Latinos. And since one cannot vote right now without being a citizen, one cannot vote, I think that finally the moment arrives when one is up to here [he gestures over his head] with all the horrible things that they do to Latinos. No, I did not do it before because, like I told you, I did not plan to become a citizen, I was going to remain a [permanent] resident here. It's because before they didn't, well, they have always attacked Latinos, but never in the ways that they have recently, or so frequently. I say no, well, I am already, well [I think] that's an abuse. And the more timidly one acts, the worse it gets.

The men, then, saw citizenship as the first step in a larger fight to keep themselves, and their racial group, from being taken advantage of. Here we see the men in this sample defining political conflict as a personal issue, one that is about the exercise and denial of their "rights."[66]

The women were also concerned about their racial group but tended to frame their answers differently. When talking about their reasons for becoming citizens, the women did not speak about protecting themselves but rather about making sure that their children were not hindered by their parents' citizenship status. A number of women said they wanted to become citizens to make certain that their children were not denied opportunities for education or financial aid for college:

> Why [did I become a citizen]? For my children also. Well, as far as I understand it, and I'm not certain if it's true, regularly people who are not citizens their children, the children of noncitizens, do not have the opportunity to receive as advanced an education as is possible. Because their parents are not citizens, they cannot receive a higher education. For them [my children], I made myself a citizen. (Ester)

> So, if I am going to stay in this country, then I have to make the effort to be able to do something in this country. I want to be, to do everything, because my children are all going to stay here, we [the family] are going to stay here. (Herminia)

Other women mentioned that they were becoming citizens because they wanted to bring their family members to the United States and had lower priority as permanent residents. This is an interesting finding, since it has generally been assumed that men naturalize at higher rates than women because they are responsible for bringing family members from the home country.[67] In this sample at least, the men seemed more concerned about job opportunities and the women with the status of children and family reunification. This indicates that perhaps men's higher naturalization rates are linked more to their economic roles than to their familial ones and that women's familial roles are driving them to become citizens so as to protect their families.

The need for self-protection is a direct product of the socioeconomic, political, and racial environment in California at the time of the inter-

views. Until the 1990s, permanent residents had most of the rights of citizens. They could own property, make political contributions, and receive
financial aid and were entitled to most constitutional protections. In
some jurisdictions, they even have the right to vote in local elections.[68]
But Proposition 187 and the 1996 welfare reform bill opened the door to
differential treatment of U.S. residents based on their citizenship status.
That trend has only increased since September 11, 2001. Thus, the calcu-
lations of immigrants with regard to naturalization have changed. The
cost of remaining a noncitizen is now seen as higher than that of going
through the process and risking failure. These immigrants are turning to
naturalization as a first step to achieve power—the ability, to vote, to
count, or to "do something" here in the United States.

IDENTITY, EFFICACY, AND VOTING

Given the first-generation respondents' view of voting as a way literally
and figuratively to count in the United States, it follows that they would
feel positive about electoral participation overall. All the first-generation
respondents said they felt voting was important. Both the men and the
women thought it was crucial to pick the right president and the right
community leaders. Others mentioned that voting was an important way
for people to express themselves and, ideally, change things for the better.

> Yes, when I become a citizen of course I will [vote]. That is a very impor-
> tant political power in this country. I hope that many people would think
> the way that I do. Because if all those immigrants that already went to be-
> come citizens felt the same way that I do, I would say that another, our
> [Latinos'] luck would be different. . . . We would have power, access to
> the vote, because here live thousands, perhaps millions of Latinos. If we
> all had the vote we could all really, well at least stop what the politicians
> are trying to do that is against our community. Because if we come to this
> country and work and pay taxes, we should have the same rights that a
> normal citizen has in this country. (Javier, first-generation Mexican)
>
> I hope that my vote will help for resolving, that it be a help for many of
> the [problems]. I hope that being a citizen I would have also the ability

to vote, and that I would have a greater ability to do something for the community, well at the political level, because that is the way that I can [do something]. First by going to school and later in that way. (Alba, first-generation Mexican)

In general, these respondents were very positive about the impact that voting can have, nationally and locally. Their strong positive feelings make it likely that they will vote once they become citizens.

The positive attitudes of first-generation respondents are also reflected in the reported levels of registration and voting among those who were eligible. Considering the women's general disinterest in politics, their participation in electoral activity is not what would be expected. Overall, of those who were eligible, the women in the sample were 50 percent more likely than the men to be registered and twice as likely to have voted. This finding is attributable mainly to the strong political engagement of the first-generation women. They gave the same kinds of reasons for voting as they had for naturalization: to protect their families and their community. Their identities, as both women and Latinas, are facilitating their incorporation into political activity.

These identities were activated by the Spanish-language media. Many of the women mentioned hearing on Spanish-language television that if you were not a citizen in this country and could not vote, then you did not count. Nancy, a first-generation Mexican, said:

Because, well, lots of people say that the only difference [when you become a citizen] is getting a passport and voting, or for the monetary benefits that you can have. In reality I am not interested in any monetary benefit, because I, because I'm preparing myself and studying in order to value myself for myself, not for the money that the government, at the expense of other people, can give me. Okay, why does citizenship interest me? Because, like they say on the television, if you don't vote, you don't count, you don't exist. And I want to exist, I want to be there, I want them to know what I think, that I am in favor of that person, or that I am of that party, or I participate in that action. It's a way to express that you're interested, that you're present here.

The responses of Myrna, a first-generation Guatemalan, and Herminia, a first-generation Mexican, also show the degree to which these women consider that voting is related to establishing a sense of "place" for themselves in the U.S. political community:

> [I want to be a citizen] to vote. Some things that I disagree with, these propositions that they propose every time there is an election, well once you're a citizen you can study the issues, and if you don't agree, you vote, and if not, you don't vote for a particular party. . . . [L]ike they say in a commercial, that for them to take you into account, you have to vote and become more or less informed about what is happening here, because we live here. We already have spent many years here, one should make herself part of the community, no? (Myrna)

> I decided to [become a citizen] to be, I want to, how do you say, to count in this country. To help them to see that one does count. One can't vote because each time they say you should vote for this or for that, you have to go register to vote or something. And then, so many years that I have lived here, and I cannot do any of that. (Herminia)

On average, most of the first-generation women had been in the United States for 19.1 years. Most of them had only recently considered naturalization. Their decision to become citizens, and by extension to exercise their right to vote, is a reaction to the hostile political context that existed at the time. But what made that reaction possible were their mobilizing identities as Latinas and as women and their use of already existing social networks for political ends. María de Jesus is a good example of this. Because she was uncomfortable about making voting decisions on her own, she got together with a group of her friends to decide how to vote:

> For me the experience was very interesting because I read the entire practice ballot, all of the book that they send, and I spent time asking friends and acquaintances so see if we spent time discussing which person we wanted to represent us and who we thought would help all people, especially Latinos. And [with that] I tried to pick the best [candidates].

This approach worked for two reasons. First, the larger political climate was so extreme that all the women were in agreement about acting on behalf of their group. Second, the women already had a social network in place—which they could turn to political ends. This bodes well for future organization because it is likely that this network was transformed by the experience and will continue to be more politically oriented than it was in the past.

The finding that women made voting decisions as a collective relates to one of the longest-standing debates in feminist political theory: the public/private dichotomy.[69] Feminist theorists have argued that historically women have been forced to operate mainly in what has been defined as the private realm. They argue that the definition of politics needs to be expanded to include the areas of the private sphere where power and patriarchy operate, areas such as the family and reproduction and that studies of participation should also be expanded to include informal, nonelectoral kinds of activities so as to more fully capture women's political activity. The Latinas in this sample, such as María de Jesús, seem to be moving beyond these public/private, informal/formal distinctions to develop a more holistic vision of activity, even if they do not define that activity as "political." As a result, their private-family roles are motivating them to act on behalf of their group(s), and for them, acting in the public realm of politics is simply an extension of their private, collectively oriented identity. They do not see boundaries between the two; they are doing what they need to do to protect their community of interest.[70] In a similar vein, Hardy-Fanta has argued that women's emphasis on collectivity and connectedness makes them especially suited to nonelectoral activity.[71] Here we see Latinas maintaining that sense of collectivity in the context of electoral participation and thus blurring the lines between the two categories.

Unlike the first-generation respondents, those from the second generation do not have any formal impediment to voting besides registering. Yet this group's propensity to vote is as yet untested, because at the time of the interviews many of these respondents were high school seniors, under the age of eighteen, and not yet eligible to vote. While any conclusions about their future participation are by definition speculative, there are a few facts about this group that make a discussion of their political attitudes useful. First, all except two were going to turn eighteen within a year of their interviews, so they were close enough to voting age that it is reasonable to assume that their current attitudes will affect their political actions in the near future. Second, most students who will drop out of high school do so by the tenth grade. The respondents were all at least high school seniors and thus were likely to finish high school. Because high school graduates are more likely than dropouts to vote, any bias in this sample would be toward greater future participation on the part of these respondents than for Latinos of their generation as a whole.

Of the second-generation respondents who were eligible to vote, 60 percent were registered at the time of their interviews, and they were equally distributed between males and females. Most of them had registered because someone had approached them and asked them to, most often in order to fight a local political battle. One young man from Montebello had registered because the city council had voted to tear down his housing tract and the adjoining park to build condominiums. A young woman from East Los Angeles registered because there was a Latina running in the local school board election. Both respondents said that they would probably have registered otherwise but that these local issues gave them an additional impetus to get involved. This demonstrates the impact that mobilization can have on individual political activity. The respondents who were eligible to vote but who had not yet registered said either that they did not realize that registering was necessary or that they had to find out more about the process before they would feel comfortable registering. Thus, a lack of knowledge and understanding of the political system is present in the second generation and likely is due to the lack of political information available in their neighborhoods or social networks.

It is with the second- and third-plus-generation respondents that we begin to see differences between Montebello and East Los Angeles in terms of their attitudes toward electoral politics. Almost all the second-generation respondents, who were high school seniors when interviewed, said they believed that voting had an impact nationally and locally. The main difference was the degree to which they felt voting would affect their racial group specifically. The East Los Angeles respondents were the only ones who said that Proposition 187 had mobilized them and their friends into electoral politics. Zali, a fourth-generation Mexican from

East Los Angeles, said, "[The Proposition 187 campaign] did wake up Mexican Americans, which I thought was maybe one of the best things that ever happened from that." Ana, a second-generation Mexican from East Los Angeles, said she forced her friends to vote during the campaign and now would like "to get more involved, like with campaigns and stuff [and giving] out flyers and stuff." Linda, a second-generation East Los Angeles Mexican, said that after the 187 campaign she thought about politics more and that kids her age talked about it more.

In contrast, none of the Montebello respondents mentioned ongoing interest in politics as a result of their participation in the Proposition 187 campaign. Although they said that they believed voting would make a difference, most said they believed this because a teacher had told them so. None said they had heard this from their families or friends. The East Los Angeles respondents, in contrast, tended to make direct connections between voting and helping their community. Luly, a 1.5-generation Mexican, said, "[I want to] vote [for] somebody that's gonna help minorities. Just not Mexicans, [all] minorities, and not somebody that's gonna put us down or something." Hilda, a second-generation Mexican, said she voted so that she could elect a Chicana to the local school board. Javier, a first-generation Mexican, said he felt voting was a very important power in this country and that if more Latinos voted, "*otra sería nuestra suerte* [our fate would be different]." Norma, a second-generation Mexican, said that Latinos need to "get in a group" and vote in order to make a difference. Jesús, a second-generation Mexican, said, "You have to vote to make a difference in this world." All these respondents feel that change needs to happen and that electoral participation is an important part of making that change. Many made direct connections between voting and improving the situation for Latinos.

This is consistent with what Marschall calls the "ethnic community" hypothesis. This theory is based on the idea that "those in a given ethnic community develop a consciousness of each other and hence cohesiveness because of pressures exerted on them by outsiders."[72] Thus, Marschall finds that Latino respondents with low levels of trust and high levels of political efficacy were more likely to participate in politics.[73] This could be what is happening in East Los Angeles and again shows the importance of the interaction between collective identity and social context. The native-born Latinos in East Los Angeles and Montebello agreed that events such as the campaign surrounding Proposition 187 showed that their group was under attack. But because the East Los Angeles Latinos had a positive attachment to their group and therefore felt their group is worthy of their efforts, they were mobilized to act, particularly in response to issues that directly affected their group. The Montebello respondents, on the other hand, felt they were under attack but did not have this sense of individual or group efficacy.

The third generation's attitudes toward voting look very similar to those of the second generation. Yet in terms of registration and voting, their reported participation is higher than expected given their negative attitudes about politics in general.[74] Of those third-plus-generation respondents who were eligible to vote, 40 percent reported being registered.[75] Of those registered, 83 percent reported having voted in the 1996 primary or national election.[76] Thus, similar to other findings among Latinos, registration seems to be a greater hurdle than actual voting.[77] This indicates that social context factors, such as the presence of political information and discussion within family and social networks or the presence of political information and/or mobilization in their neighborhoods, seem to be affecting these Latinos' integration into politics, at least in terms of encouraging them to register to vote.

Interestingly, even those third-plus-generation respondents who said they had voted also reported having limited political information available to them. They tended to express uncertainty and confusion about the voting process. One of the women, who reported voting for Bill Clinton in the 1996 presidential election, did not know that he had won. She said she had followed the *Los Angeles Times* voting recommendations because she did not feel she knew enough to decide for herself. In total, 60 percent of the third-plus-generation voters said the process of voting was confusing, and they all had some kind of outside help making the decisions, be it a parent or the media. When questioned further about specific propositions that were on the ballot, none of the third-plus-generation voters knew the specifics, and many said they had just left those blank on the ballot because they were too confusing. Though reliance on these meth-

ods for making political decisions is not unique to this group, it is important to note that these are linguistically and socioeconomically the most
integrated Latinos. Clearly, that socioeconomic and linguistic integration
has not translated into comfort in the political sphere.

The sense of a general lack of political information was true in both
areas, but especially Montebello, and relates in important ways to attitudes toward voting. Many of the respondents said they believe it is
important to vote, but they did not want to do so until they were certain
about what they were voting for. For them, it was very important to make
the "right" decision, to pick the best leader. They said that it would be
better not to vote at all than to make a mistake:

> See, that's the thing—you register to vote, but you don't know what
> you're voting for. That's why I tell my mom, "*¿Por qué voy a ir a votar?
> ¡No sé ni qué voy a votar!*" [Why should I go vote? I do not even know
> how I am going to vote!] . . . If we could be more informed about what
> we're gonna vote for, or who we're voting for, then that would be a lot
> easier for us. . . . It's like, I ask my friends, "Hey, have you voted?" and
> they're like, "Yeah, I'm registered to vote, but—" and I say, "Yeah, you're
> registered to vote, but you never vote." (Juan Carlos, second-generation
> Mexican)

> You don't know anything, you know. Only what you see on TV, that's it.
> You wanna go vote. You have to go to a certain school or something, I
> think. I don't even know where to go to vote. My parents don't know
> where they're gonna vote. A lot of people like me, they don't know
> where to go, this and that. They don't take the time to find out. That's
> why they don't go. I don't think it's lazy. It's just, everyone is just
> afraid. (Manny, second-generation Mexican)

> Well, some of them can't [vote]. But, some of them don't even know the
> process of voting also. I don't know if they're not educated in like how
> to vote, where they go, if they're afraid to vote, but for some reason, we
> just, a lot of them don't vote. I know that for sure. Like my whole neigh-
> borhood, I know most of them don't vote. (María, second-generation
> Mexican)

Asked why young people do not vote, Chris, a fourth-generation Mexican, said, "I think they're just kinda worried about being responsible for

voting up something that might hurt them, or, you know, hurt us long term. . . . I think they don't know enough about what they're voting on it, and that they might vote up something that could be against them, but they're not too sure about that. I guess they think it's better to just keep out of the situation." Desiré, a fourth-generation Mexican, expressed similar concerns: "If I don't understand something, I won't vote either way on it. I don't want to make a bad decision." Again, though members of the fourth generation are among the most integrated Latinos in the United States, their concerns about their political knowledge keeps them from feeling comfortable about participating in politics.[78]

Some East Los Angeles respondents also reported hostility toward politics because politicians cannot be trusted. A number of the male respondents said politicians would promise anything during an election but then go back on their word when they were in office. Many gave this as the main reason for not liking politics.

> A lot of presidents say that they'll do this, or politicians say that they'll do this for us, and then, you know, once the camera's off them, or whatever, it'll be a different story. They'll be proposing laws against us. Like Pete Wilson has been doing it, says he's gonna help us or whatever, and time goes on he gets better, he gets more money, more power, he's all putting us, this law against us [187]. (Jesús, second-generation Mexican)

> And when it comes to politics, it's like, say you want to vote for somebody, because socially he's doing something for our race. But then he turns their back. That's why I hate politics. I don't like that. If you're gonna say something, you'd better know what you're saying—you'd better know what you're telling those people. That's why if I went into politics, and I say, "Well, we're gonna cut down the border and there aren't gonna be no more walls, you know, oh, you can just come through." If I say that, all these people are gonna start hoping. And let's say I win, and then I turn my back, and I don't do what I said, it's gonna look bad on me, and people are gonna say, "You lied to us." That's why I don't like politics. It's like the stab behind your back, you know, you might be fine face-to-face but turn your back. (Juan Carlos, second-generation Mexican)

As we have seen previously, these men personalized politics and tended to see behavior on the part of politicians as personal betrayals. They believe that once individuals become part of larger power structures, they use that power against Latinos as a group. They see politicians, and by extension political institutions, as betraying not only themselves but also their racial group. This could help to explain why political trust seems to decrease between the immigrant and native-born generations.[79]

The native-born Montebello respondents took these concerns one step further, saying they did not want to be involved in politics because they have no power over the outcome. Juan, a third-generation Mexican, said he does not bother to vote because "something's gonna go wrong, no matter what, no matter which side you fall on. Something's gonna get screwed up. . . . Everybody that gets in office has a chance to screw up something, so why bother with it?" Others said they believed their votes did not count because the government determined the outcome in any case:

> I had always told myself I wasn't gonna vote. Either it's nothing differ-
> ent or they promise things and never keep their promises. A vote's not
> gonna count, I mean, they know who's gonna come out on top. That's
> what I think, you know. They always have everything planned out,
> how it's gonna go. [Who's "they"?] The government, the people that
> are in office, you know. My friend says, you know, it's all a plan just
> to make us think we're gonna get what we want. The government
> already has everything under control. They just wanna have us think
> we're gonna put a person up there and have them. It'll never happen.
> It's the government that's making us think that. There's no way you
> could change things. Some people change things, but they're the ones
> that have power. The government has power. No matter what you do—
> you burn your city [referring to the 1992 L.A. riots], you're gonna get
> screwed. . . . I don't think there's a way you could change things at all.
> (Juan, second-generation Mexican)

> The government's not gonna listen to anybody. They just say, you know,
> we the people. You know, we're supposed to be the government. Well
> that's, that doesn't exist anymore. . . . The government is gonna do what
> they want to do. You can get a bunch of petitions signed but that's not
> gonna do you any good. Have they listed to us before? If they did, what
> did they do? Can't change anything. (Miguel, second-generation Mexican)

> To me it's like, what are you gonna do? Can't do nothing about it.
> Something's voted in, yes, what can we do? It's the people that are

voting. The government just says, oh well, look how many votes we got, better for us. . . . You can't stop them because they have more power than the people do. (Johnny, fifth-generation Mexican)

Abraham, a third-generation Mexican from Montebello, said, "I always was predisposed to thinking, oh, like government is all corrupt and stuff . . . so it [voting] doesn't really interest me." Roberto, a second-generation Mexican who is also from Montebello, said he thinks candidates are "just trying to BS their way into office," so why vote?

Among all the respondents, the discussions about formal politics were shorter and less animated than the discussions about volunteer work and other kinds of nonelectoral activity. Respondents from both areas show the lack of political information and comfort with the political system that comes from living in areas that contain few regular voters and as a result are the targets of little political mobilization. Few respondents reported seeing lawn signs or political activity at the time of the 1996 presidential election. Given their political context, a general pessimism about electoral politics is not surprising. What is surprising is that the most pessimistic respondents are those who are most well off socioeconomically—the ones from Montebello. Their comments show that they feel little ability to influence the political system. The native-born East Los Angeles respondents and those from the first generation, on the other hand, while expressing discomfort with the electoral system, seem to have been politicized by the events in California during the 1990s. The difference lies in the affective attachment they have to their racial group, which in turn gives them a stronger sense of political efficacy with regard to electoral politics.

The differences I find in this sample could help to explain why there was increased electoral participation among Latinos in East Los Angeles during the 1990s. Figure 2 summarizes electoral turnout in both Montebello and East Los Angeles from the general election of 1990 to the June 1998 primary election, as reported by the Los Angeles County Registrar. We see that at the beginning of the decade, turnout in Montebello was about 10 percent higher than in East Los Angeles. But over the course of subsequent elections, this gap narrowed and finally reversed itself in the

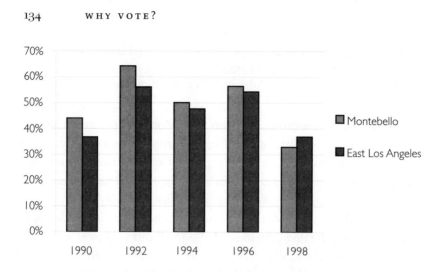

Figure 2.   Percentages of voter turnout in Montebello and East Los Angeles, 1990–1998. Source: Election returns recorded by the Los Angeles County Registrar of Voters, 1990–1998, compiled by the author.

1998 June primary election when Proposition 227 was on the ballot.[80] This indicates that the increasing naturalization rates, political mobilization, and general tumult increased Latino political participation in East Los Angeles, especially among the foreign born. These findings are consistent with those from Ricardo Ramírez's longitudinal quantitative analysis of Latino turnout in California during the 1990s. He found that mobilization increased among native- and foreign-born Latinos and that those who registered during the 1990s were the most likely to remain mobilized.[81]

It is interesting to consider why the same hostile political climate would not have had the same effect on political participation levels in Montebello. Granted, Montebello began the decade with higher levels of registration and voting than East Los Angeles, so a greater change in overall turnout would need to happen there for their numbers to change to the same extent. But it does raise some concern when a middle-class area begins to have lower turnout than a working-class area. What we have seen regarding identity, group cohesion, and attitudes toward participation and what we see in Figure 2 in terms of overall turnout for both areas during the 1990s could be reflections of differences in how the

Latinos in these two areas identify racially and the degree to which those identities include an affective group attachment and feelings of group worth. Though the Latinos in both areas express high levels of racial identification, they define that identity differently. The Montebello respondents are less likely to talk about their group identification as connected to a particular community or collective group of people. As a result, they experience all the negative aspects of social stigma—feelings of separation, of alienation, and of being negatively stereotyped by the dominant culture—without the positive aspects of feeling a part of a well-defined group they can take pride in. Because they do not have a positive affective attachment to their social group, the hostile racial climate leaves them feeling pessimistic and disempowered.

The East Los Angeles respondents' positive attachment is what makes them feel empowered to get together and make a difference for their group. As a result, their identities have motivated them to overcome their insecurity and discomfort with the political system and vote. The increases in electoral turnout for East Los Angeles as a whole during the 1990s suggest that the respondents in this sample are not the only people in East Los Angeles who have been affected in this way. If these feelings of collective purpose and mobilization continue in East Los Angeles, they are likely to have a positive impact on Latino formal and informal activity in that area over the long term. Conversely, if the Latinos in Montebello begin to develop a more positive attachment to their group, their feelings of efficacy may be enhanced, leading them to become more positive about their ability to effect change through their political actions.

CONCLUSION

We have seen that race, class, and gender affect how and when particular groups can become mobilized to participate in politics. We have also seen that the effects of these identities are mediated by, and interact with, the social context. Because Latino social networks, like those of other racial groups, are highly homogeneous, they are unlikely to entail the exchange of political information or engage network members in political discussion. In addition, these Latino respondents live in areas with little outside political mobilization. The result is that those in the more socio-economically well off area are not noticeably more positive about their political efficacy than those from the working-class neighborhood. As has been found in African American communities, neighborhoods and local institutions structure Latino political attitudes and engagement in important ways.[82]

These findings also show that when two group identities are activated simultaneously, in this case that of Latinas as women and as members of a particular racial group, the result can be a strong movement toward mobilization. The 1990s in Los Angeles were a decade of riots, natural disasters, and hostility among racial and ethnic groups. The respondents in this sample, across both genders, clearly felt that Latinos in particular were being targeted. While informal and grassroots organizing among women has had a long history in East Los Angeles, it seems now to be shifting into the electoral arena.[83] The nature of the measures that were being proposed—kicking illegal immigrant children out of school, denying medical care to the elderly, decreasing Latinos' opportunities to attend college—appealed directly to these women's roles as the caretakers and protectors of their families and neighborhoods and served as effective catalysts for their incorporation into the electoral arena. It is likely that so long as issues of education, health care, and community well-being remain at the forefront of the political agenda in Los Angeles, these Latinas will remain involved in electoral and nonelectoral politics.

FIVE

Community Problems,
Collective Solutions

Without a struggle, there can be no progress.

Frederick Douglass

The term *nonelectoral politics* refers to any community or collectively oriented activity the respondents engaged in. This included volunteer work
such as cleaning up their neighborhoods, removing graffiti, engaging in
church activities, helping to improve local schools, or assisting local children. Most studies of political behavior focus on voting behavior; however, political participation is multidimensional, with many different
modes of activity, including community activism, contacting government officials, protests, and communicating with community members.[1]
Employing a broader definition of participation is especially important
when studying groups that historically have not participated in electoral
politics. Robert Wrinkle and colleagues argue that nonelectoral political
activity is "essential to minority empowerment" as an alternative or a
supplement to voting.[2] Brady, Schlozman, and Verba point out the significance of nonpolitical voluntary activity for those groups that have
faced limited opportunities in the workplace.[3] They argue that volunteer

activity is an important way for minority groups to develop political skills and consciousness, which can counteract the effect of negative socioeconomic indicators.[4]

A broader definition of political activity is important also because, as many feminist theorists argue, the separation between the public and private spheres is an artificial one, and an individual's activity does not have to be explicitly political to be considered as such.[5] In fact, according to Verba, Schlozman, and Brady, involvement in nonpolitical institutions often lays the groundwork for formal political activity: "Both the motivation and capacity to take part in politics have their roots in the fundamental non-political institutions with which individuals are associated throughout the course of their lives. The foundations for future political involvements are laid early in life—in the family and in school. . . . [T]he factors that foster political activity . . . are stockpiled over the course of a lifetime, frequently conferring additional advantage on the initially privileged."[6] Thus, feelings of efficacy regarding nonelectoral activity may have important implications for the political incorporation of marginal groups.

Political scientists have long recognized that feelings of efficacy are important for political participation, but they have tended to measure only whether or not it "exists" in individuals.[7] The focus has not been on the source of these feelings but rather the effect their presence has on subsequent political behavior. For members of racialized groups, the contextual sources of efficacy become important. Their efficacy is not only the result of their individual capacities but also of their group identities and experiences of social stigma. Because stigma is intimately related to issues of power (i.e., only those without power in a particular context can be stigmatized), it likely has a negative effect on individuals' feelings of personal and group power and therefore on their sense of efficacy. What is efficacy if not having feelings of personal power in a particular political context?

If this is true, then the nature of the political context also could have important effects on feelings of personal efficacy. This might explain why Latinos, especially those of Mexican and Puerto Rican origin, have been found to be more likely to participate in nonelectoral activity such as marches and protests than in formal political activity such as voting.[8]

It is possible that they are more likely to feel powerful in a nonelectoral context than in an electoral one. This might also explain why the findings regarding what drives Latinos to participate in nonelectoral activity have been mixed. Though socioeconomic status—income, education, and occupation—has been found to be important, it does not explain fully Latino nonelectoral activity.[9] The differences may lie in the fact that, unlike formal electoral activity where the collective is predefined as the state or the nation, nonelectoral activity gives individuals the power to define their community of interest however they choose. This provides them with more contextual flexibility and with the ability to choose to act on behalf of those social groups with whom they feel a stronger sense of identification. Here I am imagining people's social identities within the nation-state as a series of concentric circles. On the local level, it may be easier for group members to see and identify with other members of the smaller bounded circle. Though they may understand themselves as also being situated within the larger bounded circle of the nation, that understanding of collectivity is more distant, and therefore it may be less salient to their everyday lives.

NONELECTORAL PARTICIPATION: PROTESTS, COMMUNITY WORK, AND EFFICACY

I began the discussion of the respondents' nonelectoral activity by asking them what kinds of activities they participated in and whether they saw this activity as effective. Respondents were asked about two areas: marches or protests and community work. *Community work* refers broadly to any group activity undertaken to assist a larger collective entity, however defined. This includes work for churches, schools, and other organizations whose mission may not be explicitly political. The respondents themselves also did not need to define the work as "political" for me to include it in this discussion. After discussing whether or not they engaged in these kinds of activities, I asked whether they thought that their participation could make a substantive difference for their neighborhoods.

In both East Los Angeles and Montebello, the campaigns against Proposition 187, the 1996 welfare reform, and Proposition 209 gave the respondents many opportunities to participate in marches or protests. This was especially true among the high school respondents. One of the main forms of protest against Proposition 187 was a series of walkouts that were symbolic of what opponents saw as the proposition's goal of preventing undocumented students from attending school.[10] In November 1994, the *Los Angeles Times* reported that more than ten thousand high school students in southern California had participated in the walkouts.[11] The walkouts sometimes turned into marches or other kinds of rallies to show opposition to the measure.[12] It was estimated that students from more than thirty schools participated in these protests. Two of those schools were Garfield High School and Montebello High School.

The respondents in the high school sample were sophomores at the time, and it would have been relatively easy for them to engage in these protests. But it is also important to note that their involvement in the protests was affected by how their schools dealt with the problem. At Garfield High School, because the Latino student population was very large, both school administrators and public officials joined forces to keep students from leaving school. As an alternative to walking out, the school held a teach-in at which community leaders talked about Proposition 187, and students were given the opportunity to use the microphone and say publicly how they felt about it. Los Angeles County Supervisor Gloria Molina was present at this event and encouraged the students to stay in school. All the respondents from Garfield who did not walk out said they attended the teach-in. Montebello High School held no such "alternative" action, and thus many more of the students chose to walk out.

Overall, the female respondents and those from Montebello were most likely to report having participated in protest activities. This was the product of the social context at the time, a context that motivated these respondents to take action.[13] However, this participation did not lead to greater feelings of empowerment among the Montebello participants. In fact, it may have led to a deeper sense of alienation. Thus, a mobilizing context alone may be a necessary but not sufficient precondition for political mobilization. As we will see from the East Los Angeles respondents, it seems that for members of marginal groups, a positive group identity and a sense of group worth are also necessary parts of this process.

Those respondents who were not in high school during these campaigns also were likely to have participated in marches or rallies. Overall in the sample, the largest differences in participation fell across gender lines. The Latinas were about twice as likely as the men to have participated in marches or other kinds of political protests. This was true regardless of generation or area. This is in keeping with Wrinkle and colleagues' study of nonelectoral activity, which found Chicanas more likely to participate than Chicanos.[14] In my sample, 50 percent of the women from East Los Angeles and 40 percent of the women from Montebello had participated in this kind of nonelectoral political activity. Among the men, 22 percent of those from East Los Angeles and 17 percent of those from Montebello had participated. Most of the protests were organized against Proposition 187. Because the female respondents felt this proposition would hurt children and people who need medical care, many of them talked about their participation as a logical extension of their roles as mothers. They described their action as an attempt to protect the weakest members of the community, much as they protect their families. Again, we see their gender identity interacting with their racial identity to motivate them to act on behalf of their community of interest.

This is similar to Hardy-Fanta's findings among Latina political activists in Boston: the women in her sample did not consider politics and the community separate from their families. They tended to define politics more holistically than the men and saw their actions as building families, and by extension, the community.[15] The women in my sample also talked about their activity in terms of helping to protect other families and to build social community. Two first-generation women who participated in the marches against Proposition 187 with their families said they had done so because they identified with the people who would be affected by the proposition and wanted to help them:[16]

> [I participated] because we also came like that, we came as immigrants and if now we [had] not . . . if my children had not been born here, they would not be able to have an education. I put myself in the place of those people who don't, who are here illegally, because I too was illegal.

> I also arrived that way; so did my husband. The majority of the ones that came here came that way. Like I said, how are they going to take away education from the children, their medical care, also medicine from those that are ill? That's not right. (Mercedes, first-generation Mexican)

> I went to the march, with my church. We walked with my children, my husband. I felt very good, because there was a great deal of support from people, not only Latinos but people from other nationalities. I can only hope that that action meant something. It's simply a march, but [it's important that Americans] see things, that they see us. (Alba, first-generation Mexican)

These women said they felt very positive about this kind of action and about Latinos and members of other groups getting together to support each other. They saw this activity as a form of help, of mutual support that they did as a family to help other families like theirs.

These women's family roles also facilitated their engagement when they felt the need to protest school or government officials about a particular policy issue. For example, two women in the sample got very involved in actions relating to their children's educations. Mary, a fifth-generation Mexican from Montebello, wrote letters and attended protests in order to stop the school board from closing her daughter's preschool. She was a working single parent and was concerned about losing this inexpensive day care option. She also felt her daughter was receiving high-quality care and did not want her to have to become accustomed to a new environment. These two factors motivated her to become involved in this struggle. She and other mothers protested at school board meetings, organized letter-writing campaigns, and talked to elected officials. Though they were unsuccessful in keeping the school open, they managed to have the closing date postponed.

María, a first-generation Mexican from East Los Angeles, told a similar story. She began to get more involved with the schools when she wanted to remove her daughter from a bilingual program in which she had been placed. María met with the principal, attended school board meetings, wrote letters, and talked to administrators. The school administrators told her they could not put her daughter in an English-only program because of district policy. She continued to contact school officials for more than a year but with no success. She finally stopped when her daughter entered a new grade where there was no bilingual teacher and thus was taken out of the bilingual program by default.

In both these cases, women who had not been politically active were motivated to become involved in nonelectoral political activity because they felt their children's well-being was at stake. María talked about how embarrassed she had always been to speak English to school officials. What she perceived as a threat to her daughter's educational well-being was sufficient inducement to get her to overcome her embarrassment, contact school officials, and even protest her treatment by them. Unfortunately, neither of these women felt their efforts had been successful.

Their experience, and those of the high school students generally, highlights why both group identity and social context are important to the development and maintenance of political efficacy. A number of recent studies have emphasized the role that mobilization can play in political participation, especially in minority communities.[17] For the high school students, the overall mobilization around Proposition 187 facilitated participation. For Mary and María, the motivation was the perceived threat to their children and the appeal that made to their identities as women. Yet, in the absence of any other direct political mobilization in the community, this activity did not lead them subsequently to become more involved in politics, either electoral or nonelectoral. Mary has only voted in one election in her life, and that was at her daughter's urging. María is becoming a citizen but now feels that administrators and elected officials do not really listen when people complain. Like many of the Montebello High School students who walked out, in the end they remain pessimistic about their ability to change things. Had there been more institutions present in the community to channel these women's concerns about their children and keep them mobilized, perhaps they would have become more involved politically overall.[18]

In contrast to the women, the male respondents who had participated in either marches or protests did not mention family issues when discussing why they participated. They did talk about community but primarily in terms of actions that were necessary to protect their social group and defend themselves from attacks. A number of men from

Montebello said they participated in the actions against Proposition 187 because they thought the measure was anti-Mexican, and they wanted to respond to what they saw as attacks on Latinos. They saw the attacks as an attempt by Anglos and the government to "put them down" and disrespect them. Again, the male respondents conceptualized the political problem in terms of their feelings and needs as individuals rather than as part of a collective.[19] As we saw with regard to electoral activity, these men saw politics in more adversarial terms than the women did, and that affects how they conceptualized their political activity. In this sample, their gender identity as men motivated them to act when they felt they were being attacked.

The gender differences I found in the cases of both voting and protest activity contradict many gender stereotypes. Many Chicana feminist writers complain about characterizations of Chicanas as subservient because of their acceptance of traditional gender roles.[20] Within these gender roles, men are seen as having more power than women because they have greater physical and economic power. But my results raise the possibility that this conceptualization of power among Latinos is too one-dimensional.[21] As Pierrette Hondagneu-Sotelo points out, "While women's motives for becoming political actors and neighborhood community activists may be rooted in their traditional identities as mothers, their actions provide a rich source of support for fundamental changes in multiple arenas."[22] In my sample, the women's "traditional" roles seemed to be facilitating their participation. Many of them mentioned that they dragged their husbands and children with them to protests. One woman laughingly said that she threatened not to feed her husband and sons if they refused to go with her. In addition, though their husbands earned the money in their households, many of the female respondents mentioned that they were the ones who decided how to spend it. An understanding of power within the family as based on economics is too simplistic and ignores the many ways that these "traditional" women exercise power within their families and their communities.

It also is important to emphasize what kind of activity these women were engaging in: protests. These are the same women who, in their interviews, often expressed uncertainty about their own opinions. Yet they were willing to take to the streets to make their voices heard. It is the strong connection they feel to their larger racial group—one that they see as an extension of their roles as mothers—that motivates them to overcome their discomfort and act. Here, as we saw with electoral activity, their gender and racial identities combine to motivate them to participate. As I discuss below, that combination also propels them to do other kinds of collective work on behalf of their social group(s).

In addition to their participation in marches and protests, the respondents were asked about their volunteer work. It is in the discussion of community work that I find unexpected differences between the respondents from the two areas. In general, political scientists have found that more socioeconomically well off individuals are more likely to participate in voluntary organizations and do volunteer work.[23] This is intuitively logical given that those with more economic resources tend to have more time available to engage in this activity. However, it is unclear whether these findings apply to the Latina/o experience. On the one hand, that Latinas in general are less educated and earn less than Latinos would lead us to expect that they would be less likely to engage in this activity. Or at the very least we would expect that both the Latino men and women from Montebello, because they are better off economically, would be more likely to volunteer than those from East Los Angeles. However, women's familial roles and their need for connectedness would lead us to expect that they would be more comfortable with volunteer work than with formal electoral activity.[24] These contradictions highlight the difficulties inherent in "fitting" the experiences of Latinas and other women of color into established theoretical frameworks.

Contrary to expectations, the Latinas in this sample were very involved in volunteer work. The Latino men from East Los Angeles were very engaged in this kind of activity as well. The women from East Los Angeles were most likely to do volunteer work, with 64 percent reporting taking part in some community activity. By far the most common activity reported was directly or indirectly related to children and schools. As we saw with marches and protests, the women's family roles, especially regarding children and education, played a large part in motivating them to engage in volunteer activity. In contrast, only 20 percent of the Montebello women said they volunteered. Considering that the women from both areas had similar levels of participation in marches and protests, it seems strange that the difference in community activity would be so great.

One possible explanation for these differences is the degree to which it was their gender and racial identities that motivated them to act. Most of the marches and protests the women had participated in were against Propositions 187 and 209. The women from both areas said they were against these propositions because they adversely affected children. Specifically, they felt the propositions limited Latino children's opportunity for a good education. In addition, they said that the media campaigns surrounding the propositions, especially the border-crossing images during the 187 campaign, made them feel that Mexicans specifically were targeted.[25] These two factors, their need to defend children and feelings of racial attack, motivated them to participate in the marches and protests.

But because of differences in affective group attachment between Latinos in the two areas, that same level of motivation and efficacy was not present when the focus of the activity was the "Latino community." The Montebello respondents, in part because of the particular characteristics of Montebello as a suburban middle-class area, had less of a sense of themselves as a part of any particular "community." When asked about community problems, the Montebello respondents were five times more likely to ask me to define the word *community* for them. This was despite the fact that all but one of the Montebello respondents described themselves as having a racial identity and that the Montebello women involved in the marches identified themselves as "Mexicans" in the abstract. The problem was that on the local level they did not feel they had a concrete geographically based social group to which they could attach that identification. As a result, they had more difficulty determining what tangible collective group they belonged to. The East Los Angeles respondents, on the other hand, because of that area's long history as a "Mexican" neighborhood, had a stronger sense of community and as a result a more positive group identity. We saw in the previous chapter how this provided them with the efficacy necessary to participate in electoral politics; the same is true for their volunteer work.[26]

That positive racial group attachment is what led the male respondents from East Los Angeles to have high feelings of efficacy regarding the potential impact of community activity and to engage in that activity at high rates. These men were much more involved in community work than in electoral politics. In general, the men showed relatively high rates of community involvement: 50 percent of the men from East Los Angeles and 30 percent of the men from Montebello. But the nature of their work was different from that of the female respondents. Male respondents were more likely to work with parks and recreation programs or with church youth groups doing community cleanup. None of them worked with schools, children, or the elderly. Traditional gender roles, then, affect the nature of the community work that these Latinos do.

That the men from East Los Angeles are more involved in community work than the women from Montebello raises the question of what drives volunteer activity. In their answers, the female respondents from both areas had a more collective interpretation of the political situation than did the male respondents, and the latter tended to define issues in more personal and adversarial terms. Yet the East Los Angeles men took that perceived personal animosity and used it as motivation to get involved in their community; to some extent, the Montebello men and women did not. This suggests that perhaps women's focus on "connectedness" is the result of their stigmatized, subordinate position within a racialized, patriarchal society and the need to develop a positive sense of "collective place" within that society. The men from East Los Angeles, because they too are marginalized from the dominant culture, may, like women generally, have a stronger need to look for connections with others than do other men. Their low socioeconomic status and sense of social stigma could be leading them to take on more "feminine" characteristics in how they relate to collective action. Again, we are seeing how identity and social context interact to affect the development of racial identities. In this case, the East Los Angeles men's gender identity is not following "traditional" lines because of the other ways in which they are subordinated in the United States. Here, class, race, and gender are interacting, and power, historical context, and social institutions structure that interaction. The result is that the more socioeconomically marginalized men are showing "feminine" characteristics in how they define their group identity(ies) and in their propensity to engage in collective action.

The low levels of nonelectoral engagement among the Montebello respondents could be a product of the idiosyncrasies of Montebello as a community. Many of those who live in Montebello moved there from East Los Angeles. Being able to live in Montebello has been considered a sign of "making it" by those in East Los Angeles. Thus, it is possible that Montebello residents are a self-selected group of Latinos who want to distance themselves from their racial group and who place more emphasis on their middle-class identity than on their group identity. Aída Hurtado, Patricia Gurin, and Timothy Peng found that Mexican Americans with a stronger middle-class identity were less likely to identify with their group culture.[27] This may be what is happening in Montebello. If Montebello respondents identify with their socioeconomic status more than with their racial group, it will be difficult for them to develop an affective attachment to that group. Yet, given the racialized environment in the United States, they have little choice regarding their inclusion in that stigmatized group, regardless of their personal level of group attachment. That lack of group attachment, in turn, could decrease their sense of efficacy in the political sphere. The key is how Latinos internalize their perceptions of social stigma and how that internalization affects the feelings they have about their racial group.[28]

In terms of gender differences among these respondents, these findings are important in relation to future mobilization within the Latino community. The respondents' answers indicate that the issues and tactics that would mobilize the collective identities of women would not necessarily mobilize those of men, and vice versa. If both Latinas and Latinos are to get involved in politics, these differences need to be considered when designing mobilization strategies for Latinos. They also need to be considered when designing surveys or research projects on Latino participation. As Hardy-Fanta points out, Latinas have generally been absent in studies of Latino participation.[29] None of these women described their volunteer activities as political, and only four of the women in the sample expressed a general interest in "politics." So it is likely that their community activity would not come up in a discussion that was framed as being about "politics." When studying political activity, researchers must be aware of how a particular group defines what is political. Among Latinos, looking only at what respondents define as political could result in missing much of the nonelectoral political activity that is actually occurring.

These identity-driven differences in how the respondents related to community-level activity become even more clear when looking at how efficacious they felt that activity was. As was the case with electoral activity, the first-generation respondents were the most positive about their ability to make a difference through collective action, and the native-born respondents from both areas felt that the government and those in positions of power were not going to help their racial group. The respondents from Montebello, many of whom had participated in Proposition 187 protests, remained pessimistic about the effectiveness of those actions given the power of government. The East Los Angeles respondents also felt that the government was powerful, but they said that nonelectoral activity was important because it made their racial group more visible to those in power. And, as we will see in their discussion of area problems, this motivated them to help their group unite to solve its own problems.

The respondents were asked how effective they felt nonelectoral activity was overall. This included marches, protests, and community work. As was the case with electoral activity, the men were more positive about their feelings of efficacy than their actual participation would indicate. But this finding is largely due to the combined effect of quite high feelings of efficacy among the male respondents from East Los Angeles and very low feelings of efficacy among the females in Montebello. The first serves to inflate the numbers for the men and the second to depress those for the women. Thus, the main differences among respondents in terms of their feelings of efficacy about nonelectoral activity fall along geographic lines. Because of their more positive attachment to their racial group, the respondents from East Los Angeles, both male and female, were much more positive about the effectiveness of these kinds of actions than were the respondents from Montebello. Eighty-two percent of the female respondents and 86 percent of the male respondents from East Los Angeles said they felt that nonelectoral activity could make a difference. Of the Montebello sample, 64 percent of the women and 47 percent of the men felt that they could have an impact. This finding is surprising considering that the differences in actual activity were not as great between the areas, especially among the men.

Those respondents who said they believed these kinds of activities made a difference gave similar reasons across genders and areas. The respondents often expressed concern about establishing a "place" for themselves within the larger political environment. As a result, the most common answer respondents gave about nonelectoral activity was that they felt protests are effective because they "get our voices heard." Most of the respondents from both areas seemed to feel that their racial group and its needs were invisible to the outside world. As a result, they believed it was important to have ways of expressing their opinions and forcing the outside world to see how they felt about issues. They reported a general sense that other Americans did not know what was going on in their neighborhoods. They believed that the protests were beneficial because they forced other Americans to become aware of how Latinos felt about issues, especially those who were against the propositions:

> Make people, like, more aware. Just talk about what's going on, letting people know that it's just not right, we're all part of America, you know, and letting people know that. (Ana, second-generation Mexican)

> Yeah, it got noticed. You know what people are thinking. They are against it. It got noticed in the news and everything, so it really made an impact. It got the word, the message through. (Miguel, second-generation Mexican)

> It showed the government, the state, and everything, how kids are against it [Proposition 187]. I mean, some kids, they did the walkouts because they didn't like it, you know. (Julian, second-generation Mexican)

Others talked about how the protests, in addition to raising awareness, showed group strength and made Anglos take Latino issues more seriously:

> [During the walkouts] there [were] people that really were into it, that were really against it, and really wanted to tell white people you know.

People felt like, we have to show them that we're not just gonna stand here and cross our hands, you know. (Vilma, first-generation Salvadoran)

If we would all unite, if we would all speak, all vote, all go out into the street and tell them, "You know what? We don't like this! We want that!" If we Latinos all were really united, then we would really be able to [change things] because they would listen to us. (María, first-generation Mexican)

As we saw in the discussion of their interest in politics, these respondents talked about feeling separate from what was happening politically, being ignored by "them"—the government, the state, "those people" who have the power to affect what happens to them. As a result, they felt a strong need to have a way to be heard. Marches and other kinds of protests provided an outlet for those needs and are effective in making the outside world see, hear, and understand their needs.

Interestingly, the Montebello respondents who did not think nonelectoral activity was effective also focused their reasons on issues of being heard, particularly being heard the "wrong way," which they believed would foster more negative images of Latinos. The Montebello men tended to say they wanted to be heard but in the "right" way. Many said it was better to let elected representatives speak for the community than to take to the streets:

Marches make a difference because people will know, but they also have to go talk to the people in the government and stuff. They have to speak out. They just can't march and say, "Yeah, we don't want it, and we're marching for that." You have to speak up and tell them why you don't want it. (Pedro, second-generation Guatemalan-Mexican)

Oh, for one thing, I don't think, you don't have to go and have a protest walking up and down the street, all you have to do is get a Hispanic member for Congress, Gloria Molina.[30] All they had to do was get her to speak out, you know, they didn't have to have a bunch of people. I mean, when that happened I was at Shurr [High School] and when 187 passed they went crazy at Shurr and started leaving school. So I thought that was kinda ridiculous. All the kids were just getting pissed off over something which they didn't know about. You know, at that time, like I said, I didn't know much about it either, so that gave me a reason not to get involved in it, because, um, I didn't know what it was about. But everyone else, all the other kids were like, "Oh! If everyone else is gonna protest why can't we?" (Chris, fourth-generation Mexican)

These respondents were concerned that protests would serve as another source of social stigma for their group. This concern about stigma, and their general feeling that power is located in the government and outside their group, led them to focus on the government for solutions. Unfortunately, the result is that they felt that they could not have a direct impact on their group's concerns, either individually or collectively.

In addition to wanting to let their representatives speak for them, the Montebello respondents tended to say that instead of protesting, it would be more effective to write letters or petitions to government officials:

No, no, I didn't participate [in the protests against 187]. I watched them on television and everything, but no, I didn't participate. And in my opinion that, that is, in my personal opinion I think that that is worthless, well, that's what I think, because it makes people look bad. That's how I saw it, for me I see it as a mode of expression that is not appropriate. I think that there are other methods that are better for expressing things[,] . . . for example, you could send letters, or I don't know, other methods so that the Anglo community knows that we exist here, that we are a strong community and that we can move forward. (Federico, first-generation Mexican)

Marches, they are more riot than march, because I have seen that in some places they have made things worse. I am an enemy of those things. . . . [F]or example, collecting signatures and sending them directly to the interested party [is better], that's how a person wants to be heard, and say what is happening. Those other methods I don't feel that they bring anything good. (Rafael, first-generation Mexican)

The Montebello respondents were concerned about their group's ability to express its interests. But, as discussed in chapter 3, they were also concerned about how they would be perceived by the government, elected officials, and Americans in general. Their negative feelings about the effectiveness of marches and protests stemmed from their belief that these actions would not be taken seriously by the government and would worsen Latinos' group image. By leaving the "voice" to the representatives, they felt Latinos would be able to express themselves in a way that would be less stigmatizing and thus more effective.

This reliance on official channels and government representatives to speak for them is problematic because many Montebello respondents showed little familiarity with their elected officials. Another contradiction was that the respondents from Montebello were overall less trusting of government than those from East Los Angeles. The Montebello respondents were more likely to say that the government does what it wants and that people have no power to change anything. These respondents' thoughts were representative:

What did you think about the marches?

They don't really make a point, you know, they didn't make anything, they didn't make no difference.

What do you think would have made a difference?

Leave it up to the people, the politics, you know, there's nothing we can really do.

Do you feel like people can't really change things?

Stuff like walking out, protesting, doing stuff like that, that ain't really gonna change anything. (Angela, third-generation Mexican)

Do you think it made a difference that people protested?

I don't think so. I mean, it's all in the government's hands. They have to pass through all those, the people that have the power are the ones that make the difference not us. (Eduardo, second-generation Mexican)

I don't know. Most of the people that [are] over here, and like, there's like a lot of people here that think that Mexicans should stay where they're at. A lot of people have that opinion, like people like Mexicans don't come over here . . . I don't know. I don't think that [protesting] makes a difference. I don't [think] that makes a difference, whether you go or not. It'll be the same thing. (Sergio, second-generation Mexican)

Though Montebello respondents were more likely than East Los Angeles respondents to feel that Latinos should depend on representatives and formal government channels, they were also more likely to say people cannot influence what the government chooses to do. They did feel the government and representatives can change things, but they did not necessarily trust them to change things for the good of their group. Marschall found that low trust in government combined with high feelings of efficacy lead to Latino political participation.[31] Here we see low trust combined with low efficacy leading to disengagement. These low feelings of efficacy stem from the Montebello respondents' experiencing stigma but having no positive group attachment with which to counteract it.

COMMUNITY PROBLEMS, COMMUNITY SOLUTIONS

The differences in identification and feelings of collectivity are present in the respondents' approaches to solving community problems. It is possible that much of what I found regarding protest and community activity was artificially skewed by the extreme political environment in California at the time. The discussion of respondents' communities cannot be removed from that larger context, but it does reflect how the respondents felt about the ongoing problems facing their neighborhoods and whether or not they felt the political system provided the best institutional structures for solving those problems.

I began this discussion by asking the respondents to define the main problems facing their communities. I did not define what I meant by "community" but let the respondents determine that for themselves. Once they had identified a problem, I asked them to tell me what they thought was the best way to solve it. The respondents tended to frame the problems in very concrete terms. They saw their community's most pressing problems as gang activity and crime and a lack of opportunities for employment. Only one mentioned discrimination as the biggest problem. Though many respondents spent a significant amount of time during their interviews discussing anti-Latino sentiment in the state and discrimination, they did not tend to mention those issues when asked what they felt were the community's greatest problems. For them, what constituted a "problem" was something that directly affected their daily lives, such as gang violence in their neighborhood and the lack of good jobs.

Overall, 64 percent of the respondents from both areas, men and women, and all the generations named gangs as the biggest problem facing their communities. One area of variance was that concern about gangs increased across generations, with 55 percent of the first generation naming gangs as the biggest problem, 70 percent of the second, and 79 percent of the third-plus generation. This could be because gangs are a problem rooted in U.S. society and thus possibly have less relevance for the first generation, except from a neighborhood standpoint. The second- and third-plus-generation respondents were more likely to have had personal involvement in gangs, or a personal connection to someone who was a gang member. Another possibility is that this is a reflection of the socioeconomic status of each group, since 27 percent of the first generation were more concerned about jobs than about gang activity.

Interestingly, the respondents from the two areas did not vary as much as expected in their discussion of community problems. Because Montebello is a middle-class community, one would expect that it would have fewer problems. To some extent, this was the case. Fourteen percent of Montebello respondents said there were no community problems that needed solving. In contrast, none of the East Los Angeles respondents said there were no problems. Yet that means that 86 percent of Montebello respondents did identify problems. Forty percent of those expressed concern about gangs and 20 percent about job opportunities. This could be because Montebello is located near working-class cities that have gang problems. Or it could reflect the fact that Latinos, even if middle class, are more likely than Anglos to have friends or family members living in poverty. This makes them more aware of these sorts of problems, even if they are not directly affected by them. This could affect, in turn, their policy concerns and relative feelings of security regarding their socioeconomic status.

This finding reminds us that even ostensibly "objective" measures such as socioeconomic status have different meanings, and effects, in different social contexts. As Jan Leighley and Arnold Vedlitz emphasize, we cannot assume that the same level of education provides the same privileges and feelings of security for a Latino as it does an Anglo.[32] In addition, Dalton Conley has emphasized that income alone cannot measure the other sources of wealth, or "cultural capital," that Anglos have access to, and which are generally unavailable to members of minority groups.[33] The Montebello respondents' economic concerns indicate that economic insecurity remains even in middle-class Latino areas.

While the respondents across areas, genders, and generations agreed that gangs were the largest problem their areas faced, they differed in how they conceptualized that problem. These differences were attributable not to gender or area but to generation. The male and female first-generation respondents in both cities tended to see gangs as the result of an inability on the part of parents and the local community to control and take proper care of their children. They saw this as due in part to a lack of education among the parents and to the government's laws regarding child abuse. They felt these laws were giving children too much power over their parents. They said that the fact that parents were not allowed to use corporal punishment meant that the government was hindering parents' ability to control their children. Marta's feelings in this regard were typical:

> [Youth get involved in gangs] because the parents work. The children grow up with other people. And because the government and the police do not let you tell them [your children] anything. For example, if you slap your child, now that is bad. If you punish them, now that is bad. They don't allow the parents to say anything to their children because they [the government or police] say that it is abuse and not acceptable. That's fine if the parents are about to kill the children but not if the children need a spanking.

José Luis spoke about the fear that made people join gangs and how they need help and support to find their way out of that life:

> [Young people get involved in gangs] because of a lack of education, a lack of guidance, on the part of the parents and the community. Of course we need to have in the community people who are trained, psychologists, that can help people to overcome a problem that they have, because they have a problem. Good folks, good people find themselves caught up in that [gangs] because they feel obligated to. It's a fear. And by joining up

with so many friends, they feel good. But alone, they're trembling [with fear]. [They need] someone that will help them overcome that [fear].

The first-generation respondents interpreted the gang problem as being caused by a lack of cooperation and education. They felt that the problem was caused by insufficient support for parents on the part of both government and community. They felt that if there were more cooperation, more economic and educational help and support for parents, gangs would not be a problem. Here the first generation was emphasizing the need for support and unity within their racial group and interpreting community problems as the result of the lack of those things.

The second-generation men and women from both East Los Angeles and Montebello also saw gangs as the largest problem but with a difference. They felt the existence of the gangs adversely affected how non-Latinos perceived Latinos. As we saw in chapter 3, the native-born respondents were concerned about negative community stereotypes and social stigma. They resented that gangs affect the images Anglos and others have of them. Regardless of income, many of these respondents mentioned feeling that Anglos assume that all Mexicans are *cholos*.[34] This negative image affected how they were treated in stores and in Anglo neighborhoods. These respondents, especially the ones from Montebello, were very concerned about how this image affected their chances for jobs and other career opportunities. Miguel's concerns were typical:

> [The problem is] Chicanos are fighting Chicanos. It's giving us a bad reputation. I think that's the biggest problem. Chicanos do this to other Chicanos and it comes out on the news all the time, that's basically all the things that's hurting us, just Chicanos fighting Chicanos, and Chicanos getting a bad reputation from other races, you know. Other races say, like, well, Chicanos are no good, they're violent, Hispanic people, and they're always fighting on each other, you know. Whenever you wanna, say for instance you go to a job and they see you, they see a Chicano person, and they don't wanna hire you 'cause they think you're a gang member, you know.

Ironically, Miguel was a former gang member. He said that he thought it was reasonable for Anglos and other groups to have a negative image of Latinos because some Latinos did act stereotypically. He, like many others in the second generation, said that gangs increased the social stigma attached to group members. Even those who said that they had friends who had been shot or killed as a result of gang violence did not point to violence itself as the problem. Instead, they focused on how the existence of gangs affects how people see them. These respondents directed their anger at members of their own group instead of at the people of other races who were acting on stereotypes. Instead of seeing the problem as negative stereotyping by Anglos and others, they saw it as a few Latinos ensuring that the stereotype continued to exist and, as a result, hurting the image of the entire community through their actions.

The third-plus generation tended to describe stereotyping as a separate issue from the problem of gangs. For male and female third-plus-generation respondents from both areas, gangs and violence were a problem in and of itself, instead of an image problem, like they were for the second generation. This may be due to the fact that one-fourth of this group had actually been involved in gangs, more than any other group of respondents. Those third-plus-generation respondents who had not been gang members also reported more experience with gang culture, either among their friends or within their families. Possibly, this is because these respondents simply have had a longer history in the United States and their families have had more opportunities to become involved with gangs or to have contact with others who have. In any case, as a result, the third-plus-generation respondents were more concerned about the gang problem than the first or second generation.

Because they had more direct experience with this issue, the third-plus-generation respondents' discussion of the gang problem was less abstract and much more personal than that of the other respondents. They talked very specifically about the human cost that gang activity can have on the families and friends of those who are involved. Three of these respondents had been in prison because of their gang activity and talked about how that experience had affected their lives. Al, a seventeen-year-old gang member from Garfield High School, said that he was planning to enter the military immediately after high school because he knew that if he stayed in East Los Angeles he would most likely end up dead or in jail. He said that he knew himself well enough to realize that he does not have the willpower not to "do bad stuff," as he put it, when he is near his friends, so he wanted to remove himself from the area. He saw that as his only way out. For the third-plus generation, then, gangs were not an abstraction but had direct and negative effects on their lives.

How these respondents defined the gang problem varied more by generation than by gender or area. Because the gangs had affected the respondents differently, the nature of the gang problem was seen differently by the different generations of respondents. The first generation, because they were generally older and parents, were concerned about gangs in reference to their children and their neighbors' children. The second-generation respondents, because they are generally younger, were concerned about the negative images created by gang members and how those images affected how they were treated and their overall life chances. The third-plus generation, while also concerned about negative images, were more cognizant of the direct impact that gangs have on youth and their families. So the different life experiences and life cycles of these respondents create a filter through which they interpret and understand group problems. But it is important to keep in mind that those contextual filters are similar across generations, regardless of the respondents' socioeconomic status.

The second most common problem mentioned by the respondents was salaries and opportunities for jobs. As discussed in chapter 3, salaries and a lack of job opportunities because of language limitations were seen as one of the most common forms of discrimination faced by the first generation. Similarly, the first- and third-plus-generation respondents were the most likely to mention the availability of high-quality jobs as one of the most important issues facing their racial group. Just over one-fourth of the first-generation respondents and one-fifth of the third-plus-generation respondents mentioned this as a problem. This is probably due to the fact that these respondents were on average older than the second-generation respondents and therefore likely to have had more direct experience with the labor market. The surprising thing was that many of the second-generation high school seniors also mentioned this problem, though they had yet to enter the workforce full time. For example, a seventeen-year-old second-generation woman from East Los Angeles talked about people lining up at 4:00 A.M. outside of Burger King when the restaurant advertised that it was hiring. She saw this as a sign of how desperate people in the area were to find work. Many people also mentioned their anger that police were cracking down on the street venders selling oranges on corners and at freeway exits. In their view, the vendors were entrepreneurs trying to make a living in a difficult economy and examples of how difficult it is for Latinos to survive economically in Los Angeles.[35]

The consistent mention of jobs as an important issue across generations, genders, and areas could reflect the fact that economic uncertainty remains in Latino communities even after significant socioeconomic and generational integration. In a recent study of the economic integration of immigrants in California, Kevin McCarthy and Georges Vernez found that of all immigrant groups in California, Mexicans and Central Americans are the slowest to achieve wage parity with Anglos.[36] They also found that Mexicans receive the lowest wage return of any group per year of education.[37] The economic uncertainty expressed by this sample could be a product of being an immigrant community in addition to being a racial group that historically has had high levels of poverty and low levels of education and has experienced wage discrimination. The McCarthy and Vernez study indicates that over time Latinos in California remain worse off economically than any other immigrant group. This could be the reason why so many of these Latinos, even in the second and third-plus generations, remain concerned about finding secure, well-paid employment.

Almost all of the respondents proposed the same solution for these problems: education. The differences were the degree to which they felt the solution had to come from inside or outside the community. This finding may be the result of sample selection. Because my sample came from educational institutions, it is most likely biased toward people who feel that education is important. But the number of people who mentioned education was so overwhelming and so consistent across genders, areas, and generations that it is reasonable to assume it has some relationship to overall sentiment in the community. In public opinion polls, Latinos "consistently cite education as their top policy concern."[38]

Additionally, the 2004 Pew Hispanic Center/Kaiser Family Foundation "National Survey of Latinos" found that 95 percent of Latino parents thought it was important for their children to get a college education, compared to 78 percent of white parents.[39] These findings contradict arguments that have been made to explain low levels of educational attainment among Latinos, especially Mexican Americans. A number of studies have argued that low attainment is attributable to Latinos' lack of cultural emphasis on education.[40] These respondents' strong feelings about education, feelings that were true across the entire sample, contradict this assumption. It is not a lack of emphasis on education that is responsible for low attainment levels among Latinos but other issues such as immigration status, the educational level of parents, and socioeconomic indicators.[41]

The first-generation respondents from both areas placed a great deal of emphasis on education as a solution to community problems. When these respondents talked about the importance of education, they meant it in terms of the Spanish word *educación*. The literal translation is "education," but in Spanish this word has a broader meaning. It refers to years of actual schooling and also to the quality of one's upbringing, having good manners and a strong sense of propriety. So in Spanish an uncouth college graduate would not be considered *educado* in the broader sense of the word. This distinction must be kept in mind when considering what these respondents meant when they said that education is the answer to solving community problems.

In terms of their emphasis on education, the first-generation female respondents were slightly more likely than the males to mention education as a solution for the community's problems, but in general the first-generation respondents' answers were surprisingly consistent across genders as well as areas. The most common complaint was a lack of *orientación*, or guidance, among children and their parents. They saw parents as not educated or knowledgeable enough to steer their children in the right direction and felt that there were not enough resources outside the home for children to turn to for help. Many suggested activities for children and programs for adults to teach them how to cope with problems and keep their children out of trouble. When respondents were asked what was needed to solve these problems, José Luis's suggestions were typical:

> [We need] more help, more help for the community. Not money—poverty does not go away by handing money to people. It goes away by helping the people, educating them, informing them about how they can obtain more. If the government gives help to the people involved with drugs, alcohol, gangs, if you give them help, it is possible to begin to change the ideas and, together with the parents, work to help these people. But in addition the parents need education.

Like Alba and María de Jesús, many of the women emphasized the need for educational and after-school programs to keep youth off the streets and out of trouble:

> There should be lots of programs, it should be possible for all kids of a certain age to be involved in something that they like, to keep them busy in whatever interested them, but in a positive way. Perhaps fixing a car, if that is what they like, or painting something. There are programs now, but I think that there should be many more. (Alba)

> I think that that [the gangs] will end. Not completely, but it would decrease significantly if all the people would help a little more supporting the programs that they have in the parks, the programs that they have in the schools, playing sports or for example where they can study. They should give the children opportunities to study, to play sports after school, where one does not have to pay, because many times the parents, we don't have the money to pay for classes. And in almost the majority of cases, if the children are going to study for something, someone has to pay. And many of the parents now cannot because either the father works or the mother works, or if they both work they only earn the minimum [wage] and they do not have enough left over to pay for classes for their children. As a result, the children often end up staying home alone, because the father and mother go to work, they have to go to work, and that is when the children go out into the street they get involved with the wrong kind of people, and things fall apart. But I think that if there were programs, if there were higher salaries for the parents so that only one would have to work and the other could be in charge of the children, I think that perhaps that [the gang problem] would decrease substantially. (María de Jesús)

Because for the first generation the problem is multifaceted, so are their proposed solutions. They feel that if parents made more money and had more neighborhood and government support, they would be able to dedicate more time to their children, which would be beneficial overall.

The first generation also sees a strong role for the government in helping to solve the community's problems. Like José Luis, who is quoted above, many felt government should not provide direct monetary assistance but instead fund services such as psychologists and other professionals to teach people how to solve their own problems. Other respondents said they felt it was important for people to get together to solve problems and for the government to facilitate that process:

> I don't know but I imagine that, for example, first you could put forth a project, an idea. Then [you find] people who agree with you, that you know can support and help you, that they have a way to get around, to do this. Once you have enough people that agree with you and you think it can work, I don't know if you take it to the level of the law, to the vote, or to the politicians, I don't know, but we'll assume that we have all of that squared away. [Then] look for companies to promote the idea, and that give money. That is, the government gives money for arms or money for welfare, for WIC [Women, Infants, and Children food program], for a number of things. The government has money for many things. But if the issue is education, then the government doesn't have any money. AmeriCorps [which she is involved in] has money, but the program is new. [In general,] there isn't money for all that [education]. So use rich companies. All the companies are rich: Coca-Cola, Toyota, all the cars. So, so many companies, all of them are rich, they all have money. So I'm not certain how all that would go, but you can ask for donations, or explain the programs. I know that Toyota gave money for the day care center [at the adult school]. And that is a good thing. (Rosa, first-generation Mexican)

Here Rosa is expressing her uncertainty about how one appeals to official government channels. Yet she is able to gloss over that uncertainty by emphasizing the power of people uniting around a good idea. Her belief in the efficacy of that collective process increases her confidence in her proposed solution, despite the fact that she clearly does not feel she understands how politics or government work.

As with electoral activity, the first generation's solutions for community problems reflected their strong feelings of individual efficacy coupled with their overall faith in the U.S. government. This is not surprising given that they chose to come here and take part in this system. As a result, they suggested combining the efforts of their racial group with those of the government. They saw the gang problem and other corollary problems such as alcohol and drug abuse as stemming from a general lack of available education and information. They said that if people had more access to activities and programs for youth and families and were more informed about the resources available, many of these problems would be solved. They saw government, along with the local community and private sector, as playing important roles in both facilitating and funding this process.

Though their definitions of the problems were similar to that of the first generation, the second-generation respondents from East Los Angeles and Montebello had different approaches to community solutions. Like the first-generation respondents, the second-generation respondents from East Los Angeles had a strong collective orientation and saw education as a key component in finding solutions for community problems. In addition, they stressed the importance of communication. But they did not consider formal political institutions part of the solution. When asked how to solve the problems, they said that people not only had to educate themselves but also to go out and talk to each other in order to build consensus and find collective solutions. Unlike the first generation, a number of these second-generation respondents explicitly said that the government and police should not be depended on to solve these problems but that it is up to their local neighborhoods. Juan Carlos talked about the importance of communication and Latinos taking care of themselves:

> [You should] reach out to people and make them realize a lot of things. *No con coraje,* not with anger, but talk to people. I guess make them feel at home, make them feel that you're determined about them. . . . You cannot wait for the president to come by and say, "We're gonna take these kids and these gang members here and get them out of here." We gotta do [it], we gotta take action. . . . It's real hard to reach out to people. They think that, well, if one person falls, then they think, I'm gonna fall too. Instead of saying, "You know what? If that person falls, why

not just pick them up?" And tell them, "You know what? If you do, come on and I can help you out." And that's what we need.

Some, like the second-generation respondents quoted below, felt strongly that Latinos need to come together in order to move forward and that they should not wait for help from Anglos, government, or the police, which they see as outside, and in some ways hostile to, Latinos.

> They're the ones that can make the change. No white person's gonna come here and make the change for them, for our community. Why do I wanna do it? If we're not gonna do it, who is? And the people that go away, well they just forget. They don't wanna remember how it was, how they lived, and they don't wanna be part of their culture. They just want to live the illusion of the American Dream. . . . I'm gonna come back and help my community, and work in my community, work for the people and not for myself. I think that's important. (Hilda)

> I just, I think that like, Chicanos need to help themselves because others aren't gonna help them. And, if people will help them, it's very few. So we need to think about progressing and showing all these people that put us down that we don't fit the stereotype of dumb field-workers or whatever, that we're baby machines. (Verónica)

> If you want your community cleaner, safer, you know, let's have a meeting, let's set up a group that will do that, you know. 'Cause, I mean, the people around here think the city should do all this. They city's not gonna do nothing, you know, they have their own problems to worry about. They don't either have the money or the time, you know, and what's gonna happen is the community has to get involved to change the community. You can't just expect the city to do it . . . I think that's the best way, you know, talk to people and tell them that we can make a difference, you know. (Bernie)

Many of the East Los Angeles respondents mentioned that East Los Angeles has a "bad image" or a "bad rep" and that that was one of the reasons they needed to get together to improve their community. As Jesús put it, when discussing why much of the housing where he lives is substandard, "Like the city, they don't want to do nothing about it, like, [they think] it's a bad community, so why fix it?"

Like the first-generation respondents from both areas, the second-generation respondents from East Los Angeles felt a strong sense of group identity and of social stigma. In some ways, their feelings of being attacked by the government and other institutions seemed to be motivating them to adopt a self-help approach to problem solving. Thus, while they may feel strongly about the importance of education, communication, and collective solutions, they also feel strongly that the government is not going to serve as a positive force for change within their group. Their sense of stigma is similar to what we saw among the Montebello respondents regarding the effectiveness of protest activity. The difference is that their strong sense of local community and group worth, which likely is a product of East Los Angeles's long history as a Latino area and location for Latino mobilization, gives them a positive identity that makes them feel efficacious and motivates them to engage in collective action to solve area problems.

In contrast, most of the solutions proposed by the second-generation respondents from Montebello were to be implemented by government. They suggested hiring more police, enforcing the curfew, and providing more activities to keep people off the streets. Two suggested that the community should communicate more to make people feel better about themselves and to make Anglos see that not all Mexicans are cholos. In general, their answers to these questions were much shorter and less animated than those from East Los Angeles. This may simply be due to the fact that these respondents live in an area where gang violence is not as prevalent. They think someone else, like the government, should try to fix it but do not see the need for collective or community-based solutions. The respondents from East Los Angeles have a more collectively grounded vision of their racial identity(ies), see the gang problem as a very real threat to their area, and feel strongly that the community can and must get together to take care of its own problems. They see that as the only real solution.

The perception on the part of these respondents that government institutions are hostile to them is likely a product of the negative political environment prevalent in California during the period when these interviews were conducted and the larger historical experiences of Latinos in these areas. What is interesting is that not all these Latinos reacted in the same way to the same negative environment. The second-generation East Los Angeles respondents used government disinterest in community problems as a catalyst for a community-based program of self-help. They may feel somewhat alienated from Anglo society, but they feel connected to their racial group and derive feelings of efficacy and empowerment from the strength of that group. The Montebello respondents, in contrast, had no positive group attachment to counteract the negative effects produced by the larger environment. The result is that they are pessimistic about the possibility that things can change for the better.

These differences in identity and community orientation are even more striking among the third-plus-generation respondents. All of the third-plus-generation East Los Angeles respondents said that the best solution for these problems is for people to get together, talk to each other, and decide how best to fix things. One woman mentioned the story of a public housing project the County of Los Angeles had tried to build next to the adult school where she was being interviewed. She said it made her feel good that the people in the neighborhood had gotten together to fight it and that they had won. She was hoping that these kinds of things would happen more in the future. Two of the men were also very involved in church activities and programs to try to reform gang members. They both felt very strongly that it was possible to change things, to make a difference in people's lives and get them away from gang life. They felt what mattered was talking to people and showing them love and respect. Jay, a fifth-generation respondent, described his participation in a recent rally he had helped to organize:

> We had a big rally and we blocked off the street and had to get permission and we just put food out there for everybody to eat, you know, for the community. And we had a balloon for the little kids to jump in. And there was some singing and stuff like that, you know, for the church, and they were just trying to compel them to come out and to associate with them and just be a part of what they had there, to like, to try to follow. To deal with their troubles, and stuff, they were just trying to get them to come out and try something new, you know, 'cause it's kinda hard for people in our community to be different. They see something

like, through all the gangs and stuff you see a lot of young people that see gangs and think, oh yeah, that's cool, I wanna go do that, you know. They get attention, they get respect. There's not a lot of people that see that being different, to have like a purpose, or a cause, they don't think that's as effective. . . . [I like j]ust the little events that we have. Singing or eating or whatever. Or the parks or whatever, we get to clean them. And I like doing the things with people, to like, all their normal every-day that they're caught up in. Every day is like the same routine for them, or whatever, at their house or whatever, like the cholos every day with their homeys kicking back in their house and we say, "Why don't you come and try this?" And they're there with their violence or their drugs or whatever and we try to take them out of it.

Like the second generation, these third-plus-generation East Los Angeles respondents were saying explicitly that government cannot be expected to solve Latinos' problems, but Latinos themselves can. Further, they were certain that, working collectively, the local community could solve its own problems; it was simply a matter of communication, coordination, and commitment among neighbors and parents.

The third-plus-generation Montebello respondents were very pessimistic about the chances of anything changing for Latinos. Some explicitly said that people cannot change anything because it is the government that decides how things are and that it will not allow people to make things better. Some of them said they felt that the government had purposely caused Latinos' problems. The following exchange with Juan, a third-generation tattoo artist, reflects these general feelings.

Do you feel there's any way to solve those problems?

Yeah, there is, but it's not going to.

How come?

Politicians won't let it.

How could it change?

What situation are you talking about now? There's a lot of things that need change.

Like what?

Well, there's a lot of things. It's, there's a lot of things going wrong, such as dealing with the Native American Indian. [The] government's not gonna give them back their land, that's not gonna happen. Hawaiians are fighting over their own, you know, they want their country back, that's not gonna happen either. What the government takes, they take, they're not gonna give it back. They can promise you a bunch of things, but it's not gonna happen. The government is all for the government. They want to benefit first.

Do you think the common people ever benefit?

Depends on the situation. So far nobody's benefiting. The government can say, "Hey, we're doing great right now." But nobody's doing great. When they tell you you're doing bad, hey, then we're going good. They play head games with people. It's not right, it's not correct.

Do you think people like you can do anything about that?

Well, everybody can, you know, say something about it. But how long have the people been saying things, trying to speak up, and the government will hear it, but they're not gonna do anything about it. The government is for the government.

Johnny expressed similar feelings when asked if he saw any way to solve Latinos' problems:

You can't. I wish you could. I wish we could make it better. Like I say it's all the government that's doing everything. They're the ones that want all the minimum wage or benefits put down, or something. Like they're trying to take the benefits away from the retirement people. They shouldn't take it away. They've been here all their lives and worked for all that money. Now you want that money for something else? That ain't right.

Other Montebello respondents proposed government action, in the shape of stricter laws and sentencing of criminals, as the only solution. Some suggested locking up gang members for life; two suggested simply having them all killed. Underlying these extreme suggestions was a sense of futility. They felt that maybe tougher laws would do something about the current generation of gang members, but there would always be another group ready to take their place.

Considering the historical experience of the Latino community with institutions of the U.S. government, it seems reasonable for the respondents to feel this way. Combine that with their general feelings of being different from and stigmatized by Anglos, and their alienation and pessimism make sense. The second- and third-plus-generation respondents from both areas agreed with each other to the extent that they expressed little faith in the government's ability to solve their group's problems. The difference among the East Los Angeles respondents is that they did have faith in Latinos' ability to do so. Their affective attachment to their group and feelings of group worthiness served as a mobilizing force in their participation because it allowed them to channel their frustrations into working on behalf of the group. The Montebello respondents did not have the same mobilizing impetus. Although they felt separate from Anglo society—and by extension, government institutions—they did not feel a connection to any collective that was more meaningful and powerful than themselves as individuals. Because they had no constructive outlet for their frustration, all that is left is feelings of alienation and futility.

SEGREGATION AND COMMUNITY ACTIVITY

This analysis has shown that the factors influencing and motivating Latinos' feelings about nonelectoral participation are complex and interactive. Women seem more willing than men to protest on behalf of their racial group, especially when they see the issues as relating to family. The respondents from East Los Angeles place more emphasis on community-based solutions to problems and feel more positive about success. The differences among the respondents cut across gender, area, and generational lines. This suggests that intragroup differences, along with gender and contextual issues, need to be taken into consideration when analyzing Latino involvement in nonelectoral activity.

These findings raise a number of other issues. One is that none of the major community problems, as the respondents defined them, was political. Though it is true that the first-generation respondents mentioned throughout their interviews the current political situation and anti-immigrant sentiment as problems, in the end their most pressing concerns were the violence in their neighborhoods and their economic well-being. One of the female first-generation respondents said that all Latinos have is *la honradez y el trabajo* — honor and work. She resented the movement to take away community services because she felt it meant that Americans were saying that Latinos had no honor and wanted to take away their right to work. So her concern with what was in many ways a political problem stemmed from how she saw it affecting her ability to work and support her family. Looking at these interviews, one is reminded that the Latino community is at heart a working-class, immigrant community. People want to be able to work, receive a decent salary, take care of their children, and live with dignity. Gangs and jobs are seen as the biggest problems because they keep people from accomplishing those things and interfere directly with their quality of life. In this context discrimination is important but secondary. Because they live in highly segregated neighborhoods, they see how Anglos feel about them "out there," outside the neighborhood, as important but not crucial to everyday life.

It is this separation between the community and the rest of American society, the "social apartness" that Martha Menchaca describes, that creates a separation between the Latino community and "politics."[42] This was also true for the middle-class Montebello community because racially its residents are as segregated as those from East Los Angeles. It is important that none of these respondents described their community activity as political. Even the youth who had been most involved in actions against Proposition 187 did not see this activity as political. As we also saw in chapter 4, they define politics as separate from them and something located outside their group. A number of respondents who said that they were not involved in politics or interested in it went on to talk about local political fights they had been involved in. One woman fought to keep her child's preschool open. A young man organized to keep his house from being torn down by real estate developers. There are other examples. Yet they did not define this activity as political. The respondents who did volunteer work or community outreach do not define that work as political either. For them, there is a strict line between politics and the community, just as there is a clear geographic line separating them from Anglos.

This geographic segregation has an effect on their feelings of political "separateness." A number of respondents mentioned residential segregation as an important issue, which they saw as having both political and cultural repercussions. For example, Ana said:

> We're not aware; we just do our own thing. We just think that, oh East L.A., and that's it. We don't look outside the doors of East L.A., we don't look outside our stuff just right here. We just stay here and do our own thing, let others decide for us, like people off in Congress and stuff. Like even Governor Wilson and stuff, we just let them do their own thing over there in Sacramento and we just sit here.

Ramón believed segregation allowed Anglos to ignore the issues that affect Latinos:

> [Segregation is both] good and bad. Good, because I guess it's easier to get along with your kind. There's no really, well, there is conflict, but there's no conflict having to do with maybe, white people living here and then white people not liking Hispanics. That's really it. The bad part is that we don't get, we don't get the representation that we need and we don't get, what I've heard, if we're kept or segregated in a little place, who are we gonna talk to? If we talk to someone outside they might hear us once as far as something getting done, they don't do anything. Maybe if it was mixed, or if it was, if there was someone that cared—I know there's people that care, but it's just hard sometimes to get stuff done, I understand that. But if they really saw that it needed to be done, I mean, if we pushed them, they would do it.

David felt segregation limited economic opportunity and kept people from being exposed to other races and cultures. He thought this increased racial tension among groups:

> Like, they [Latinos] all stay in, roughly segregated like in the same area. Not a lot of Hispanics live around L.A. County. And like East L.A., a lot of them are usually there, and they're afraid to like move out to different places, to like where it's more white populated, or more black populated. They like, they just wanna stay with each other. And I think that

might affect us later on. 'Cause you might not be able to get a job outside of this, like certain L.A. County. You go somewhere and you might
not even get a job. And I think, I think, maybe [it would be] very excit-
ing, it would be more everybody, just like, it would be more integrated.
People really feeling like, it might just be like [a] better community.
They'll stop a little bit more of the racial. Get to know each other. It'll
be like [when people say,] "Oh man the blacks are all this, and the Mexicans this," they'll know each other [so they will be able to say,] "No, it's
not true, you know, this and that."

In the previous chapters, we have seen how the homogeneity of
Latino social networks and the fact that they are not usually sites of
political discussion have a negative effect on Latino political engagement. This homogeneity is largely driven by their geographic segregation. Therefore, for these respondents, segregation is both good and bad.
On the one hand, it helps them to feel more positive about their racial
group. Many respondents mentioned that it was very comfortable always being around people like themselves. There was conflict, but it
was generally not racialized. On the other hand, this separation keeps
Latinos from seeing formal political institutions as related to community problems, keeps representatives from having to address group
needs, limits economic opportunity, and increases interracial tensions in
Los Angeles.

CONCLUSION

Consistent with the findings from the Latino National Political Survey,
the Latinos in this sample were more comfortable with nonelectoral political activity than with participation in electoral politics.[43] Their answers
to these questions were longer and more animated than those in response
to questions about electoral politics. In general, they felt more comfortable about these topics and more confident in their ability to participate
in these kinds of activities. This is largely because they can see clear connections between nonelectoral activity and addressing group problems.
When it came to electoral politics, these connections were more difficult

for the respondents to see. Their general sense of separateness from Anglo society, and by extension formal politics, decreased their level of comfort with the electoral system.

This sample also shows some important positive trends among Latinos. The high level of nonelectoral participation among Latinas and the strong positive feelings the respondents from East Los Angeles have about nonelectoral activity in general bode well for future levels of participation among both Latinas and Latinos in East Los Angeles. This suggests that the grassroots political activity that has occurred historically in the area has had a positive effect on the residents' feelings of efficacy and their sense of group attachment. It is possible that their positive feelings about the efficacy of nonelectoral political activity mean that the East Los Angeles men could become much more active in the future. It also indicates that the same kind of political organizing could have a positive effect on the racial identification and group orientation of Latinos in Montebello. And in the long term, this nonelectoral activity should serve as an educational process that ideally will increase Latinos' confidence in their ability to participate in other forms of politics. As a result, over time this activity on the part of both Latinas and Latinos should translate into increased electoral and nonelectoral political participation.

The findings for both electoral and nonelectoral activity show that racial identification per se is not what really matters for marginal groups but the degree to which it includes a positive affective attachment to the racial group, including feelings of group worthiness. All these Latinos were aware that they were living in a period of racial threat. Most felt strongly that Latinos faced important problems that needed to be addressed. Yet their belief that they had both the skill and the capacity to respond positively to that threat and act collectively to solve those problems varied. The importance of context and identity to this process shows the degree to which members of subordinate groups need a positive group attachment to counteract their feelings of social stigma. Once in place, that positive identification makes them feel that they have the ability to effect change in their community of interest. Without that sense of personal agency, they are left with feelings of social distance and political alienation.

Fluid Borders

LATINOS, RACE, AND
AMERICAN POLITICS

In order to get beyond racism, we must first take account
of race. There is no other way.

U.S. Supreme Court Justice Harry Blackmun

Political engagement requires that individuals have particular understandings of themselves vis-à-vis the political system. For members of
subordinate groups, affective attachment to their social group forms an
important part of that understanding. Thus it is the content of their collective identities that determines whether or not a particular campaign,
political movement, or social issue will mobilize group members to
become engaged in politics and how they will choose to be engaged.
These collective identities are constructed by individuals' experiences of
stigma, by their social context, and by the social networks in which they
are engaged. History matters, including past political experiences and
the organizational and institutional makeup of the particular geographic
space where individuals live. The interaction between the individual
and the social context is what makes identities fluid and changeable. The
result is that there are multiple possible identities individuals can possess, and individuals possess multiple identities (simultaneously) over

the course of their lifetimes. These identities and contexts provide individuals with psychological and contextual capital that they may draw from to enhance their political engagement.

These findings raise an important cautionary note. The positive group attachment felt by the East Los Angeles respondents could be characterized as what Wendy Brown calls an identity of "shared injury."[1] In other words, these Latinos felt a strong sense of identification with their group and local area because they felt that both were routinely attacked and criticized by the outside world. That sense of shared attack is what, in part, drove them to want to work to help their group and to improve their community. But, as Alejandro Portes points out, success stories undermine group cohesion if that cohesion is based on a common story of adversity.[2] If a person is successful, that success contradicts the group narrative of shared injury, and the only option left to that person is to exit the group. As a result, "solidarity grounded in a common experience of subordination can help perpetuate the very situation it decries."[3] If this is true, then the collective identity present in East Los Angeles may have a mobilizing effect only until it reaches a certain point of success. At the very least, we should not assume uncritically that all positive group attachments are beneficial across all contexts.

Beyond this cautionary note, there are important methodological considerations that arise from my findings. Scholars of political behavior need to incorporate more nuanced measures of group identity into their studies. The attitudes of my respondents show the degree to which identity is situational and socially constructed. In terms of politics, we have seen that the same identity (i.e., "I am a Latino") can have very different effects on political attitudes and activity depending on whether that identity includes an affective attachment to a particular social group. In addition, people hold multiple identities at any given time. It is likely that no measure can grasp all aspects of this complex question, but political scientists could do much better than they have up until now. We need better measures for identity, measures that include the effect that the intersection of multiple identities—race, gender, class, sexuality—can have. Such measures would need to (1) allow individuals to express multiple group memberships; (2) allow individuals to express the degree to which they believe their fate is linked to that of each group and the affective attachment they have to those groups; and (3) allow individuals to report the amount of stigma they believe applies to each group.

The importance of allowing individuals to express multiple group memberships is important given this study's findings regarding how race, class, and gender identities interact. But there are some caveats. Such an understanding must not see these group memberships as additive or hierarchically ordered. It may be true that particular memberships, for important political and historical reasons, are more salient with regard to certain issues and contexts. This has been found to be true in terms of racial versus gender identities in the U.S. context.[4] But any extant ordering is likely a *political* product rather than any "natural" ordering of these identifications.[5] As the intersections literature shows, we need to treat individuals as whole people with multiple identifications rather than try to separate out, and hierarchically order, particular identifications.[6]

Also, the acceptance of multiple potential memberships should keep scholars open to the potential for multiple experiences both within and among different groups. Many contemporary commentators point to the lack of a universal "Latino," "gay," or "female" experience as justification for ignoring these categorizations altogether. Part of what has allowed this and other "color-blind talk" to take root in American political discourse has been scholars' inability to show how this multiplicity of experience is in fact the direct result of inequality of opportunity in American society across multiple dimensions. As hooks points out, all forms of oppression support one another.[7] Rather than attempt to generalize across what are very different experiences, a more flexible model of collective identity would allow scholars to see how marginalization is cross-cutting and how it expresses itself differently across groups, contexts, and experiences. Thus, as we try to measure multiple identities, we cannot forget that all are related and mutually constitutive of one another, even within one individual.

In addition to including the possibility of multiple group identities, collective identity measures must incorporate some understanding of what Michael Dawson calls "linked fate"—the extent to which the individual sees his or her (social, economic, and/or political) as related to the fate of the larger group—and his or her affective attachment to that group.[8] Dawson convincingly shows the importance of this factor for African Americans, but little has been done to look at the role of linked fate in the attitudes of members of other racial groups. Cathy Cohen's work on gays in the black community would lead us to expect that feelings of linked fate vary significantly across multiple marginalities, but these questions need to be explored further.[9] In addition, measures of linked fate must be coupled with measures of individuals' affective group attachment. This study's findings suggest that feelings of group connection tell only part of the identification story; understanding the positive or negative attributions individuals attach to those connections is important as well. The combination of these two measures of group identification will provide a more accurate picture of how identities may vary within and among groups. It will also provide important information about how individuals' group affinities relate to their perceptions of external negative group attributions.

The issue of external group attributions reminds us that we must include a measure of social stigma along with measures of group identity. While it would be difficult if not impossible to measure "actual" levels of stigmatization in a particular society across all possible dimensions, it is possible to arrive at some sense of individuals' feelings of personal stigma and relate those feelings to their group identification(s) and feelings of linked fate. Stigma is a relational concept, one that is more about perception than concrete experience. To contend with multiple group memberships, scholars should construct questions that address the relative stigmatization respondents may feel across different group memberships. Such a framework would allow scholars to see how feelings of stigma can exist along multiple dimensions, and how they may vary, for different reasons, both within and among marginal groups. For example, a Latino man is marginalized in terms of his racial identity but dominant in terms of his gender. In this study we have seen that Latinas' racial and gender identities interact in important ways and affect their political activity. A model that looks at intersection must allow for a more complex picture of how power operates both within and among groups. Such a model would provide a more accurate picture of how inequality, marginalization, and feelings of social stigma interact in American society and affect the life experiences of members of both marginal and dominant groups.

Social psychologists have developed a number of scales that hold promise as potential measures of this question.[10] For example, in his work on party identification, Steven Greene provides a useful critique of the standard National Election Survey(NES)/Michigan measure of partisanship, much of which is applicable to other measures of group identification. He suggests the use of a psychologically based measure of group identity, one that contains measures of group affinity, linked fate, and feelings of group stigma.[11] Jean Phinney has created a model of ethnic identity development that is based on a fourteen-item Multigroup Ethnic Identity questionnaire. It includes measures of group attachment, feelings of belonging, and group behaviors.[12] Kathleen Either and Kay Deaux use a combination of qualitative and quantitative measures to look at social identity and the meanings it holds for individuals.[13] Though quite involved, portions of their method could be incorporated into studies of political behavior. Finally, Riia Luhtanen and Jennifer Crocker have developed a "collective self-esteem" scale that measures senses of stigma both individually and for the group, in addition to general group identification.[14] This is not meant to be an exhaustive listing of all the measures available for group identity but to show that social psychologists have been working to develop quite sophisticated measures of identity and stigma and that it would be relatively easy for political scientists to incorporate these more complex measures into studies of political behavior.

In addition, this study, along with many others, suggests the need for scholars of political behavior to take more seriously the effects that social context has on individual attitudes and activity. We have seen in this study that this is especially true in terms of the politicization of social networks and an area's organizational history.[15] Other studies have highlighted the importance of poverty, mobilization, and racial heterogeneity to political outcomes. For example, in their study of poverty in the African American community, Cathy Cohen and Michael Dawson found that neighborhood poverty has a significant effect on political attitudes and behavior.[16] In her comparative analysis of the voting behavior of Anglos, African Americans, Asian Americans, and Latinos, Leighley found that contextual factors, such as mobilization and the size of the racial community, play an important role in the participation patterns of racial groups.[17] Similarly, in his analysis of the role of state-level racial heterogeneity in political conflict, Rodney Hero showed that states' racial makeup has important effects on state politics and public policies.[18] Hero recently applied his racial heterogeneity model to an analysis of community social capital and found that more unequal and racially heterogeneous communities have less social capital, whereas more homogeneous communities have more.[19] All these findings strongly suggest that the factors driving politics and political behavior in the United States are multidimensional and entail variables beyond the scope of the individual. To reflect more accurately the factors driving participation, political behavior studies need to do a better job of incorporating contextual measures into their models.

This study's findings also indicate a need to return to the study of political socialization. Socialization studies were popular during the 1960s and early 1970s in political science but have since lost favor.[20] To a large extent, this is because it was believed that this area of inquiry had been played out. The assumption was that there were no new insights to be drawn from it. However, since much of this work was done, the United States has undergone significant demographic, economic, and technological change. This study suggests that we should reopen the study of political socialization from two directions: how individuals become socialized into politics and how particular institutions, organizations, and/or local contexts socialize individuals into politics. The two are related yet distinct areas of inquiry.

In terms of the socialization of the individual, the political socialization literature had a number of conceptual and methodological problems, which I will not get into here.[21] I am interested in discussing the relevance of this literature to the study of new immigrant groups in the United States. As Wendy Tam Cho points out, most of the work on political socialization and participation in the United States was done at a time when the U.S. population was quite homogeneous.[22] Therefore, the socioeconomic theories that came out of these analyses tell us little about the socialization or participation processes of the diverse racial-ethnic groups now present in the United States. Cho argues, "Because immigrant groups are socialized through different channels and thus bring unique experiences to bear upon the political perspective in America, they provide a new degree of variation to the participation data."[23] Thus, though socioeconomic status provides skills that ease participation, "if these [socioeconomic] variables do not concurrently socialize an individual into stronger beliefs about the efficacy of voting and democratic ideals, they will not result in the expected higher participation levels."[24] In addition, Cho contends that "if minorities have informational and social networks that provide unique political information and a different source of political socialization, they may not derive the same sort of satisfaction from affirming allegiances to the political system."[25]

We have seen in this study that Latino informational and social networks are highly homogeneous, suggesting that Latinos will experience the differential socialization trajectory Cho hypothesizes. Also, my findings indicate that these networks can vary significantly even within communities, further increasing the complexity of the socialization process. Yet, as James Gimpel, Celeste Lay, and Jason Schuknecht point out, "surprisingly little research has been done on the role of the local context in the political socialization process."[26] In *Cultivating Democracy*, these scholars do an excellent job of integrating individual-level and contextual factors into their analysis. However, the findings from their work and this study show that many questions remain unanswered. For example, previous work on political socialization has emphasized the role parents play in this process.[27] We know that in immigrant families it is often the case that the children socialize the parents into the norms of the host country, rather than the other way around. So we need to know more about how the parental role varies in immigrant versus nonimmigrant households. Also, the segmented assimilation model in sociology suggests that immigrants can follow very different trajectories in their acculturation processes.[28] Yet we know little about how those varied trajectories relate to political incorporation. Currently, one in five Americans is either an immigrant or the child of immigrants. Given the size and political significance of this population, it is important that scholars find out more about how political socialization occurs across groups and how that process varies both within groups and among localities.

Political participation studies have also paid little attention to the other half of the socialization equation—political mobilization.[29] This is largely due to the influence of Robert Dahl's vision of pluralism on the study of American politics.[30] In the pluralist model, the political system is made up of multiple competing groups that must vie with each other in order to gain political support. Because all groups must gain popular support in order to be successful in terms of public policy, it is assumed that all members of a democratic system will eventually be targeted for mobilization. The work of scholars such as E. E. Schattschneider and Anthony Downs leads us to believe that the most likely entities to do this mobilization work are political parties.[31] This is because parties continually need to forge majority coalitions. Any group not organized by one party, it is assumed, will be the focus of mobilization by the other. Yet Paul Frymer has shown that this assumption does not hold in the case of racial groups.[32] In fact, because of the stigma attached to African Americans as a group, he found that both major political parties in the United States have continually tried to distance themselves from issues that would lead to their identification with blacks. Also, we know that in the era of advanced technologies for targeted mail, telephone, and in-person get-out-the-vote efforts, campaigns can focus on likely voters and virtually ignore new voters or nonhabitual voters. Thus, the assumption that the mobilization of all groups will be driven by political interest is not borne out by much of what we know about how parties decide on their coalition partners and how political campaigns expend their limited resources.

The lack of political mobilization in East Los Angeles and Montebello, despite the fact that Montebello is a middle-class area, speaks to the need for scholars to better understand why some groups (or areas) are the targets of mobilization more often than others and the differential effects that may have. Some recent experimental work is encouraging in this regard. In their study of political mobilization of youth in different states, Alan Gerber and Donald Green have found that the effects of get-out-the-vote contact vary depending on the type of contact and whether it was peer-to-peer.[33] Applications of this model, with important modifications, to Latino and Asian American voters suggest that contactability, in addition to the voter's racial-ethnic political context, is an important factor.[34] These studies also indicate that the relative effect of contact can vary among groups as well as within them. This kind of research provides important information about how mobilization happens and how and when it is most effective. A complement to these studies would be more information regarding how and why political campaigns or parties choose to mobilize in some areas rather than others and how those determinations relate to questions of group stigma and political power.

This study's findings suggest the need for important changes in how we conceptualize and conduct political behavior research in the United States. They also indicate the need for important practical changes in how we work to foster group political incorporation. If we believe that a positive group attachment, politicized social networks, and community-level organization are important to the political incorporation of marginal groups, it is important to consider how we would go about fostering their creation. I have three suggestions: (1) encourage the development of positive collective identities by decreasing stigma and increasing group members' opportunities to encounter positive images of their group; (2) enhance the politicization of social networks by reconceptualizing how we teach civic engagement; and (3) work to build local organization by organizing around group and context-relevant issues.

FOSTERING A POSITIVE GROUP IDENTITY

This study found that the key question for the respondents was not whether or not they had a group identity but what kind of affective attachment and feelings of group worth was part of that identity. It also found that the development of a positive group attachment is intimately related to experiences of negative stereotypes and social stigma.[35] Therefore, the most direct way to facilitate this kind of attachment is to lessen the amount of stigma a group experiences. Currently, the most common approach to addressing stigma is to target a specific practice, for example, employment, and encourage employers to hire members of stigmatized groups. The assumption is that encouraging ongoing interaction among members of different groups will lead to a change of attitude and a decrease of stigma. Unfortunately, this approach is doomed to fail because it ignores the fact that stigma is created and reinforced by a larger context that exists beyond the scope of a particular employment environment. That larger context serves to reinforce the negative attitudes of the dominant group, which eventually will erode any positive effects that arise from the change in hiring practices.

Because of this, Link and Phelan argue, any attempt to change stigma must be multifaceted and multileveled and must address the fundamental causes of stigma. They contend such an approach should be "multifaceted to address the many mechanisms that can lead to disadvantaged outcomes . . . and multilevel to address issues of both individual and structural discrimination[,] . . . [and] it must either change the deeply held attitudes and beliefs of powerful groups that lead to labeling, stereotyping, setting apart, devaluing, and discriminating, or it must change circumstances so as to limit the power of such groups to make their cognitions the dominant ones."[36] To adequately respond to stigma, we must choose interventions that "either produce fundamental changes in attitudes and beliefs or change the power relations that underlie the ability of the dominant group to act on their attitudes and beliefs."[37]

This study suggests that while working toward this long-term goal, there are some things that can be done in the short term to help members of stigmatized groups feel more positive about their own group. Studies of second-generation immigrant youth have found that "how these youths think and feel about themselves is critically affected by the parents' modes of ethnic socialization and by the strength of the attachment that the child feels to the parents and to the parents' national origin."[38] Similarly, in this study I find that those respondents who had a strong grounding in their cultural history, from their parents, school, or the local area, had a more positive group attachment. Those from East Los Angeles regularly mentioned that people having mariachis give *serenatas* to neighbors or attending the 16th of September parades made them feel positive about their culture and their traditions.[39] Many of the East Los Angeles respondents also had taken a Chicano Studies course in high school, which gave them much of this historical information. In Montebello, in contrast, these traditions were not as visible, and the only offering in the high school curriculum was a multicultural studies class, which did not seem to have as great an impact on the respondents' feelings of group attachment.[40]

The importance of having an attachment to the history and culture of the social group could be a reflection of the fact that, in a stigmatized context, having a positive group identity requires that individuals be able to construct for themselves an alternative narrative to the dominant one. That narrative would include a positive sense of the group's history, accomplishments, and place in society. Many pundits dismiss the inclusion of multicultural curricula and development of a broader spectrum of positive role models for youth as simply superficial "political correctness" and argue that it does little to improve group relations. Though it is true that these kinds of efforts are largely symbolic, that symbolism may have important effects on self-esteem and collective identification within stigmatized groups. At the very least, the findings from this and other studies of immigrant youth indicate that encouraging parents to talk about their culture and history with their children and encouraging schools and localities to add curricula and hold events that create positive images of stigmatized groups could go a long way toward reducing feelings of stigma and encouraging youth to feel good about themselves and their social group. That positive group attachment could, in turn, facilitate their acculturation into American society on a number of different levels.

POLITICIZING SOCIAL NETWORKS

Among these respondents we have seen that the absence of political information and discussion within their social networks has detrimental effects on their political engagement. Gimpel, Lay, and Schuknecht found similar processes occurring among youth in urban and suburban Maryland.[41] One simple way to encourage the politicization of social networks is to incorporate these concerns into school curricula. As Richard Niemi and Jane Junn have pointed out, schools are one of the most important links between education and citizenship.[42] The premise is that if youth see politics as relevant to their lives and discuss it with their friends at an early age, it is more likely that these kinds of discussions will continue to be parts of their networks later in life. In addition, findings from the Kids Voting program show that civic engagement activities that include parental discussions with children about politics had positive, and unexpected, socialization effects *on the parents*.[43] Michael McDevitt and colleagues found that this program has a circular effect. It increases peer-to-peer political discussion and enhances political exchange at home, and then the products of the home conversations are shared with peers, creating a "loop of influence in which the family and the school enliven the political discussion of each other."[44] Particularly of relevance to this study is their finding that participation in these programs significantly narrows the political engagement gaps between Anglo and Latino students. Thus, the implementation of new programs and approaches to encouraging student political engagement could have significant positive effects on adult political socialization as well.

But how do we do this most effectively? A recent report, *The Civic Mission of Schools*, reviews the extant literature on civic education and makes six recommendations for what schools can do to ensure the political engagement of their students: (1) provide instruction in government, history, law, and democracy, because having this subject matter taught has been shown to increase engagement, so long as it is not done in a rote fashion; (2) incorporate discussion of current events (local, national, and international) into the classroom, and frame these discussions around issues that young people see as relevant to their lives; (3) provide opportunities for students to perform community service that is linked to formal classroom curriculum and instruction; (4) offer extracurricular activities; (5) encourage student participation in school governance; and (6) encourage student participation in simulations of democratic processes and procedures, such as voting, trials, legislative deliberation, and diplomacy.[45]

This is not to suggest that a one-size-fits-all civic education program would be appropriate. Jonathon F. Zaff and colleagues caution that programs to promote citizenship among youths of color must focus on the "information interactions in youths' lives, such as with parent and peers, and on the culture in which youth are raised."[46] They found that "ethnic-related experiences and attitudes that are salient or matter to the youths' self-concepts appear to be important predictors of later citizenship engagement."[47] Gimpel and colleagues also emphasize the importance of the larger school environment—in particular, the students' perception of the school as "fair"—to the effectiveness of any civic education program.[48] Thus, a successful approach to youth civic engagement would have to be context-specific and include in its curriculum programs and projects that are relevant to the life experiences and collective identities of the youths involved.

This kind of approach to teaching civic engagement would be very different from the situation today. In California, students are required only to take one semester of U.S. government in order to graduate from high school. Only twenty-nine states in the United States currently require some kind of civics course. Most of the assessment tests students must take to receive the high school diploma contain no civics or social studies questions. Many states have adopted community service requirements for high school graduation, but many of those programs are not in any way connected to actual coursework or curricula. So we are a long way from what has been found most effective.

There is reason to believe that such a program could work. Whereas studies have found that today's youths are less interested in voting, political discussion, and political issues than their predecessors, they have been found to be highly involved in community service, and they express strong support for the principles of tolerance and free speech.[49] Of course, such a program would require significant investment of resources at a time when public schools are being asked to do more with less. For this kind of program to become an academic priority, we would need to reconceptualize the role schools play in preparing youths to be members of the polity. In addition, as a society we would need to accept responsibility for ensuring that we have an engaged and participatory citizenry.[50] Though it will be difficult to create such a consensus, the potential payoffs are too great to be ignored.

BUILDING COMMUNITY SOCIAL CAPITAL

My findings demonstrate that organizational mobilization, even if not explicitly political, can have long-term positive effects on feelings of efficacy in the nonelectoral arena. So how do we go about building mobilization and organizational capacity in communities? First, we need to focus organizational efforts on the specific needs and experiences of local communities. Studies, as well as the experiences of political organizers, show that the best way to mobilize people is to organize around something very specific that is important to them. This is the core of Saul Alinksy's model of organizing: ask the group to tell you what is important to them, organize around that, and work from there.[51] In his study of Mexican American political organizations, Benjamin Márquez found organizations that emphasize particular racial and class-based identities are more successful at organizing than those that depend simply on shared ethnicity and experiences of racial discrimination.[52] Thus, organizational efforts that appeal to particular collective identities will likely be most effective. As we saw in the case of the Mothers of East Los Angeles, organization that arises in response to a particular threat, in this case a prison construction project, can grow into something very different, yet remain effective.[53] The Mothers have successfully blocked construction of a toxic incinerator project in a nearby city, and now candidates and environmental organizations regularly seek their endorsement of policy programs and proposals.

Second, we need to make efforts to ensure that more political mobilization occurs in immigrant communities. Because models of political party behavior assume that parties will, because of self-interest, mobilize all potential voters, it has largely been left up to the political parties to do this kind of work.[54] Yet bringing new voters into the political system is not necessarily in the parties' best interest. They would be spending limited resources on engaging individuals who may or may not vote and, even more important, may not vote for *them*. Parties would much rather spend their time and resources on political "sure things"—likely, partisan voters. In addition, the tendency in American politics has been for congressional and state legislative districts to become "safer." In these safe districts, parties have no real incentive to spend resources; the majority party is almost assured of victory, and the minority party knows they have little chance of winning. The minority party would rather focus its efforts on races that are competitive.[55] The result is that in immigrant communities there are large numbers of people who need to be brought into electoral politics at any given time—and no institution in society whose interests lay in continually mobilizing these new voters. If the United States is serious about being a participatory democracy, as a society we need to create institutions and programs that will foment this kind of mobilization. But, again, a one-size-fits-all solution is not likely to work. To be effective, that program would have to be contextually specific and historically and culturally relevant to the particular community.

For the sake of clarity, I have listed these recommendations separately. Yet they are highly interrelated. For example, as Frymer points out, one of the main reasons why the political parties have not targeted African Americans for mobilization has been the social stigma attached to the group.[56] So decreases in social stigma could also have a positive impact on party mobilization among African Americans and other racial groups. Similarly, the politicization of social networks will likely lead to greater political interest in general, which could make community organizational efforts more effective. And the effectiveness of all these efforts will depend, to a large extent, on their ability to appeal to and mobilize individuals' group identity(ies). Because they are so interrelated, movement on only one front will not have as great an impact as movement along all three fronts.

By making these recommendations, I am skirting close to the line of normatively driven social science. My efforts here are driven by two concerns. First, I believe it is imperative that social scientists make their work politically relevant, as well as constructive. It is very easy to find flaws and problems in programs and in society. It is much more difficult to find ways to address the problems identified. Second, and related to the first, one of the things that is sometimes missing from political behavior studies is a reminder of why scholars do this work in the first place, why we care either about democracy or about participation in democracy. When John Locke and other Enlightenment theorists were trying to imagine a form of government that satisfied the laws of nature but was no longer ruled by a monarch, their goal was to create a better and more just society.[57] That Locke and his contemporaries denied women and people of color any formal political voice in the new society is a problem but does not negate the fact that their goal was to expand political rights and freedoms beyond those under monarchy. The idea was that, in the end, society would be more just because its government was more just.

Yet over the past one hundred years in the United States income inequality has increased, and levels of political participation are decreasing.[58] Thus, the question is whether our democracy is creating a more just society. One of the main problems with the current state of political participation in the United States is that "policy makers are hearing less from groups with distinctive needs and concerns arising from their social class and group status."[59] One assumes that if the voices were more representative, the resulting policies would also be more reflective of the needs of society as a whole. Based on the findings from this study, I would argue that the best way to reach a more inclusive politics is through acknowledging and encouraging the development of positive identities and group attachments among social groups. In other words, for members of stigmatized groups, establishing a positive attachment to their social group may be a necessary first step toward their attachment to the political community as a whole.[60] It is only after they develop a positive sense of purpose and place within their social group that they are able to see a place for themselves within the larger U.S. political community. Conversely, a less positive attachment may make it more difficult for group members to identify with the larger society.

This vision is in stark contrast to those who argue that acknowledgment of the existence of race in the United States will lead to increased conflict and "balkanization."[61] Instead, I am arguing in favor of what Iris Young calls a "politics of difference," in which political movements are organized around the presumption that "justice is best served by acknowledging the cultural and structural social groups differentiating a society, and by attending to how differences of culture or structural social position produce conflict and condition relations of privilege and relative disadvantage."[62] As such, "accommodating and sometimes compensating for the consequences of social differentiation are necessary for achieving equal respect and genuinely equal opportunity for every person to develop and exercise her or his capacities and participate in public life."[63]

This position assumes that by talking about difference, we can actually increase societal understanding rather than decrease it.[64] A politics that recognizes and values those differences is not subject to fragmentation, as other authors have argued. Difference per se is not the real concern but the fact that in the United States racial differences have been constructed into a hierarchical racial order. In this context, difference by definition implies stigma. Of course, I am not suggesting that increasing minority group participation automatically will benefit democracy as a whole and is guaranteed to make democratic politics more inclusive and egalitarian. There are other structural changes that must occur as well. As Jane Junn cautions, increased participation on the part of minorities can change the structures of inequality in society only if those institutions of democracy are indeed neutral and if the common understanding of agency and citizenship is fluid.[65] If these assumptions are not met, more participation will only, on the one hand, reinforce and legitimate existing structures of domination and, on the other, force groups who are different from the norm to either assimilate or exit the system.[66] Ignoring that reality only serves to justify and maintain an unequal ordering of social relations.[67]

This study's findings have highlighted some of structural considerations that need to be included in analyses of stigmatized groups in American society. The analysis I have presented is antithetical to the idea that the United States can "move beyond" race. Racialization has affected Latinos in Los Angeles from the day the Southwest became part of the United States, and it affects Latino immigrants from the day they step onto U.S. soil. That racialization, and the stigma that accompanies it, affects how they constitute themselves and their social group. It affects how they define their community of interest and how they choose to act on behalf of that interest. When analyzing the political participation of Latinos and other marginal groups, that reality cannot be ignored. Only by understanding the complexity and multiple layers of internal and external border crossings underlying the Latino experience can we understand how, why, and when Latinos incorporate themselves into the political system. Integration into politics requires a shift in Latinos' borders; these borders are constituted by forces of power within the individual and the larger society. This process is complex and fluid, but sifting through the multiple layers is necessary if we are to understand fully the Latino political experience in the United States.

APPENDIX A Study Respondents

This appendix lists all study respondents. "Age," "Years in U.S.," and "Citizen" refer to the respondent's age, length of time in the United States, and citizenship status at the time of the interview. In the "Generation" column, 1 = foreign born; 1.5 = foreign born but immigrated to the United States as a child; 2 = first generation, born in the United States; 3 = second generation, born in the United States; and 4 = third or third-plus generation, born in the United States. Some of the respondents' parents had arrived in the United States at different times. So, for example, "3 mother/2 father" means that the respondent is third generation on the mother's side and second generation on the father's. Schools are listed to indicate the location of the interview and the respondent's area of origin. Four schools were used for the interviews: Garfield Adult School (GAS) and Garfield High School (GHS) in East Los Angeles and Montebello Adult School (MAS) and Montebello High School (MHS) in Montebello.

Name	School	Gender	Age	Nationality	Generation	Interview Language	Years in U.S.	Citizen
Javier	GAS	Male	28	Mexican	1	Spanish	9	No
Mercedes	GAS	Female	40	Mexican	1	Both	25	Yes
Alfredo	GAS	Male	68	Mexican	1	Spanish	37	Yes
María	GAS	Female	38	Mexican	1	Spanish	25	No
Alba	GAS	Female	28	Mexican	1	Spanish	10	No
Jaidy	GAS	Female	43	Honduran	1	Spanish	25	No
Herminia	GAS	Female	52	Mexican	1	Spanish	21	No
Arturo	GAS	Male	27	Mexican	1	English	15	No
José Luis	GAS	Male	39	Mexican	1	Spanish	10	No
Roberto	GAS	Male	23	Mexican	1	Spanish	3	No
Rosa	GAS	Female	35	Mexican	1	Spanish	17	No
Lilia	GAS	Female	24	Mexican	1.5	English	21	No
Luly	GAS	Female	24	Mexican	1.5	English	20	No
María	GAS	Female	34	Mexican	1.5	English	26	No
Guillermina	GAS	Ferrale	15	Mexican	2	English	15	Yes
Hilda	GAS	Female	20	Mexican	2	English	20	Yes
Ramón	GAS	Male	24	Mexican	2	English	24	Yes
Bernie	GAS	Male	19	Mexican	2	English	19	Yes
Juan Carlos	GAS	Male	19	Mexican	2	Both	19	Yes
César	GAS	Male	19	Mexican	2	English	19	Yes
María Josefina	GAS	Female	25	Mexican	2	English	22	Yes
John	GAS	Male	60	Mexican	3	English	60	Yes
José	GAS	Male	41	Mexican	3	Both	41	Yes

Name	School	Gender	Age	Ethnicity	Generation	Language		Yes/No
Zali	GAS	Female	17	Mexican	4 mother/1.5 father	English	17	Yes
Gilbert	GAS	Male	44	Mexican	4	English	44	Yes
José	GHS	Male	17	Mexican	1.5	English	12	Yes
María	GHS	Female	18	Mexican	1.5	English	13	No
Vilma	GHS	Female	17	Salvadoran	1.5	English	16	No
Salvador	GHS	Male	16	Mexican	2	English	16	Yes
Teresa	GHS	Female	17	Mexican	2	English	17	Yes
Verónica	GHS	Female	17	Mexican	2	English	17	Yes
Will	GHS	Male	16	Mexican	2	English	16	Yes
Fernando	GHS	Male	18	Mexican	2	Spanish	8	Yes
Ana	GHS	Female	17	Mexican	2	English	17	Yes
Miguel	GHS	Male	17	Mexican	2	English	17	Yes
Jonathan	GHS	Male	17	Mexican	3	English	17	Yes
Arturo	GHS	Male	17	Mexican-Salvadoran	2	Both	18	Yes
José	GHS	Male	17	Mexican	2	Both	17	Yes
Agustín	GHS	Male	17	Mexican	2	English	17	Yes
Ana	GHS	Female	17	Mexican	2	English	17	Yes
Norma	GHS	Female	19	Mexican-Salvadoran	2	Both	15	Yes
Armando	GHS	Male	18	Mexican	2	English	18	Yes
Linda	GHS	Female	17	Mexican	2	English	0	Yes
Jesús	GHS	Male	17	Mexican	2	English	17	Yes
Araceli	GHS	Female	17	Mexican	2	English	15	Yes
Abby	GHS	Female	17	Mexican	2	English	15	Yes

Name	School	Gender	Age	Nationality	Generation	Interview Language	Years in U.S.	Citizen
Laura	GHS	Female	17	Mexican	3	English	17	Yes
Miledy	GHS	Female	16	Mexican	3 mother/2 father	English	16	Yes
Al	GHS	Male	17	Mexican	4	English	17	Yes
Jay	GHS	Male	17	Mexican	5	English	17	Yes
Martin	MAS	Male	33	Mexican	1	Spanish	17	No
Marta	MAS	Female	36	Mexican	1	Spanish	16	No
María	MAS	Female	63	Guatemalan	1	Spanish	13	No
María	MAS	Female	48	Salvadoran	1	Spanish	26	Yes
Lupe	MAS	Female	35	Mexican	1	Spanish	20	No
Artemio	MAS	Male	23	Mexican	1	Spanish	1	No
María de Jesús	MAS	Female	38	Mexican	1	Spanish	19	Yes
Hector	MAS	Male	26	Mexican	1	Spanish	0	No
Ester	MAS	Female	46	Mexican	1	Spanish	19	Yes
Carlos	MAS	Male	26	Mexican	1	Both	2	No
Adán	MAS	Male	37	Mexican	1	English	19	No
Myrna	MAS	Female	46	Mexican	1	Spanish	30	No
Nancy	MAS	Female	27	Mexican	1	Spanish	10	No
Rafael	MAS	Male	44	Mexican	1	Spanish	20	No
Juan	MAS	Male	21	Mexican-Salvadoran	2	English	21	Yes
Miguel	MAS	Male	20	Mexican	2	English	20	Yes

Name	School	Gender	Age	Ethnicity	Generation	Language	Age	
Jonathon	MAS	Male	19	Mexican	2 mother/3 father	English	19	Yes
Enrique	MAS	Male	19	Mexican	2 mother/3 father	English	19	Yes
Michelle	MAS	Female	24	Mexican	3	English	24	Yes
Cassandra	MAS	Female	18	Mexican	3	English	18	Yes
Juan	MAS	Male	40	Mexican	3	English	40	Yes
Adela	MAS	Female	30	Mexican	4	English	30	Yes
Chris	MAS	Male	18	Mexican–Native American	4	English	18	Yes
Desiré	MAS	Female	22	Mexican	4	English	22	Yes
Collette	MAS	Female	42	Mexican	4	English	42	Yes
Emma	MAS	Female	38	Mexican	4	English	38	Yes
Johnny	MAS	Male	21	Mexican	5	English	21	Yes
Mary	MAS	Female	52	Mexican	5	English	52	Yes
Federico	MHS	Male	18	Mexican	1	Spanish	5	No
Caroline	MHS	Female	17	Colombian	1	English	10	No
Jesús	MHS	Male	17	Mexican	1.5	English	13	No
Israel	MHS	Male	18	Mexican	1.5	English	8	Yes
Araceli	MHS	Female	17	Mexican	2	English	17	Yes
Roberto	MHS	Male	17	Salvadoran	2	English	17	Yes
Sergio	MHS	Male	17	Mexican	2	English	17	Yes
Francisco	MHS	Male	17	Mexican	2	English	17	Yes
Laura	MHS	Female	17	Mexican	2	English	17	Yes
Eduardo	MHS	Male	18	Mexican	2	English	18	Yes
David	MHS	Male	17	Mexican	2	English	17	Yes

Name	School	Gender	Age	Nationality	Generation	Interview Language	Years in U.S.	Citizen
Pedro	MHS	Male	18	Guatemalan-Mexican	2	English	18	Yes
Julian	MHS	Male	17	Mexican	2	English	17	Yes
Yessica	MHS	Female	17	Mexican	2	English	17	Yes
Angela	MHS	Female	18	Mexican	3	English	18	Yes
Abraham	MHS	Male	17	Mexican	3 mother/2 father	English	17	Yes
Richard	MHS	Male	17	Mexican-Colombian	3 mother/2 father	English	17	Yes
Celina	MHS	Female	17	Mexican	3 mother/2 father	English	17	Yes
Cynthia	MHS	Female	17	Salvadoran	3	English	17	Yes
Julianna	MHS	Female	18	Mexican	3	English	18	Yes
Marianna	MHS	Female	17	Mexican	4	English	17	Yes
Corrine	MHS	Female	16	Mexican	4	English	16	Yes

APPENDIX B Interview Questionnaire

Because the interviews were semistructured, the questions were not always asked in the same order, except for the first question, with which I began all the interviews. But I attempted to ask each respondent all of the questions that applied to him or her. This version of the questions is written as if the respondent were Mexican; for other Latinos, the questions would be worded to refer to the group they belonged to.

1. How did you (or your family) come to be in the United States?
2. Have you (or your parents) ever had any negative experiences because you were Mexican?
3. Do you think there is discrimination against Mexicans in Los Angeles?
4. When you think of the word *discrimination,* what kinds of experiences does that bring to mind?
5. [For second generation and beyond] Are you glad you (or your parents) immigrated here?
6. Do you speak Spanish at home?

7. Would you want your children to learn Spanish? Why?
8. Does your family maintain Mexican culture? Why?
9. How do you identify yourself?
10. Do you think you could define yourself as more than one of these terms at the same time?
11. Do you think Mexicans have things in common with Salvadorans, Guatemalans, and other people of Latin American descent? What things?
12. Do you think most Americans can tell the difference between a Mexican and a Salvadoran? Why, or why not?
13. Do you think that some Americans have a negative image of Mexicans? What is that image?
14. Where do you think that image comes from?
15. Do you think it will ever change?
16. Do you watch TV in English and Spanish? Have you noticed any differences between the two?
17. Are you interested in politics? Why?
18. Did you pay any attention to the presidential campaign last November?
19. What are your general feelings about the political system in this country?
20. Are you a citizen?
21. If yes, are you registered to vote? Why?
22. Did you register with a particular party, or independent? Why?
23. If no, do you plan on becoming one? Why?
24. During the campaign, do you feel like you received enough information from the parties and about the issues in order to make your decision?
25. Do you think your vote matters?
26. Do you think people like you can affect what government does?
27. Why do you think so many Latinos, even if they're citizens, don't vote?
28. Did you have any opinion about Proposition 187?
29. Did you feel the proposition was directed at any group in particular?
30. Have you ever participated in walkouts, marches, or other kinds of protests?
31. Did you think these actions were good ideas? Do you think they made a difference? What kind of activity do you think would have made a difference?
32. If Proposition 187 gets enforced, do you think it will affect the community? What about legal immigrants?

33. Do you think 187 will keep people from immigrating here?
34. Have you heard about Proposition 209? What do you think about it?
35. What do you think are the good things about living in this community?
36. What are the bad things?
37. Can you think of any way to resolve these problems?
38. Do you do any volunteer/community work?
39. Do you think if more people volunteered, it would make a difference in the community? What do you think would make a difference?
40. What do you think is the biggest problem facing your community today? How would you solve it?
41. Is there anything that we haven't talked about that you think is important, or that you would like to add?

For those who went to high school in the United States:

42. Do you feel like you've gotten a good education here? In what ways?
43. Do you think the teachers have high expectations of the students? Why?
44. Did you ever take a Chicano Studies or Minority Cultures course? If so, did you like it?
45. Have you taken Government? Did you like it? After taking it, were you more interested in politics in general?

For those who said they were not citizens:

46. Are you planning to become a citizen? Why?
47. How long have you been in the United States?

Notes

CHAPTER 1. LATINO POLITICAL ENGAGEMENT

Epigraph: Frederick Douglass, "An Address on West India Emancipation," in John W. Blassingame, ed., *The Frederick Douglass Papers*, series 1, *Speeches, Debates, and Interviews, 1855–63* (New Haven: Yale University Press, 1979).

    1. I define *political engagement* broadly, to include not only political activity, which includes both electoral and nonelectoral participation (voting, marching, protesting, community work, etc.), but also interest in politics. This broader definition is appropriate because Mexican Americans and Puerto Ricans have been found to be less likely than Anglos to vote, but more likely to engage in activities such as marches and protests. See Sidney Verba, Kay Lehman Schlozman, Henry Brady, and Norman Nie, "Race, Ethnicity and Political Resources: Participation in the United States, *British Journal of Politics* 23 (1993): 453–97; Robert D. Wrinkle, Joseph Stewart Jr., J. L. Polinard, Kenneth J. Meier, and John R. Arvizu, "Ethnicity and Nonelectoral Participation," *Hispanic Journal of Behavioral Sciences* 18 (1996): 142–53; Natasha Hritzuk and David K. Park, "The Question of Latino Participation: From an SES to a Social Structural Explanation," *Social Science Quarterly* 81 (2000): 151–66.

2. Vicki L. Ruiz, *From Out of the Shadows* (New York: Oxford University Press, 1998), xv.

3. The study's respondents came from many Latin American countries, including Mexico, El Salvador, Colombia, Guatemala, and Honduras. Although I discuss my findings in terms of "Latinos," more than three quarters of my respondents (83 percent) were Mexican or Mexican American. When discussing the experiences of particular individuals, I use their national origin identifier.

4. Economic sociologists such as Alejandro Portes have developed a large literature that shows the importance of ethnic enclaves and social context to the ability of immigrants to experience socioeconomic mobility in the United States. For an overview, see Alejandro Portes, ed., *The Economic Sociology of Immigration: Essays on Networks, Ethnicity, and Entrepreneurship* (New York: Russell Sage Foundation, 1995).

5. Rogers M. Smith provides an in-depth discussion of this need for psychological attachment to the nation and the narratives that arise from it. See *Stories of Peoplehood: The Politics and Morals of Political Membership* (Cambridge: Cambridge University Press, 2003), esp. chap. 1.

6. See, e.g., John R. Logan, Brian J. Stults, and Reynolds Farley, "Segregation of Minorities in the Metropolis: Two Decades of Change," *Demography* 41 (2004): 1–22; Richard D. Alba and John R. Logan, "Minority Proximity to Whites in Suburbs: An Individual-Level Analysis of Segregation," *American Journal of Sociology* 98 (1993): 1388–1427; Richard D. Alba, John R. Logan, and Brian J. Stults, "The Changing Neighborhood Contexts of the Immigrant Metropolis," *Social Forces* 79 (2000): 587–621; Richard D. Alba, John R. Logan, Wenquan Zhange, and Brian J. Stults, "Strangers Next Door: Immigrant Groups and Suburbs in Los Angeles and New York, " in Phyllis Moen, Donna Dempster-McClain, and Henry A. Walker, eds., *A Nation Divided: Diversity, Inequality and Community in American Society* (Ithaca: Cornell University Press, 1999).

7. Suzanne Oboler, "It Must Be a Fake! Racial Ideologies, Identities, and the Question of Rights," in Jorge J. E. Gracia and Pablo De Greiff, eds., *Hispanics/Latinos in the United States: Ethnicity, Race, and Rights* (New York: Routledge, 2000), 127.

8. For historical overviews of these experiences, see Leonard Pitt, *The Decline of the Californios: A Social History of the Spanish-Speaking Californians, 1846–1890*, 2d ed. (Berkeley: University of California Press, 1994); Tomás Almaguer, *Racial Fault Lines: The Historical Origins of White Supremacy in California* (Berkeley: University of California Press, 1994); Rodolfo Acuña, *Occupied America: A History of Chicanos*, 3d ed. (New York: HarperCollins, 1988); Martha Menchaca, *The Mexican Outsiders: A Community History of Marginalization and Discrimination in California* (Austin: University of Texas Press, 1995); Martha Menchaca, *Recovering History, Constructing Race: The Indian, Black, and White Roots of Mexican Americans* (Austin:

University of Texas Press, 2003); James Jennings and Monte Rivera, *Puerto Rican Politics in Urban America* (Westport, Conn.: Greenwood Press, 1984).

9. Just one example is the fact that U.S. immigration policy varies significantly by country of origin, particularly among those petitioning for political asylum. Once granted asylum, political exiles, like Cubans, have a much easier and more streamlined process for being granted citizenship than do asylum seekers from other countries. Immigrants seeking political asylum from countries with whom the United States has good relations, like those from Central America in the 1980s, have found it very difficult to normalize their status in the United States, regardless of their personal desire to do so.

10. *Merriam-Webster's Collegiate Dictionary*, 11th ed. (Springfield, Mass.: Merriam-Webster, Inc., 2003).

11. See Mustafa Emirbayer and Jeff Goodwin, "Network Analysis, Culture, and the Problem of Agency," *American Journal of Sociology* 99 (1994): 1411–54.

12. Yen Le Espiritu, *Home Bound: Filipino American Lives across Cultures, Communities, and Countries* (Berkeley: University of California Press, 2003), 1–2.

13. E.g., see Suzanne Oboler, *Ethnic Labels, Latino Lives: Identity and the Politics of (Re)presentation in the United States* (Minneapolis: University of Minnesota Press, 1995).

14. Iris Marion Young, "Structure, Difference and Hispanic/Latino Claims of Justice," in Gracia and De Greiff, eds., *Hispanics/Latinos in the United States*, 153.

15. Ibid.

16. Jorge J. E. Gracia and Pablo De Greiff, introduction to *Hispanics/Latinos in the United States*, 10.

17. For an overview of these perspectives, see Judith A. Howard, "Social Psychology of Identities," *Annual Review of Sociology* 26 (2000): 367–93.

18. Ibid., 388.

19. For an overview of studies of the effects of stigma on behavior, see Bruce G. Link and Jo C. Phelan, "Conceptualizing Stigma," *Annual Review of Sociology* 27 (2001): 363–85. To understand the effects of stereotypes on self-image, see M. A. Hogg and J. C. Turner, "Intergroup Behaviour, Self Stereotyping and the Salience of Social Categories," *British Journal of Social Psychology* 26 (1987): 325–40.

20. Jennifer Crocker, Brenda Major, and Claude Steele, "Social Stigma," in Daniel T. Gilbert, Susan T. Fiske, and Gardner Lindzey, eds., *Handbook of Social Psychology*, 4th ed. (New York: McGraw-Hill, 1998), 504–53, quote on 505.

21. Link and Phelan, "Conceptualizing Stigma," 367.

22. Hogg and Turner, "Intergroup Behavior"; and Crocker, Major, and Steele, "Social Stigma."

23. Angus Campbell, Phillip E. Converse, Warren E. Miller, and Donald E. Stokes, *The American Voter* (New York: John Wiley and Sons, 1960).

24. See Sidney Verba and Norman H. Nie, *Participation in America: Political*

Democracy and Social Equality (Chicago: University of Chicago Press, 1972); Steven J. Rosenstone and John Mark Hansen, *Mobilization, Participation, and Democracy in America* (New York: Macmillan, 1993); Raymond Wolfinger and Steven J. Rosenstone, *Who Votes?* (New Haven: Yale University Press, 1980); Sidney Verba, Norman H. Nie, and Jae-on Kim, *Participation and Political Equality: A Seven-Nation Comparison* (Cambridge: Cambridge University Press, 1978); and M. Margaret Conway, *Political Participation in the United States*, 2d ed. (Washington, D.C.: Congressional Quarterly Press, 1991).

25. Verba, Schlozman, and Brady expand on the SES model and analyze the myriad resources (occupational experience being only one example) and civic skills that arise from SES. Sidney Verba, Kay Lehman Schlozman, and Henry Brady, *Voice and Equality: Civic Voluntarism in American Politics* (Cambridge, Mass.: Harvard University Press, 1995).

26. Mancur Olson, *The Logic of Collective Action: Public Goods and the Theory of Groups*, 2d ed. (Cambridge, Mass.: Harvard University Press, 1971).

27. For an overview of this literature, see Francesca Polletta and James M. Jasper, "Collective Identity and Social Movements," *Annual Review of Sociology* 27 (2001): 283–305.

28. Michael C. Dawson, *Black Visions: The Roots of Contemporary African-American Political Ideologies* (Chicago: University of Chicago Press, 2001), 4.

29. Polletta and Jasper, "Collective Identity and Social Movements," 285.

30. The term *collective identity* "denotes those aspects of the self concept that relate to race, ethnic background, religion, feelings of belonging in one's community, and the like." Riia K. Luhtanen and Jennifer Crocker, "A Collective Self-Esteem Scale: Self Evaluation of One's Social Identity," *Personality and Social Psychology Bulletin* 18 (1992): 302–18, quote on 302.

31. See Kimberlé Crenshaw, "Mapping the Margins: Intersectionality, Identity, Politics, and Violence against Women of Color," *Stanford Law Review* 43 (1991): 1241–99; Patricia Hill Collins, *Feminist Thought: Knowledge, Consciousness, and the Politics of Empowerment*, 2d ed. (New York: Routledge, 2000); and Kimberlé Crenshaw, Kendall Thomas, Neil Gotanda, and Gary Peller, eds., *Critical Race Theory: The Key Writings That Formed the Movement* (New York: New Press, 1995).

32. For a discussion of the importance of relational analyses in social science, see Mustafa Emirbayer, "Manifesto for a Relational Sociology," *American Journal of Sociology* 103 (1997): 281–317. For a look at how identity has been conceptualized and measured by social psychologists, see Luhtanen and Crocker, "A Collective Self-Esteem Scale"; and Marilynn B. Brewer and Rupert J. Brown, "Intergroup Relations," in Gilbert, Fiske, and Lindzey, eds., *Handbook of Social Psychology*.

33. My understanding of race as a socially constructed concept comes from Michael Omi and Howard Winant, *Racial Formation in the United States from the 1960s to the 1990s* (New York: Routledge, 1994).

34. European social psychologists use the term *social identity* to refer to what I am calling *collective identity*. My definition of *collective identity* is the same as that of social identity, as defined by Henri Tajfel and J. C. Turner. See "The Social Identity Theory of Intergroup Behavior," in Stephen Worchel and William G. Austin, eds., *Psychology of Intergroup Relations* (Chicago: Nelson-Hall, 1986); and "An Integrative Theory of Intergroup Conflict," in William G. Austin and Stephen Worchel, eds., *The Social Psychology of Intergroup Relations* (Monterey, Calif.: Brooks/Cole Books, 1979).

35. Min Zhou and Carl L. Bankston III, "Social Capital and the Adaptation of the Second Generation: the Case of Vietnamese Youth in New Orleans," *International Migration Review* 28 (1994): 821–45, quote on 821. See also Kathryn Harper, "Immigrant Generation, Assimilation and Adolescent Psychological Well-Being," *Social Forces* 79 (2001): 969–1004.

36. Sociologists use the term *human capital* to denote resources that belong to the individual, such as educational level or job skills. For a discussion of the relationship between social capital and human capital, see James S. Coleman, "Social Capital and the Creation of Human Capital," *American Journal of Sociology* 94 (1988): S95–S120.

37. Rubén Rumbaut, "The Crucible Within: Ethnic Identity, Self-Esteem, and Segmented Assimilation among Children of Immigrants," *International Migration Review* 28 (1994): 748–94, quote on 756.

38. María Eugenia Matute-Bianchi, "Ethnic Identities and Patterns of School Success and Failure among Mexican Descent and Japanese-American Students in a California High School: An Ethnographic Analysis," *American Journal of Education* 95 (1986): 233–55.

39. For a detailed overview of this history, see Rogers M. Smith, *Civic Ideals: Conflicting Visions of Citizenship in U.S. History* (New Haven: Yale University Press, 1997).

40. Katherine Tate's finding that descriptive representation among African Americans does affect their feelings of trust and efficacy in government supports this proposition. See Katherine Tate, *Black Faces in the Mirror: African Americans and Their Representatives in the U.S. Congress* (Princeton: Princeton University Press, 2003).

41. Michael Dawson uses the term *linked fate*. Katherine Tate calls this "common fate." They are largely describing a sense that one's fate is tied to that of other group members. See Michael Dawson, *Behind the Mule: Race and Class in African-American Politics* (Princeton: Princeton University Press, 1994); and Katherine Tate, *From Protest to Politics: The New Black Voters in American Elections* (Cambridge, Mass.: Harvard University Press, 1994), 90–92.

42. Dawson, *Behind the Mule*; and Tate, *From Protest to Politics*, 90–92.

43. One could argue that such feelings would be captured by traditional mea-

surements of political efficacy. Yet it would be useful to know more about where those feelings of efficacy come from and whether the sources vary among and/or within groups. Such an analysis is difficult using current measures. Thus, looking at group attachment and feelings of stigma may prove a fruitful avenue of inquiry.

44. In *Voice and Equality*, 355, Verba, Schlozman, and Brady also argue that measurement problems may explain in part why they did not find that group consciousness had an effect on the participation patterns of the racial groups in their study.

45. See David Easton and Jack Dennis, *Children in the Political System: The Origins of Political Legitimacy* (New York: McGraw-Hill, 1969); M. Kent Jennings and Richard G. Niemi. "The Transmission of Political Values from Parent to Child," *American Political Science Review* 62 (1968): 169–184; and M. Kent Jennings, Laura Stoker, and Jake Bowers, "Politics across Generations: Family Transmission Reexamined," Working Paper (Institute for Governmental Studies, Berkeley, Calif., 2001).

46. Chicano Studies was offered at Garfield High School and Multicultural History was offered at Montebello High School. Those were the only explicitly "multicultural" course offerings available to the respondents at the time of the interviews.

47. These celebrations are organized yearly and are the largest in the southern California area. They recognize Mexico's independence from Spain.

48. This idea of counternarrative is similar to Michael Dawson's idea of black "counterpublics." But, given the relatively recent nature of Latino political organizing, I do not believe the community has developed ongoing movements that could credibly be described as "counterpublics." It is reasonable to assume, however, that this kind of counternarrative, as with African Americans, is a necessary first step to contesting the political status quo. See Dawson, *Black Visions*, esp. chap. 1.

49. Zhou and Bankston, "Social Capital and the Adaptation of the Second Generation."

50. Here the ideas of agency and efficacy are related but not the same. By *efficacy*, I mean, as is found in the political behavior literature, people's perception that they can make change through their actions. This is related to feelings of agency, but it is used specifically in relation to political activity. For an overview of the literature on the relationship between efficacy and socioeconomic status, see Verba and Nie, *Participation in America*; Rosenstone and Hansen, *Mobilization, Participation, and Democracy in America*; Verba, Schlozman, and Brady, *Voice and Equality*; and Wolfinger and Rosenstone, *Who Votes?*

51. By *white*, these respondents were referring to Anglos.

52. Stephen J. Worchel, Francisco Morales, Dario Páez, and Jean-Claude Deschamps, *Social Identity: International Perspectives* (London: Sage, 1998).

53. I say "little" choice since American history is full of stories of members of racial groups that were able to "pass" as white. But, again, this is the result of phenotype differences that are an accident of birth, rather than of any conscious act on the part of the individual.

54. Robert D. Putnam, *Bowling Alone: The Collapse and Revival of American Community* (New York: Simon and Schuster, 2000). For critiques of Putnam, see Alejandro Portes, "Social Capital: Its Origins and Applications in Modern Sociology," *Annual Review of Sociology* 24 (1998): 1–24, particularly pages 17–20; and Theda Skocpol, "Unraveling from Above," *American Prospect* 25 (1996): 20–25.

55. Portes, "Social Capital."

56. Kent E. Portney and Jeffrey M. Berry, "Mobilizing Minority Communities: Social Capital and Participation in Urban Neighborhoods," *American Behavioral Scientist* 40 (1997): 632–644.

57. Janelle Wong, "Getting out the Vote among Asian Americans: A Field Experiment," paper presented at the annual meeting of the American Political Science Association, Philadelphia, Pa., September 2003.

58. This is what Meyer calls the political "opportunity structure." See David S. Meyer, "Political Opportunity and Nested Institutions," *Social Movement Studies* 2 (2003): 17–35.

59. Gerald C. Lubenow and Bruce E. Cain, eds., *Governing California: Politics, Government and Public Policy in the Golden State* (Berkeley: Institute for Governmental Studies, 1997).

60. We will see in chapter 5 that the East Los Angeles respondents emphasize the need for "self-help" at the local level. This may partly be a result of the fact that they have no local government to turn to for assistance.

61. For an overview of this literature, see Portes, "Social Capital." See also Pierre Bourdieu, "The Forms of Capital," in J. G. Richardson, ed., *Handbook of Theory and Research for the Sociology of Education* (New York: Greenwood Press, 1985), 241–258; and Coleman, "Social Capital in the Creation of Human Capital."

62. Portes, "Social Capital," 8.

63. For a review of this literature, see Miller McPherson, Lynn Smith-Lovin, and James M. Cook, "Birds of a Feather: Homophily in Social Networks," *Annual Review of Sociology* 27 (2001): 415–444.

64. Lee Sigelman, Timothy Bledsoe, Susan Welch, and Michael Combs, "Making Contact? Black-White Social Interaction in an Urban Setting," *American Journal of Sociology* 101 (1996): 1306–1332.

65. Peter Marsden, "Core Discussion Networks of Americans," *American Sociological Review* 52 (1987): 122–131.

66. Menchaca, *The Mexican Outsiders*, 169.

67. Although the effects of interracial contact received a great deal of scholarly attention after the end of segregation, that attention has faded in recent years. In addition, little work has looked at the effects of Latino-Anglo contact. The work that has been done found little effect but also did not look at equal-status contact, which has been found to be important in the case of black-Anglo interaction. For work on Latinos, see Susan Welch and Lee Sigelman, "Getting to Know You? Latino-Anglo Social Contact," *Social Science Quarterly* 81 (2000): 67–83. For an overview of the contact literature, see Lee Sigelman and Susan Welch, "The Contact Hypothesis Revisited: Black-White Interaction and Positive Racial Attitudes," *Social Forces* 71 (1993): 781–795. For a discussion of the importance of equal-status contact, see Jerry W. Robinson and James D. Preston, "Equal-Status Contact and Modification of Racial Prejudice: A Reexamination of the Contact Hypothesis," *Social Forces* 54 (1976): 911–924; and Cornelius Riordan and Josephine Ruggiero, "Producing Equal-Status Interracial Interaction: A Replication," *Social Psychology Quarterly* 43 (1980): 131–136.

68. David Knoke, "Networks of Political Action: Toward Theory Construction." *Social Forces* 68 (1990): 1041–1063, quote on 1058. See also Kathryn Ray, Mike Savage, Gindo Tampubolon, Alan Warde Brian Longhurst, and Mark Tomlinson, "The Exclusiveness of the Political Field: Networks and Political Mobilization," *Social Movement Studies* 2 (2003): 38–60.

69. Ronald La Due Lake and Robert Huckfeldt, "Social Capital, Social Networks, and Political Participation," *Political Psychology* 19 (1998): 567–584.

70. Melissa J. Marschall, "Does the Shoe Fit? Testing Models of Participation for African American and Latino Involvement in Politics," *Urban Affairs Review* 37 (2001): 227–248.

71. Hritzuk and Park, "The Question of Latino Participation."

72. Ibid., 164.

73. For an overview of these historical experiences, see Almaguer, *Racial Fault Lines*; Douglas Monroy, *Thrown among Strangers: The Making of Mexican Culture in Frontier America* (Berkeley: University of California Press, 1993); Matt García, *A World of Its Own: Race, Labor, and Citrus in the Making of Greater Los Angeles* (Chapel Hill: University of North Carolina Press, 2002); George J. Sánchez, *Becoming Mexican American: Ethnicity, Culture and Identity in Chicano Los Angeles, 1900–1945* (New York: Oxford University Press, 1993); and Rodolfo Acuña, *Anything but Mexican: Chicanos in Contemporary Los Angeles* (New York: Verso Press, 1997).

74. For a recent work that reviews findings on family political socialization from the 1960s to the 1990s, see Jennings, Stoker, and Bowers, "Politics across Generations." With regard to immigrant political socialization, part of the problem is that there has been so little work on this topic. See Alex Stepick and Carol

Dutton Stepick, "Becoming American, Constructing Ethnicity: Immigrant Youth and Civic Engagement," *Applied Developmental Science* 6 (2002): 246–257.

75. For a historical overview of these processes of segregation, see David G. Gutiérrez, *Walls and Mirrors: Mexican Americans, Mexican Immigrants, and the Politics of Ethnicity* (Berkeley: University of California Press, 1995), chaps. 3, 5, and 6. For a discussion of Latino residential segregation, see Douglas Massey and Nancy Denton, "Trends in the Residential Segregation of Blacks, Hispanics, and Asians, 1970–80," *American Sociological Review* 52 (December 1987): 802–825. Massey and Denton found that Latino segregation in Los Angeles was increasing over time, which was contrary to what was happening with black segregation in Los Angeles during the same period.

76. By *third-plus-generation*, I mean individuals who are third, fourth, or fifth generation. *Second-generation* refers to individuals who were born in the United States to immigrant parents. The term *1.5-generation* describes individuals who are foreign born but migrated to the United States at a young age. *First-generation* applies to the foreign-born respondents.

77. Zhou and Bankston, "Social Capital and the Adaptation of the Second Generation," 825.

78. Two exceptions are José E. Cruz, *Identity and Power: Puerto Rican Politics and the Challenge of Ethnicity* (Philadelphia: Temple University Press, 1998); and Carlos Muñoz, *Youth, Identity, Power: The Chicano Movement* (New York: Verso Press, 1989). Some examples of works from other disciplines are Ruiz, *From Out of the Shadows*; Antionette Sedillo-López, ed., *Historical Themes and Identity: Mestizaje and Labels* (New York: Garland, 1995); Menchaca, *Recovering History, Constructing Race*; Gracia and De Greiff, eds., *Hispanics/Latinos in the United States*; Mary Romero, Pierrette Hondagneu-Sotelo, and Vilma Ortiz, eds., *Challenging Fronteras: Structuring Latina and Latino Lives in the United States: An Anthology of Readings* (New York: Routledge, 1997); Andrés Torres, ed., *The Puerto Rican Movement: Voices from the Diaspora* (Philadelphia: Temple University Press, 1998); Rubén G. Rumbaut and Alejandro Portes, eds., *Ethnicities: Children of Immigrants in America* (Berkeley: University of California Press, 2001); Alejandro Portes and Rubén G. Rumbaut, *Legacies: The Stories of the Immigrant Second Generation* (Berkeley: University of California Press, 2001); Roger Waldinger and Mehdi Bozorgmher, *Ethnic Los Angeles* (New York: Russell Sage Foundation, 1996); Martha E. Bernal and George P. Knight, eds., *Ethnic Identity: Formation and Transmission among Hispanics and Other Minorities* (Albany: State University of New York Press, 1993); William V. Flores and Rina Benmayor, eds., *Latino Cultural Citizenship: Claiming Identity, Space, and Rights* (Boston: Beacon Press, 1997); Latina Feminist Group, *Telling to Live: Latina Feminist Testimonios* (Durham, N.C.: Duke University Press, 2001); Ed Morales, *Living in Spanglish: The Search for Latino Identity in America* (New York: St. Martin's Press, 2002).

79. See Verba, Schlozman, and Brady, *Voice and Equality*; Verba and Nie, *Participation in America*; Rosenstone and Hansen, *Mobilization, Participation, and Democracy in America*; Wolfinger and Rosenstone, *Who Votes?*; Verba, Nie, and Kim, *Participation and Political Equality*; and Conway, *Political Participation in the United States*.

80. Some examples are Cathy J. Cohen, *The Boundaries of Blackness: AIDS and the Breakdown of Black Politics* (Chicago: University of Chicago Press, 1999); Dawson, *Black Visions*; James S. Jackson, Patricia Gurin, and Shirley J. Hatchett, *The 1984 Black Election Study* (Ann Arbor, Mich.: Interuniversity Consortium for Political and Social Research, 1989); Andrea Simpson, *The Tie That Binds: Identity and Political Attitudes in the Post–Civil Rights Generation* (New York: New York University Press, 1998); and Tate, *From Protest to Politics*.

81. Louis DeSipio, *Counting on the Latino Vote: Latinos as New Electorate* (Charlottesville: University Press of Virginia, 1996), 4–5.

82. Carol Hardy-Fanta, *Latina Politics, Latino Politics: Gender, Culture and Participation in Boston* (Philadelphia: Temple University Press, 1993). See also Mary Pardo, *Mexican American Women Activists: Identity and Resistance in Two Los Angeles Communities* (Philadelphia: Temple University Press, 1998).

83. See F. Chris García, introduction to *Pursuing Power: Latinos and the Political System* (Notre Dame: Notre Dame University Press, 1997), and "Inputs into the Political System: Participation," 31–43; Rodney Hero, *Latinos and the U.S. Political System: Two-Tiered Pluralism* (Philadelphia: Temple University Press, 1992), chaps. 1 and 2; David Rodríguez, *Latino National Political Coalitions: Struggles and Challenges* (New York: Routledge, 2002); and Rodolfo D. Torres and George Katsiaficas, eds., *Latino Social Movements: Historical and Theoretical Perspectives: A New Political Science Reader* (New York: Routledge, 1999).

84. Putnam, *Bowling Alone*.

85. Wolfinger and Rosenstone, *Who Votes?*

86. María Antonia Calvo and Steven Rosenstone, "Hispanic Political Participation" (Southwest Voter Institute, San Antonio, 1989).

87. F. Chris García, Angelo Falcón, and Rodolfo de la Garza, "Ethnicity and Politics: Evidence from the Latino National Political Survey," *Hispanic Journal of Behavioral Sciences* 18 (1996): 91–103.

88. Verba et al., "Race, Ethnicity and Political Resources."

89. Briefly, studies have different approaches to identifying "Latino" respondents. For largely financial reasons, many studies use Spanish-surname lists rather than random- digit dialing. Or they may focus sampling on the states that contain the largest proportion of the Latino population. Both create difficulties in asserting that the sample is "truly" representative of the national Latino population as a whole.

90. From 1968 to 1972 Latinos in southern California and other areas of the

country engaged in a set of mobilizations and protests that have been called the Chicano Movement. The organization in southern California culminated in the 1970 Chicano Moratorium march, held in East Los Angeles's Belvedere Park (later renamed Salazar Park after the *Los Angeles Times* journalist who was shot by police during this event). For a history of the Chicano Movement in California, see Muñoz, *Youth, Identity, Power;* and Mario T. García, ed., *Rubén Salazar, Border Correspondent: Selected Writings, 1955–1970* (Berkeley: University of California Press, 1995).

91. See, e.g., Simon Romero, "1,500 Students Leave Class to Protest against Prop. 187," *Los Angeles Times,* 15 Oct. 1994, 3; Beth Shuster and Chip Johnson, "Students at 2 Pacoima Schools Protest 187," *Los Angeles Times* [Valley Edition], 21 Oct. 1994, 1; Fred Alvarez and Maia Davis, "1,500 Students Leave Schools over Prop. 187," *Los Angeles Times* [Ventura West Edition], 29 Oct. 1994, 1; Amy Pyle and Greg Hernández, "10,000 Students Protest Prop. 187 Immigration: Walkout in Orange and L.A. Counties Is Largest Yet," *Los Angeles Times* [Orange County Edition], 3 Nov. 1994, 1.

92. Jon D. Markman, "Prop 187's Quiet Student Revolution Activism," *Los Angeles Times,* 6 Nov. 1994, 3.

93. Dennis McLellan, "Stirring up Activist Passion in Today's Youth," *Los Angeles Times,* 4 Nov. 1994, 1.

94. Quote from UCLA education professor James Trent, as reported by Markman, "Prop 187's Quiet Student Revolution Activism."

95. For studies looking mainly at Anglos, see Campbell et al., *The American Voter;* Verba and Nie, *Participation in America;* Rosenstone and Hansen, *Mobilization, Participation, and Democracy in America.* For studies that include Latinos, see Wolfinger and Rosenstone, *Who Votes?;* Verba et al., "Race, Ethnicity and Political Resources;" García, Falcón, and de la Garza, "Ethnicity and Politics"; DeSipio, *Counting on the Latino Vote;* Verba, Schlozman, and Brady, *Voice and Equality;* and Jan Leighley, *Strength in Numbers? The Political Mobilization of Racial and Ethnic Minorities* (Princeton: Princeton University Press, 2001).

96. According to the 2000 census, East Los Angeles is 97 percent Latino, and Montebello is 75 percent Latino. The 2000 census reported a median household income of $28,544 for East Los Angeles and $38,805 for Montebello. On average, East Los Angeles households are larger than those in Montebello, 4.2 versus 3.2 persons, so the income difference is even greater. The median household incomes in my sample were similar: $28,321 and $37,877, respectively. Nationally, Latinos have a median household income of $30,735, and for Latinos of Mexican origin it is about the same, $30,400. So the income levels in the East Los Angeles sample are similar to that of Latinos nationally, and the Montebello sample is slightly better off than Latinos nationally. Also, according to the 2000 census, 43 percent of Latinos aged 25 and older in East Los Angeles had less than 9 years of education,

compared to 19 percent of those from Montebello. Only 3 percent of Latinos from East Los Angeles had a college or professional degree versus 10 percent of those from Montebello. This puts Montebello at about the national average; about 10.6 percent of Latinos nationally have a college education, compared to about 27 percent of Anglos. While we know that the sample respondents from the two areas vary in terms of income levels, a comparison along the other parameter of socioeconomic status, years of education, is more difficult to make in the context of this sample. All of the high school respondents were seniors and therefore have the same amount of education, almost 12 years. The census data indicate that it is likely that the parents of those from East Los Angeles are less educated than those from Montebello, and this should affect their children's political socialization and attitudes. But for the adult school students, especially the foreign born, it is difficult to make a direct translation of years of education in Mexico or Latin America to years of education in the United States. One of the main problems with my research design is that it does not allow for an analysis of the effect of education, and the adult school students, specifically in Montebello, may be less educated than the general population in the area. But since more of my Montebello Adult School respondents were college educated than those in East Los Angeles, and they were more likely to have white-collar jobs, I believe that the socioeconomic differences between the two communities with regard to education are still present in this sample. Forty-nine percent of East Los Angeles residents and 38 percent of Montebello residents were foreign born. Likewise, my East Los Angeles sample contained twice as many first-generation respondents as the Montebello sample, and the Montebello sample had about twice as many third-plus-generation respondents as the East Los Angeles sample.

97. One methodological problem with this study is that neither community is a "discrete" space; both are "nested" in the megalopolis that is southern California. Thus, determining boundaries and understanding their meaning is difficult. Self-selection is also an issue, in that individuals are living in these areas by choice, and the differences I found among the residents could have existed prior to their settlement in the particular area. However, as previous studies, done at the neighborhood level, have found that the density of social ties and conditions of mutual trust have important positive effects on immigrant adaptation, this level of analysis can provide important information regarding the role of local context in political socialization. These particular geographic spaces have a meaningful impact on the social networks, organizational opportunities, and community ties that the respondents experience in their day-to-day lives. These networks and resources influence the development of collective identity(ies) for residents in both communities. See Robert J. Sampson, Jeffrey D. Morenoff, and Thomas Gannon-Rowley, "Assessing 'Neighborhood Effects': Social Processes and New Directions in Research," *Annual Review of Sociology* 28 (2002): 443–478;

and James G. Gimpel, J. Celeste Lay, and Jason E. Schuknecht, *Cultivating Democracy: Civic Environments and Political Socialization in America* (Washington, D.C.: Brookings Institution, 2003).

98. For a discussion of qualitative sampling and interviewing methods, see Robert S. Weiss, *Learning from Strangers: The Art and Method of Qualitative Interview Studies* (New York: Free Press, 1994).

99. Another reason that I chose schools to find my respondents is that one of the central questions I wanted to look at was Latino identity. Choosing respondents from "Latino" organizations, even if not explicitly political, would presume a certain level of group identification. Using Latino-majority schools allowed me to find Latino respondents without requiring that they identify as "Latinos," per se.

100. The sample was made up of 100 respondents: 50 seniors from the two high schools (25 from each) and 50 adult school students from the two adult schools (25 from each). At Garfield High School the respondents were chosen from nontracked, required senior courses. At Montebello High School every fifth name was chosen from a computerized list of the senior class. The choice of respondents was less structured at the two adult schools because of the nature of the adult school population. Because people attend adult school voluntarily and because they may have conflicts that prevent them from attending class, the student population fluctuates from day to day. The adult school respondents in both adult schools were chosen from English as a second language (ESL), citizenship, vocational education, and computer classes. The sample also included a few staff people who grew up in the area where the school was located. About a third of the interviews were conducted in Spanish, and some were conducted in both Spanish and English. Participation was voluntary. A list of the respondents is available in Appendix A.

101. I conducted all of the interviews and transcribed and translated more than 85 percent of them. A bilingual research assistant completed the remainder. Here I provide only the English translation.

102. In the discussion, I present the percentage of the respondents who held a particular position to give a sense of what respondents thought relative to other respondents. I also include quotations that are representative of the general perceptions in order to let the respondents' own voices be heard.

103. Irving Seidman, *Interviewing and Qualitative Research: A Guide for Researchers in Education and the Social Sciences* (New York: Columbia University Teachers College Press, 1991), 4.

104. Anselm Strauss and Juliet Corbin, *Basics of Qualitative Research: Techniques and Procedures for Developing Grounded Theory*, 2d ed. (Thousand Oaks, Calif.: Sage, 1998), 12.

105. Ibid.

106. For a discussion of these anti-immigrant tendencies in California, see

Otto Santa Ana, *Brown Tide Rising* (Austin: University of Texas Press, 2002); and William Deverell, *Whitewashed Adobe* (Berkeley: University of California Press, 2004). For an account of the ascriptive undertones of these movements, see Smith, *Civic Ideals*.

107. DeSipio, *Counting on the Latino Vote*.

108. For the qualitative work, see Ochoa, *Becoming Neighbors*; Gary M. Segura, F. Chris García, Rodolfo O. de la Garza, and Harry Pachón, *Social Capital and the Latino Community* (Claremont, Calif.: Tomás Rivera Policy Institute, 2000), 42–52. For the quantitative studies, see Ricardo Ramírez, "The Changing California Voter: A Longitudinal Analysis of Latino Political Mobilization and Participation" (paper presented at the annual meeting of the American Political Science Association, San Francisco, September 2001); and Luis Ricardo Fraga and Ricardo Ramírez, "Unquestioned Influence: Latinos and the 2000 Election in California," in Rodolfo de la Garza and Louis DeSipio, eds., *Muted Voices: Latinos and the 2000 Elections* (New York: Rowman and Littlefield, 2004).

109. For examples of how these kinds of messages were sent by mainstream California media sources, see Santa Ana, *Brown Tide Rising*.

110. Ochoa's study of Mexican Americans in La Puente, California, during the same period presented very similar findings regarding intracommunity relations. See Ochoa, *Becoming Neighbors*.

111. This perception is a fairly accurate one, given the stratification that exists in the labor market in Los Angeles and the importance of English skills in the stratification process. See Rebecca Morales and Paul M. Ong, "The Illusion of Progress: Latinos in Los Angeles," in Rebecca Morales and Frank Bonilla, eds., *Latinos in a Changing U.S. Economy* (Newbury Park, Calif.: Sage, 1993), 55–84. For a larger discussion of immigrants in the California economy, see Kevin McCarthy and Georges Vernez, *Immigration in a Changing Economy: California's Experience* (Santa Monica, Calif.: RAND Corporation, 1997), chaps. 5–9.

112. At the time of the interviews, Matthew Martínez and Esteban Torres were the congressional representatives for Montebello. At the state level, Montebello was represented by Charles Calderón in the senate and Martha Escútia and Grace Napolitano in the assembly. At the local level, of five seats, the Montebello City Council had three Latinos: Art Payán, Kathy Salazar, and Arnold Alvarez-Glasman. Both East Los Angeles and Montebello were represented by Gloria Molina on the Los Angeles County Board of Supervisors. On the congressional level, East Los Angeles was divided between Congressman Xavier Becerra and Congresswoman Lucille Roybal-Allard. On the state level, East Los Angeles's senator was Richard Polanco, and its assemblypersons were Antonio Villaraigosa and Luis Caldera. In the Los Angeles City Council, Boyle Heights and El Sereno (both parts of East Los Angeles) were represented by Richard Alatorre.

113. As Tate cogently points out, we know little about representation in gen-

eral and descriptive representation in particular. Her work provides important insights into its impact in the African American community. Similar work needs to be done on the effects of Latino representation on Latino political attitudes and activity. See Tate, *Black Faces in the Mirror,* esp. chap. 1.

114. Hardy-Fanta, *Latina Politics, Latino Politics,* chap. 5.

115. Jimy M. Sanders, "Ethnic Boundaries and Identity in Plural Societies," *Annual Review of Sociology* 28 (2002): 327–357, 330.

116. Ibid., 329.

117. For a discussion of how to incorporate relational analyses into social science research, see Emirbayer, "Manifesto for a Relational Sociology."

118. E.g., see Peter Skerry, *Mexican Americans: The Ambivalent Minority* (Cambridge, Mass.: Harvard University Press, 1995), chap. 1; and Earl Shorris, *Latinos: A Biography of the People* (New York: Avon Books, 1992), chap. 7.

119. For an overview of the experiences of the Mothers of East Los Angeles, see Pardo, *Mexican American Women Activists.*

CHAPTER 2. LEGACIES OF CONQUEST

Epigraph: Christopher Rand, *Los Angeles, the Ultimate City* (New York: Oxford University Press, 1967), 10.

1. For an overview of these historical experiences, see Tomás Almaguer, *Racial Fault Lines: The Historical Origins of White Supremacy in California* (Berkeley: University of California Press, 1994); Douglas Monroy, *Thrown among Strangers: The Making of Mexican Culture in Frontier America* (Berkeley: University of California Press, 1993); Matt García, *A World of Its Own: Race, Labor, and Citrus in the Making of Greater Los Angeles* (Chapel Hill: University of North Carolina Press, 2002); George J. Sánchez, *Becoming Mexican American: Ethnicity, Culture, and Identity in Chicano Los Angeles, 1900–1945* (New York: Oxford University Press, 1993); and Rodolfo Acuña, *Anything but Mexican: Chicanos in Contemporary Los Angeles* (New York: Verso Press, 1997).

2. Otto Santa Ana, *Brown Tide Rising: Metaphors of Latinos in Contemporary Public Discourse* (Austin: University of Texas Press, 2002).

3. Daniel Weintraub, "State's Budget Mess: Will It Ever Clear Up?" *Los Angeles Times,* 24 Oct. 1994. California's even more severe budget crisis at the start of the twenty-first century shows the degree to which these budget problems have yet to be resolved.

4. Ronald Brownstein and Richard Simon, "Hospitality Turns into Hostility: California Has a Long History of Welcoming Newcomers for Their Cheap Labor—Until Times Turn Rough. The Current Backlash Is Also Fueled by the Scope and Nature of the Immigration," *Los Angeles Times,* 14 Nov. 1993.

5. Weintraub, "State's Budget Mess."

6. Fred Alvarez, "Rebuilding the Economy: Businesses Adapting to a New Climate. Labor: Workers Displaced by the Devastation of the Past Four Years Are Shifting Gears, Striking out on Their Own or Transferring Old Job Skills to New Professions," *Los Angeles Times,* 22 May 1994.

7. Ibid.

8. Ibid.

9. Weintraub, "State's Budget Mess,"

10. Benjamin Zycher, "Governor Wilson, Come Clean on the Tax Hike Instead of Immigrant-bashing, Let's Talk about the Catastrophe Left by His Budget 'Solution,'" *Los Angeles Times,* 22 Oct. 1994.

11. In fact, Wilson made a brief, aborted run for the presidency in 1996. His main message was his opposition to immigration and affirmative action.

12. Brownstein and Simon, "Hospitality Turns into Hostility."

13. Ibid.

14. Ibid.

15. Vlae Kershner, "A Hot Issue for the '90s: California Leads in Immigration—and Backlash," *San Francisco Chronicle,* 21 June 1993, A1.

16. Ibid.

17. Gebe Martínez, "The Times Poll; As Orange County Neighborhoods Change, Tensions Build: Ethnic Makeup of Many Communities Is Shifting. Many Fear the Change Is Not Always for the Better," *Los Angeles Times,* 26 Oct. 1993, A1.

18. Kershner, "A Hot Issue for the '90s."

19. Ibid.; and Eric Bailey and Dan Morain, "Anti-Immigration Bills Flood Legislature; Rights: Republicans See the Measures as a Way to Help the State Cut Costs. Critics See the Move as Political Opportunism and, in Some Cases, Racism," *Los Angeles Times,* 3 May 1993, A3.

20. Kershner, "A Hot Issue for the '90s."

21. Ibid.

22. Bailey and Morain, "Anti-Immigration Bills Flood Legislature."

23. Ibid.

24. Ibid.

25. Ibid.

26. As of March 2003, the Immigration and Naturalization Service, formerly located in the Justice Department, was reorganized under the Office of Homeland Security. It is now called the U.S. Citizenship and Immigration Services (USCIS).

27. For a highly detailed discussion of the metaphors used to describe immigrants during this campaign and their effects, see Santa Ana, *Brown Tide Rising.*

28. Gebe Martínez and Patrick J. McDonnell, "Proposition 187 Backers Counting on Message, not Strategy," *Los Angeles Times,* 30 Oct. 1994, A1.

29. Martínez and McDonnell, "Proposition 187."

30. Ibid.

31. Ibid.

32. Ibid.

33. Ibid.

34. Ibid.

35. Suzanne Espinosa and Benjamin Pimentel, "Anger at Immigration Overflow," *San Francisco Chronicle*, 27 Aug. 1993, A1.

36. Ibid.

37. For an overview of this story, see Luis A. Carrillo, "Perspectives on the 'Tagger Shooting': How to Kill a Latino Kid and Walk Free; The Treatment Given the Killer of an Unarmed 18-Year-Old Tagger Proves That the Real Affirmative Action Is for White Males," op-ed, *Los Angeles Times*, 27 Nov. 1995; Efraín Hernández, "Masters Will Clean Trash, Not Graffiti: Judge Changes Punishment for Gun Violations due to Concerns for the Safety of a Man Who Killed a Tagger," *Los Angeles Times*, 28 Dec. 1995; Ann W. O'Neill and Nicholas Riccardi, "Hurt Tagger Was Treated as Suspect, not Victim, Lawyer Says Crime: Police Deny Accusations That Investigation of Jan. 31 Shooting Favored the Gunman. They Cite Conflicting Stories Given by the Youth," *Los Angeles Times*, 15 Mar. 1995.

38. Carillo, "Perspectives on the 'Tagger Shooting.'"

39. O'Neill and Riccardi, "Hurt Tagger Was Treated as Suspect."

40. Mike Davis, "The Social Origins of the Referendum," *NACLA Report on the Americas* 29 (1995): 24–28.

41. Ibid.

42. Ibid.

43. O'Neill and Riccardi, "Hurt Tagger Was Treated as Suspect."

44. Carrillo, "Perspectives on the 'Tagger Shooting.'"

45. Ibid.

46. This is borne out by the fact that all racial-ethnic groups in California other than Anglos voted against Proposition 209: 76 percent of Mexican Americans, 75 percent of African Americans, and 61 percent of Asians. Santa Ana, *Brown Tide Rising*, 129.

47. R. Michael Alvarez and Lisa García Bedolla, "The Revolution against Affirmative Action in California: Politics, Economics and Proposition 209," *State Politics and Policy Quarterly* 4 (2004): 1–17.

48. Ron Unz, Roundtable presentation to the Heritage Foundation, Washington, D.C., Oct. 1998.

49. Santa Ana, *Brown Tide Rising*, 200.

50. Ibid.

51. Ibid., 247.

52. Ibid. This is similar to Schmidt's finding that language policy debates are more about competing visions of national identity than the costs and/or benefits

of particular language policy programs. See Ronald J. Schmidt Sr., *Language Policy and Identity Politics in the United States* (Philadelphia: Temple University Press, 2000).

53. Ronald Takaki, *A Different Mirror: A History of Multicultural America* (Boston: Back Bay Books, 1993).

54. Leonard Pitt, *The Decline of the Californios: A Social History of the Spanish-speaking Californians, 1846–1890,* 2d ed. (Berkeley: University of California Press, 1970), 16–17.

55. See Takaki, *A Different Mirror,* 166–169; and David J. Weber, ed., *Foreigners in Their Native Land: Historical Roots of the Mexican Americans* (Albuquerque: University of New Mexico Press, 1973), chap. 2.

56. Takaki, *A Different Mirror,* 170–172.

57. Willam Deverell, *Whitewashed Adobe: The Rise of Los Angeles and the Remaking of Its Mexican Past* (Berkeley: University of California Press, 2004), 6–9.

58. Deverell, *Whitewashed Adobe,* 2; emphasis in the original. See also William Alexander McClung, *Landscapes of Desire: Anglo Mythologies of Los Angeles* (Berkeley: University of California Press, 2000), esp. chap. 2.

59. Monroy, *Thrown among Strangers,* 208–9.

60. Mike Davis, *City of Quartz: Excavating the Future in Los Angeles* (New York: Verso Press, 1990); and Raphael J. Sonenshein, *Politics in Black and White: Race and Power in Los Angeles* (Princeton: Princeton University Press, 1993), chap. 2.

61. Robert Mayer, *Los Angeles: A Chronological and Documentary History, 1542–1976* (Dobbs Ferry, N.Y.: Oceana Publications, 1978), 112.

62. Albert Camarillo, *Chicanos in a Changing Society: From Mexican Pueblos to American Barrios in Santa Barbara and Southern California, 1848–1930,* 6th ed. (Cambridge, Mass.: Harvard University Press, 1996), 108.

63. Deverell, *Whitewashed Adobe,* 13.

64. See Camarillo, *Chicanos in a Changing Society;* and Richard Griswold del Castillo, *The Los Angeles Barrio, 1850–1890* (Berkeley: University of California Press, 1979).

65. Deverell, *Whitewashed Adobe,* 12.

66. Ibid., 25.

67. See Griswold del Castillo, *The Los Angeles Barrio,* 38; and Camarillo, *Chicanos in a Changing Society,* chaps. 3, 5.

68. Pitt, *Decline of the Californios,* 197.

69. Ibid.

70. The word *greaser* was actually included in the act until it was removed by amendment the following year. See Camarillo, *Chicanos in a Changing Society,* 108; and Pitt, *Decline of the Californios,* 197.

71. For a discussion of the economics and politics behind the original foreign miners' tax during the gold rush, see Pitt, *Decline of the Californios,* chap. 3.

72. Camarillo, *Chicanos in a Changing Society*, 108; and Pitt, *Decline of the Californios*, 198.

73. Mayer, *Los Angeles*, 110.

74. Martha Menchaca provides a detailed account of how different incentive structures encouraged Mexicans to define themselves either as Native American or as Mexican, depending on their interests and their state of residence. See Martha Menchaca, *Recovering History, Constructing Race: The Indian, Black, and White Roots of Mexican Americans* (Austin: University of Texas Press, 2002), esp. chap. 4.

75. Almaguer, *Racial Fault Lines*, chaps. 1–3.

76. The Native American population's inability to confirm their land grants was due to problems that began under Mexican rule and only worsened after annexation. For a detailed discussion of this history, see Lisbeth Haas, *Conquests and Historical Identities in California, 1769–1936* (Berkeley: University of California Press, 1995).

77. Menchaca, *Recovering History, Constructing Race*, 264.

78. Ibid., 66.

79. David G. Gutiérrez, *Walls and Mirrors: Mexican Americans, Mexican Immigrants, and the Politics of Ethnicity* (Berkeley: University of California Press, 1995), 20–25.

80. Menchaca, *Recovering History, Constructing Race*, 272.

81. Pitt, *Decline of the Calfornios*, 42–45.

82. Ibid., 45.

83. Visitors to Santa Barbara probably have seen De la Guerra Street, which is named after this prominent family in Santa Barbara. Menchaca, *Recovering History, Constructing Race*, 221.

84. Ibid., 220–21.

85. Pitt, *Decline of the Californios*, 132–33; Griswold del Castillo, *The Los Angeles Barrio*, 154.

86. Griswold del Castillo, *The Los Angeles Barrio*, 156.

87. Pitt, *Decline of the Californios*, 136.

88. Ibid.

89. The other county where the Know-Nothings were defeated was Santa Barbara. For a fuller discussion, see Pitt, *Decline of the Californios*, 137.

90. Griswold del Castillo, *The Los Angeles Barrio*, 154–55; Pitt, *Decline of the Californios*, 201.

91. Griswold del Castillo, *The Los Angeles Barrio*, 158.

92. Pitt, *Decline of the Californios*, 202.

93. Ibid.

94. For example, in his campaign for assemblyman, Spanish-language newspaper editor Francisco Ramírez won only 692 of 2,245 ballots cast. See Pitt, *Decline of the Californios*, 203–4; and Griswold del Castillo, *The Los Angeles Barrio*, 158.

95. Griswold del Castillo, *The Los Angeles Barrio*, 159.

96. Deverell, *Whitewashed Adobe*, 264 n. 47.

97. James P. Allen and Eugene Turner, *The Ethnic Quilt: Population Diversity in Southern California* (Northridge: Center for Geographical Studies, California State University, Northridge, 1997), 10; and John R. Chávez, *Eastside Landmark: A History of the East Los Angeles Community Union, 1968–1993* (Stanford: Stanford University Press, 1998), chap. 6.

98. Gutiérrez, *Walls and Mirrors*, 24.

99. Deverell, *Whitewashed Adobe*, 17.

100. Allen and Turner, *The Ethnic Quilt*, 95.

101. Mayer, *Los Angeles*, 117.

102. Allen and Turner, *The Ethnic Quilt*, 93

103. Robert M. Fogelson, *The Fragmented Metropolis: Los Angeles, 1850–1930* (Cambridge, Mass.: Harvard University Press, 1967), 188.

104. For a discussion of the history of Mexican American geographic and political isolation, see Griswold del Castillo, *The Los Angeles Barrio*, chap. 5.

105. Ibid., 26.

106. Quoted in Deverell, *Whitewashed Adobe*, 47.

107. Ibid.

108. Deverell, *Whitewashed Adobe*, 31.

109. Ibid., 149.

110. Griswold del Castillo, *The Los Angeles Barrio*, 150. In July 2003, the Mexican American Legal Defense and Education Fund filed a lawsuit on behalf of those U.S. citizens who were deported to Mexico during these campaigns. The suit requests reparations on their behalf. The outcome of the suit is still pending.

111. Mayer, *Los Angeles*, 125–26. History does repeat itself. In the Rampart scandal that erupted in the late 1990s in the LAPD, there were reports of police colluding with INS agents to deport suspected gang members, some of whom were legal immigrants who had not been convicted of any crimes.

112. For a discussion of the Mexican American experience in Los Angeles during the depression, see Francisco E. Balderrama and Raymond Rodríguez, *Decade of Betrayal: Mexican Repatriation in the 1930s* (Albuquerque: University of New Mexico Press, 1995); and Abraham Hoffman, *Unwanted Mexican Americans in the Great Depression: Repatriation Pressures, 1929–1939* (Tucson: University of Arizona Press, 1974).

113. Balderrama and Rodríguez, *Decade of Betrayal*, 2–3.

114. See Juan Ramón García, *Operation Wetback: The Mass Deportation of Mexican Undocumented Workers in 1954* (Westport, Conn.: Greenwood Press, 1980); and Rodolfo Acuña, *Occupied America: A History of Chicanos*, 3d ed. (New York: HarperCollins, 1988), 266–269.

115. For a summary of the Sleepy Lagoon incident, see Acuña, *Occupied America*, 255–57.

116. Gutiérrez, *Walls and Mirrors*, 124.

117. Ibid., 256.

118. For a more extensive discussion of the causes and effects of the Zoot Suit Riots, see Mauricio Mazón, *The Zoot Suit Riots: The Psychology of Symbolic Annihilation* (Austin: University of Texas Press, 1984).

119. Acuña, *Occupied America*, 256.

120. Ibid., 257.

121. Menchaca describes this well in her discussion of the "social apartness" of Anglos and Mexicans in Santa Paula, California, during the late twentieth century. Martha Menchaca, *The Mexican Outsiders: A Community History of Marginalization and Discrimination in California* (Austin: University of Texas Press, 1995).

122. Monroy, *Thrown among Strangers*.

123. See Weber, *Foreigners in Their Native Land*; Almaguer, *Racial Fault Lines*; and Takaki, *A Different Mirror*.

124. For a more detailed discussion of the legal and historical specifics of Mexican racial categorizations in the United States, see Ian F. Haney-López, *White by Law: The Legal Construction of Race* (New York: New York University Press, 1996); and Menchaca, *Recovering History, Constructing Race*.

125. Almaguer, *Racial Fault Lines*, 57. But, as we saw earlier in this chapter in the case of Manuel Domínquez, the limitations on the rights of "Indians" sometimes also had a negative effect on upper-class Californios. Pitt, *Decline of the Californios*, 202.

126. Gutiérrez, *Walls and Mirrors*, 14.

127. Griswold del Castillo, *The Los Angeles Barrio*, 127.

128. Ibid.

129. Ibid., 133.

130. Ibid., 134.

131. This history of East Los Angeles is based on information from Ricardo Romo, *East Los Angeles: History of a Barrio* (Austin: University of Texas Press, 1983); Leonard Pitt and Dale Pitt, *Los Angeles A to Z: An Encyclopedia of the City and County* (Berkeley: University of California Press, 1997), 129–30; and Griswold del Castillo, *The Los Angeles Barrio*.

132. See George W. Mohoff and Jack P. Valov, *A Stroll through Russiantown* (Los Angeles: G. W. Mohoff and P. Valov, 1996).

133. Romo, *East Los Angeles*, 62.

134. *Garza v. County of Los Angeles Board of Supervisors*, 918 F.2d 763 (9th Cir. 1990). J. Morgan Kousser, who provided expert testimony in the case, argues in chapter 2 of *Colorblind Justice* that the evidence of discriminatory intent against Mexicans was overwhelming. See J. Morgan Kousser, *Colorblind Injustice: Minor-*

ity Voting Rights and the Undoing of the Second Reconstruction (Chapel Hill: University of North Carolina Press, 1999).

135. Romo, *East Los Angeles*, 10.

136. Ibid.

137. For a more general discussion of the negative impact segregation can have on the socioeconomic status of communities of color, see Douglas S. Massey and Nancy A. Denton, *American Apartheid: Segregation and the Making of the Underclass* (Cambridge, Mass.: Harvard University Press, 1993).

138. Gutiérrez, *Walls and Mirrors*, 96.

139. Ibid., 97.

140. See Julie Leininger Pycior, *LBJ and Mexican Americans: The Paradox of Power* (Austin: University of Texas Press, 1997), chap. 3.

141. For an extensive description of the activities of the GI Forum, a Mexican American veterans' organization, see Pycior, *LBJ and Mexican Americans*.

142. Pitt and Pitt, *Los Angeles A to Z*, 102.

143. See Sonenshein, *Politics in Black and White*, chap. 1.

144. No Latino held a state executive office during the twentieth century in California until Cruz Bustamante was elected lieutenant governor in 1999. See Mart Martin, *The Almanac of Women and Minorities in American Politics* (Boulder, Colo.: Westview Press, 1999), chap. 3.

145. Carlos Muñoz, *Youth, Identity, Power: The Chicano Movement* (New York: Verso Press, 1989), 55–56.

146. Pycior, *LBJ and Mexican Americans*, 121.

147. Muñoz, *Youth, Identity, and Power*, 55.

148. For an overall history of TELACU, see Chávez, *Eastside Landmark*.

149. Rubén Salazar was a prominent journalist for the *Los Angeles Times* and wrote highly controversial political columns criticizing race relations in Los Angeles and the United States. For an overview of his life and work, see Mario T. García, ed., *Rubén Salazar, Border Correspondent: Selected Writings, 1955–1970* (Berkeley: University of California Press, 1995).

150. Chávez, *Eastside Landmark*, 256.

151. This discussion is based on Mary Pardo, *Mexican American Women Activists: Identity and Resistance inTwo Los Angeles Communities* (Philadelphia: Temple University Press, 1998), chaps. 2, 3, 5; and Mary Pardo, "Mexican American Grassroots Community Activists: 'Mothers of East Los Angeles,'" in F. Chris García, ed., *Pursuing Power: Latinos and the Political System* (Notre Dame: University of Notre Dame Press, 1997), 151–68.

152. Pardo, *Mexican American Women Activists*, 62.

153. Pardo, "Mexican American Women Grassroots Community Activists," 163–64.

154. *Montebello News*, 4 Sept. 1936.

155. Cecelia Rasmussen, "Community Profile: Montebello," *Los Angeles Times*, 24 Jan. 1997, 2.

156. Montebello Chamber of Commerce, "A History of the City of Montebello," pamphlet, Montebello, Calif., 1985.

157. Monroy, *Thrown among Strangers*, 208–9.

158. Deverell describes just such an instance in 1857. Whites were concerned that Mexicans would retaliate after a white deputy marshal shot and killed an unarmed Mexican over two dollars. The El Monte Boys were called in to help protect the city. Deverell, *Whitewashed Adobe*, 15–19.

159. Ibid., 23.

160. The majority of my information on the Simons Brick Plant is taken from Deverell, *Whitewashed Adobe*, chap. 4. I also gathered information from Virginia Escalante, "El Pueblo de Simons," *Los Angeles Times*, 23 Sept. 1982, 1–4. Escalante's piece was based on five years of research conducted by Montebello resident Ray Ramírez on the history of the Simons plant. See also Margarita Nieto, "Chicano History Brick by Brick," *Los Angeles Times*, 18 Sept. 1988, 3.

161. Deverell, *Whitewashed Adobe*, 137.

162. Ibid.

163. By 1905, the Simons family had already been making bricks in southern California for over two decades. They also had plants in Santa Monica and Pasadena. Deverell, *Whitewashed Adobe*, 133–34.

164. Ibid., 135.

165. Nieto, "Chicano History Brick by Brick," 3.

166. Deverell, *Whitewashed Adobe*, 140.

167. Ibid., 142–43.

168. Cecelia Rasmussen, "Brick Firm Cemented Lives," *Los Angeles Times*, 6 Nov. 1995, 3.

169. Ibid. The inability of workers to organize a union was often praised by the *Los Angeles Times* as one of the best aspects of the Simons model. See Deverell, *Whitewashed Adobe*, 141.

170. Deverell, *Whitewashed Adobe*, 149–53.

171. Ibid., 164.

172. Ibid., 166.

173. Ibid., 154.

174. Ibid.

175. Ibid.

176. City historical records, City of Montebello Public Library.

177. Gary M. Segura, F. Chris García, Rodolfo de la Garza, and Harry P. Pachón, eds., *Social Capital and the Latino Community* (Claremont, Calif.: Tomás Rivera Policy Institute), 43.

178. Deverell, *Whitewashed Adobe*, 154.

179. Ibid.
180. Ibid.
181. As quoted in Deverell, *Whitewashed Adobe,* 154.
182. Rasmussen, "Brick Firm Cemented Lives," 3.
183. Deverell, *Whitewashed Adobe,* 168.
184. Rasmussen, "Brick Firm Cemented Lives," 3.
185. Escalante, "El Pueblo de Simons," 1–4.
186. Rasmussen, "Brick Firm Cemented Lives," 3.
187. Deverell, *Whitewashed Adobe,* 169–70.
188. Nieto, "Chicano History Brick by Brick," 3.
189. Ibid., 159.
190. Ibid., 160.
191. Segura et al., *Social Capital and the Latino Community,* 43.
192. Ibid., 51.
193. Ibid., 46–52.
194. Ibid., 46.
195. Ibid., 46–47.
196. Ibid., 47.

CHAPTER 3. A THIN LINE BETWEEN LOVE AND HATE

Epigraph: Martin Luther King, Jr., "A Letter from the Birmingham Jail," in David A. Hollinger and Charles Capper, eds., *The American Intellectual Tradition,* 2d ed., vol. 2, *1865 to the Present* (New York: Oxford University Press, 1993), 327–34.

1. See, e.g., F. Chris García and Rodolfo de la Garza, *The Chicano Political Experience: Three Perspectives* (Notre Dame: University of Notre Dame Press, 1977); Rodney Hero, *Latinos and the U.S. Political System: Two-Tiered Pluralism* (Philadelphia: Temple University Press, 1992); Juan Gómez Quiñones, *Chicano Politics: Reality and Promise, 1940–1990* (Albuquerque: University of New Mexico Press, 1990); Andrés Torres and José E. Velázquez, eds., introduction to *The Puerto Rican Movement: Voices from the Diaspora* (Philadelphia: Temple University Press, 1998); María Cristina García, *Havana USA: Cuban Exiles and Cuban Americans in South Florida, 1959–1994* (Berkeley: University of California Press, 1996), chap. 3.

2. For a discussion of those that deemphasized language maintenance, see Mario T. García, *Mexican Americans: Leadership, Ideology, and Identity, 1930–1960* (New Haven: Yale University Press, 1989); for those emphasizing language maintenance, see Rodolfo Acuña, *Occupied America: A History of Chicanos,* 2d ed. (New York: Harper & Row, 1999).

3. Jennifer Crocker, Brenda Major, and Claude Steele, "Social Stigma," in

Daniel T. Gilbert, Susan T. Fiske, and Gardner Lindzey, eds., *The Handbook of Social Psychology*, 4th ed. (New York: McGraw-Hill, 1998), 504–53, quote on 505.

4. Henri Tajfel and J. C. Turner, "An Integrative Theory of Intergroup Conflict," in William G. Austin and Stephen Worchel, eds., *The Social Psychology of Intergroup Relations* (Monterey, Calif.: Brooks/Cole Books, 1979), 33–47; Henri Tajfel and J. C. Turner, "The Social Identity Theory of Intergroup Behavior," in Stephen Worchel and William G. Austin, eds., *Psychology of Intergroup Relations* (Chicago: Nelson-Hall, 1986), 7–24; and Marilynn B. Brewer and Rupert J. Brown, "Intergroup Relations," in Gilbert, Fiske, and Lindzey, eds., *The Handbook of Social Psychology*, 554–94.

5. Amado Padilla and William Pérez, "Acculturation, Social Identity, and Social Cognition: A New Perspective," *Hispanic Journal of Behavioral Sciences* 25 (2003): 35–55.

6. Ibid., 518.

7. Crocker, Major, and Steele, "Social Stigma," 519.

8. Ibid.

9. Bruce G. Link and Jo C. Phelan, "Conceptualizing Stigma," *Annual Review of Sociology* 27 (2001): 363–85, 380.

10. Crocker, Major, and Steele, "Social Stigma"; and Link and Phelan, "Conceptualizing Stigma."

11. Robert M. Krauss and Chi-Yue Chiu, "Language and Social Behavior," in Gilbert, Fiske, and Lindzey, eds., *The Handbook of Social Psychology*, 41–88.

12. Joshua A. Fishman, *Language and Ethnicity in Minority Sociolinguistic Perspective* (Philadelphia: Multilingual Matters, 1989), 6. See also Joshua A. Fishman, "Macrosociolinguistics and the Sociology of Language in the Early Eighties," *Annual Review of Sociology* 11 (1985): 113–27; and Gillian Sankoff, *The Social Life of Language* (Philadelphia: University of Pennsylvania Press, 1980).

13. Lesley Milroy, "Language and Group Identity," *Journal of Multilingual and Multicultural Development* 3 (1982): 207–16, 209–10.

14. Ibid., 209.

15. Ofelia García, José Luis Morín, and Klaudia M. Rivera, "How Threatened Is the Spanish of New York Puerto Ricans? Language Shift with Vaivén," in Joshua Fishman, ed., *Can Threatened Languages Be Saved? Reversing Language Shift, Revisited: A 21st-Century Perspective* (Buffalo, N.Y.: Multilingual Matters, 2001), 44–73.

16. Ana Celia Zentella, "Lexical Leveling in Four New York City Spanish Dialects: Linguistic and Social Factors," *Hispania* 73 (1990): 1094–2015, 1102.

17. Ana Celia Zentella, *Growing Up Bilingual: Puerto Rican Children in New York* (New York: Blackwell, 1997).

18. Bonnie Urciuoli, *Exposing Prejudice: Puerto Rican Experiences of Language, Race and Class* (Boulder, Colo.: Westview Press, 1997).

19. Donaldo P. Macedo, Bessie Dendrinos, and Panayota Gounari, *The Hegemony of English* (Boulder, Colo.: Paradigm Publishers, 2003).

20. For an overview of this history, see Ronald Schmidt Sr., *Language Policy and Identity Politics in the United States* (Philadelphia: Temple University Press, 2000), chaps. 3, 6.

21. Arthur M. Schlesinger Jr., *The Disuniting of America: Reflections on a Multicultural Society* (New York: Norton, 1992), 109–10.

22. Alejandro Portes and Rubén G. Rumbaut, *Immigrant America: A Portrait* (Berkeley: University of California Press, 1996), 194; emphasis in the original.

23. Ibid., 196.

24. For Americanization and Mexican Americans, see George J. Sánchez, *Becoming Mexican American: Ethnicity, Culture, and Identity in Chicano Los Angeles, 1900–1945* (New York: Oxford University Press, 1993), chap. 4; George J. Sánchez, "'Go after the Women': Americanization and the Mexican Immigrant Woman, 1915–1929," in Vicki L. Ruiz and Ellen Carol DuBois, eds., *Unequal Sisters: A Multicultural Reader in U.S. Women's History,* 2d ed. (New York: Routledge, 1994), 284–97; Vicki L. Ruiz, *Out of the Shadows* (New York: Oxford University Press, 1998), 33–35; Sarah Deutsch, *No Separate Refuge: Culture, Class, and Gender on the Anglo-Hispanic Frontier in the American Southwest, 1880–1940* (New York: Oxford University Press, 1987), 63–86; Gilbert González, *Chicano Education in the Era of Segregation* (Philadelphia: Balch Institute Press, 1990), 30–61. For Native Americans, see Ronald Takaki, *A Different Mirror: A History of Multicultural America* (Boston: Back Bay Books, 1993), chap. 9. For discussions of twentieth-century Americanization programs in the United States, see Richard Conant Harper, *The Course of the Melting Pot Idea to 1910* (New York: Arno Press, 1980), chap. 1; and Joseph Dorinson, "The Educational Alliance: An Institutional Study in Americanization and Acculturation," in Michael D'Innocenzo and Josef P. Sirefman, eds., *Immigration and Ethnicity: American Society—"Melting Pot" or "Salad Bowl?"* (Westport, Conn.: Greenwood Press, 1992), 93–108.

25. Richard Rodríguez, *Hunger of Memory: The Education of Richard Rodriguez* (New York: Bantam Books, 1983), 5. See also Patricia Gándara, "Learning English in California: Guideposts for the Nation," in Marcelo M. Suárez-Orozco and Mariela M. Páez, eds., *Latinos: Remaking America* (Berkeley: University of California Press, 2002).

26. U.S. Senate, Henry Cabot Lodge, "Speech to the Senate." 28th Cong., *Congressional Record*, vol. 177 (1896), 281.

27. Peter Brimelow, *Alien Nation: Common Sense about America's Immigration Disaster* (New York: HarperCollins, 1996), 89. Parenthetical statement and emphasis in the original.

28. Alejandro Portes and Robert L. Bach, *Latin Journey: Cuban and Mexican*

Immigrants in the United States (Berkeley: University of California Press, 1984), chap. 4.

29. Richard Griswold del Castillo, *The Los Angeles Barrio, 1850–1890: A Social History* (Berkeley: University of California Press, 1979), 176.

30. See Brimelow, *Alien Nation;* and Linda Chávez, *Out of the Barrio: Toward a New Politics of Hispanic Assimilation* (New York: Basic Books, 1991), introd. and chap. 1.

31. For examples of works that address this conflict, see Rodolfo de la Garza and Adela Flores, "The Impact of Mexican Immigrants on the Political Behavior of Chicanos: A Clarification of Issues and Some Hypotheses for Future Research," in Harley L. Browning and Rodolfo de la Garza, eds., *Mexican Immigrants and Mexican Americans: An Evolving Relation* (Austin: University of Texas Press, 1986), 211–229; David Gutiérrez, *Walls and Mirrors: Mexican Immigrants, Mexican Americans, and the Politics of Ethnicity* (Berkeley: University of California Press, 1995); Martha Menchaca, *The Mexican Outsiders: A Community History of Marginalization and Discrimination in California* (Austin: University of Texas Press, 1995), chap. 9.

32. Gutiérrez, *Walls and Mirrors,* 6.

33. Menchaca, *The Mexican Outsiders,* 200–202.

34. Gilda Ochoa, *Becoming Neighbors in a Mexican American Community: Power, Conflict and Solidarity* (Austin: University of Texas Press, 2004).

35. Amado M. Padilla and David Durán, "The Psychological Dimension in Understanding Immigrant Students," in Rubén G. Rumbaut and Wayne A. Cornelius, eds., *California's Immigrant Children: Theory, Research, and Implications for Educational Policy* (San Diego: Center for U.S.-Mexican Studies, University of California, San Diego, 1995), 131–60.

36. This could help to explain why some Latino parents supported Proposition 227, an initiative to end bilingual education in the state. This question is addressed in more depth at the end of this chapter.

37. Krauss and Chiu, "Language and Social Behavior," 54.

38. Schmidt, *Language Policy and Identity Politics.*

39. John Edwards, "Language in Group and Individual Identity," in Glynis M. Breakwell, ed., *Social Psychology of Identity and Self Concept* (London: Surrey University Press, 1992), 129–46.

40. Milton Gordon, *Assimilation in American Life* (New York: Oxford University Press, 1964), 81.

41. These findings are consistent with findings from the Children of Immigrants Longitudinal Survey (CILS), conducted by Rumbaut and Portes. The CILS included 4,288 respondents, all of whom were of either the 1.5 or second generation. They found that in 1995–96 only 1.2 percent of their Mexican-origin respondents and 0.4 percent of their Nicaraguan respondents reported a purely "American" identity. See the introduction to Rubén Rumbaut and Alejandro Portes, eds.,

Ethnicities: Children of Immigrants in America (Berkeley: University of California Press, 2001), 1–19.

42. For a discussion of the political process underlying the adoption of the term *Chicano,* see Acuña, *Occupied America,* 338–39.

43. It is important to keep in mind that when I say *Latino,* I mean whatever ethnic-origin identifier the interviewee used to describe himself or herself. I used the term chosen by the interviewee when I asked questions regarding how he or she defined and felt about the members of his or her racial group.

44. Again, this is consistent with findings from the Children of Immigrants Study and previous studies of Latino self-identification and language. See Rubén G. Rumbaut, "The Crucible Within: Ethnic Identity, Self-Esteem, and Segmented Assimilation among Children of Immigrants," *International Migration Review* 28 (1994), 748–94, 779–80; and Aída Hurtado and Carlos H. Arce, "Mexicans, Chicanos, Mexican Americans or Pochos . . . ¿Qué Somos? The Impact of Language and Nativity on Ethnic Labeling," *Aztlán* 17 (1987): 103–30.

45. Mahzarin R. Banaji and Nilanjana Dasgupta, "The Consciousness of Social Beliefs: A Program of Research on Stereotyping and Prejudice," in Vincent Y. Yzerbyt, Guy Lories, and Benoit Dardenne, eds., *Metacognition: Cognitive and Social Dimensions* (London: Sage, 1998).

46. Crocker, Major, and Steele, "Social Stigma," 532.

47. Cathy Cohen calls this in-group marginalization secondary marginalization and describes how it affects the African American community's response to the AIDS crisis. Her important work reminds us that we need to be aware of the existence of hierarchy among groups and also within them. See Cathy J. Cohen, *The Boundaries of Blackness: AIDS and the Breakdown of Black Politics* (Chicago: University of Chicago Press, 1999).

48. Cohen, *The Boundaries of Blackness.*

49. As noted in the introduction, this is consistent with other studies that have shown social networks in the United States to be remarkably homogeneous. For a review of this literature, see Miller McPherson, Lynn Smith-Lovin, and James M. Cook, "Birds of a Feather: Homophily in Social Networks," *Annual Review of Sociology* 27 (2001): 415–44.

50. Children Now, "A Different World: Children's Perceptions of Race and Class in Media" (http://www.childrennow.org/media/mc98/DiffWorld.html, 1998), 1.

51. Frank Gilliam, Iyengar Shanto, Adam Simon, and Oliver Wright, "Crime in Black and White: The Violent, Scary World of Local News," *Harvard International Journal of Press/Politics* 1 (1996): 6–23.

52. At the time of the interviews, gang members would speak of their gang affiliations as being "from" a particular place or gang.

53. Being shaved bald was at the time a common feature among some Latino gangs.

54. Whittier is a relatively affluent, majority-Anglo city near Montebello. "Old town" is the city's historic district, which consists of a group of restaurants, bars, and other nightlife venues along one main street. It is a popular night spot for young people.

55. Menchaca, *The Mexican Outsiders*, chap. 8.

56. For a more detailed discussion of racial and ethnic stratification in the Los Angeles labor market, see Rebecca Morales and Paul M. Ong, "The Illusion of Progress: Latinos in Los Angeles," in Rebecca Morales and Frank Bonilla, eds., *Latinos in a Changing U.S. Economy* (Newbury Park, Calif.: Sage, 1993), 55–84. For a fuller discussion of immigrants in the California economy, see Kevin McCarthy and Georges Vernez, *Immigration in a Changing Economy: California's Experience* (Santa Monica, Calif.: RAND Corporation, 1997), chaps. 5–9.

57. For a more in-depth discussion of these differences, see Crocker, Major, and Steele, "Social Stigma," 507–8.

58. For a discussion of this process among African Americans, see Hazel V. Carby, "Policing Black Woman's Body in an Urban Context," in Cathy J. Cohen, Kathleen Jones, and Joan C. Tronto, eds., *Women Transforming Politics: An Alternative Reader* (New York: New York University Press), 151–66.

59. A recent RAND study estimates that immigrants to California from Mexico and other Latin American countries have from 7.5 to 10.5 years of education. McCarthy and Vernez, *Immigration in a Changing Economy*, 38.

60. Victor M. Valle and Rodolfo D. Torres, *Latino Metropolis* (Minneapolis: University of Minnesota Press, 2000), 54–55.

61. Ibid, 54.

62. Otto Santa Ana, *Brown Tide Rising: Metaphors of Latinos in Contemporary American Public Discourse* (Austin: University of Texas Press, 2002). For an overview of how the media treats immigration in general, see Leo R. Chávez, *Covering Immigration: Popular Images and the Politics of the Nation* (Berkeley: University of California Press, 2001).

63. Valle and Torres report a 1998 study that found that Latinos make up only 2.8 percent of editorial employees in the nation's newspapers. As a result, "it is hard to imagine Latinos having much of an impact on the culture of mainstream journalism." Valle and Torres, *Latino Metropolis*, 57.

64. It is estimated that 23 percent of Latinos in California voted in favor of Proposition 187. For an overview of the proposition and the politics surrounding the campaign, see Caroline J. Tolbert and Rodney E. Hero, "Race/Ethnicity and Direct Democracy: An Analysis of California's Illegal Immigration Initiative," *Journal of Politics* 58 (1996): 806–18.

65. Although the nature of this sample makes it difficult to separate the com-

munity and generational effects, the fact that the first-generation respondents from Montebello tended to be more anti-immigrant and that the third-plus-generation respondents from East Los Angeles tended to be more pro-immigrant leads me to believe that the effect is contextual more than generational. Generational conflict does exist in East Los Angeles, but the multigenerational nature of the community and the levels of community identity and cohesion that exist there temper its effects.

CHAPTER 4. WHY VOTE?

Epigraph: Otto Santa Ana, *Brown Tide Rising: Metaphors of Latinos in Contemporary American Public Discourse* (Austin: University of Texas Press, 2002), 1.

1. See, e.g., Michael Dawson's analysis of Black feminism in *Black Visions: The Roots of Contemporary African-American Political Ideologies* (Chicago: University of Chicago Press, 2001), chap. 4. See also bell hooks, *Feminist Theory: From Margin to Center* (Boston: South End Press, 1984); Latina Feminist Group, *Telling to Live: Latina Feminist Testimonies* (Durham, N.C.: Duke University Press, 2001); Kimberlé Crenshaw, Kendall Thomas, Neil Gotanda, and Gary Peller, eds., *Critical Race Theory: The Key Writings that Formed the Movement* (New York: New Press, 1995); Audre Lorde, *Sister/Outsider: Essays and Speeches* (Freedom, Calif.: Crossing Press, 1984); and Adrien Katherine Wing, ed., *Critical Race Feminism: A Reader* (New York: New York University Press, 1997).

2. Dawson, *Black Visions*, 4.

3. Among the political scientists who do address these questions are Michael Dawson, *Behind the Mule: Race and Class in African-American Politics* (Princeton: Princeton University Press, 1994), and *Black Visions;* Jennifer Hochschild, *Facing up to the American Dream: Race, Class, and the Soul of the Nation* (Princeton: Princeton University Press, 1995); Michael Jones-Correa, *Between Two Nations: The Political Predicament of Latinos in New York City* (Ithaca: Cornell University Press, 1998); Katherine Tate, *From Protest to Politics: The New Black Voters in American Elections* (Cambridge, Mass.: Harvard University Press, 1993); and Jan Leighley, *Strength in Numbers? The Political Mobilization of Racial and Ethnic Minorities* (Princeton: Princeton University Press, 2001).

4. Jan E. Leighley and Arnold Vedlitz, "Race, Ethnicity and Political Participation: Competing Models and Contrasting Explanations," *American Journal of Political Science* 61 (1999): 1092–1114, 1095–97.

5. One of the first studies in this area was Angus Campbell, Phillip E. Converse, Warren E. Miller, and Donald E. Stokes, *The American Voter* (New York: John Wiley and Sons, 1960). See also Sidney Verba, Kay Lehman Schlozman, and Henry E. Brady, *Voice and Equality: Civic Voluntarism in American Politics* (Cam-

bridge, Mass.: Harvard University Press, 1995); Steven J. Rosenstone and John Mark Hansen, *Mobilization, Participation and Democracy in America* (New York: Macmillan, 1993); Raymond E. Wolfinger and Steven J. Rosenstone, *Who Votes?* (New Haven: Yale University Press, 1980); Sidney Verba and Norman H. Nie, *Participation in America: Political Democracy and Social Equality* (Chicago: University of Chicago Press, 1972); Sidney Verba, Norman H. Nie, and Jae-on Kim, *Participation and Political Equality: A Seven-Nation Comparison* (Cambridge: Cambridge University Press, 1978); and M. Margaret Conway, *Political Participation in the United States*, 2d ed. (Washington, D.C.: Congressional Quarterly Press, 1991).

6. Henry E. Brady, Sidney Verba, and Kay Lehman Schlozman, "Beyond SES: A Resource Model of Participation," *American Political Science Review* 89 (1995): 271–94. See also introduction to Verba, Schlozman, and Brady, *Voice and Equality.*

7. Verba, Schlozman, and Brady, *Voice and Equality*, 5.

8. Tate, *From Protest to Politics*. For Latino findings, see F. Chris García, Angelo Falcón, and Rodolfo de la Garza, "Ethnicity and Politics: Evidence from the Latino National Political Survey," *Hispanic Journal of Behavioral Sciences* 18 (1996): 91–103; and John A. García, "Political Participation: Resources and Involvement among Latinos and the American Political System," in F. Chris García, ed., *Pursuing Power: Latinos and the Political System* (Notre Dame: University of Notre Dame Press, 1997), 44–71.

9. Leighley and Vedlitz, "Race, Ethnicity, and Participation," 1094.

10. Ibid.

11. Rosenstone and Hansen, *Mobilization and Participation.*

12. For linked fate, see Dawson, *Behind the Mule;* for political alienation, see Marvin E. Olsen, "Two Categories of Political Alienation," *Social Forces* 47 (1969): 288–99; for group identity, see Tate, *From Protest to Politics;* and Carol Hardy-Fanta, *Latina Politics, Latino Politics: Gender, Culture and Political Participation in Boston* (Philadelphia: Temple University Press, 1993); for group conflict, see Henri Tajfel and J. Turner, "The Social Identity Theory of Intergroup Behavior," in Stephen Worchel and William Austin, eds., *The Psychology of Intergroup Behavior* (Chicago: Nelson-Hall, 1986), 7–24.

13. For works that look at gender differences among Latinos, see Lisa J. Montoya, "Gender and Citizenship in Latino Political Participation," in Marcelo Suárez-Orozco and Mariela M. Páez, eds., *Latinos: Remaking America* (Berkeley: University of California Press, 2002); Mary Pardo, *Mexican American Women Activists: Identity and Resistance in Two Communities in Los Angeles* (Philadelphia: Temple University Press, 1998); and Hardy-Fanta, *Latina Politics, Latino Politics.*

14. Nancy Burns, Kay Lehman Schlozman, and Sidney Verba, *The Private Roots of Public Action: Gender, Equality and Political Participation* (Cambridge, Mass.: Harvard University Press, 2001).

15. Much of this work came out of Carol Gilligan's findings regarding gender differences in moral development. See Carol Gilligan, *In a Different Voice: Psychological Theory and Women's Development* (Cambridge, Mass.: Harvard University Press, 1982); Cass Sunstein, ed., *Feminism and Political Theory* (Chicago: University of Chicago Press, 1990); and Kay Lehman Schlozman, Nancy Burns, Sidney Verba, and Jesse Donahue, "Gender and Citizen Participation: Is There a Different Voice?" *American Journal of Political Science* 39 (1995): 267–93, 268–72.

16. See, e.g., Catherine MacKinnon, *Feminism Unmodified: Discourses on Life and Law* (Cambridge, Mass.: Harvard University Press, 1987).

17. Kimberlé Crenshaw, "Mapping the Margins: Intersectionality, Identity, Politics and Violence Against Women of Color," *Stanford Law Review* 43 (1991): 1241–99; Patricia Hill Collins, *Black Feminist Thought: Knowledge, Consciousness and the Politics of Empowerment*, 2d ed. (New York: Routledge, 2000).

18. Studies commonly assume that in the U.S. context race trumps gender. But this is for historical reasons rather than any characteristic implicit in the race category itself. Jane Mansbridge and Katherine Tate, "Race Trumps Gender: Black Opinion on the Thomas Nomination," *PS: Political Science and Politics* 25 (1992): 488–92; and Claudine Gay and Katherine Tate, "Doubly Bound: The Impact of Gender and Race on the Politics of Black Women," *Political Psychology* 19 (1998): 169–84.

19. Judith R. Gordon, *Organizational Behavior: A Diagnostic Approach*, 5th ed. (Saddle River, N.J.: Prentice Hall, 1996), 266–67; Deborah Tannen, ed., *Gender and Conversational Interaction* (New York: Oxford University Press, 1993).

20. For an overview of linguistic differences between men and women, see Deborah Tannen, *You Just Don't Understand: Women and Men in Conversation* (New York: Morrow, 1990).

21. James Diego Vigil, *A Rainbow of Gangs: Street Cultures in the Mega City* (Austin: University of Texas Press, 2002).

22. hooks, *Feminist Theory*; Crenshaw, "Mapping the Margins"; and Hill Collins, *Black Feminist Thought*.

23. Cathy J. Cohen and Michael C. Dawson, "Neighborhood Poverty and African American Politics," *American Political Science Review* 87 (1993): 286–302, 287.

24. Ibid., 289. See also Cathy J. Cohen, *The Boundaries of Blackness: AIDS and the Breakdown of Black Politics* (Chicago: University of Chicago Press, 1999).

25. Cohen and Dawson, "Neighborhood Poverty," 298.

26. Melissa J. Marschall, "Does the Shoe Fit? Testing Models of Participation for African American and Latino Involvement in Local Politics," *Urban Affairs Review* 37 (2001): 227–48, 243.

27. Leighley, *Strength in Numbers*, 7–12.

28. Janelle Wong, "Getting out the Vote among Asian Americans: A Field

Experiment" (paper presented at the annual meeting of the American Political Science Association, Philadelphia, Pa., Sept. 2003).

29. Melissa Michelson, "Mobilizing the Latino Youth Vote," Working Paper 10 (Center for Information and Research on Civic Learning and Engagement, Washington, D.C., 2003).

30. David Knoke, "Networks of Political Action: Toward Theory Construction," *Social Forces* 68 (1990): 1041–63, 1058.

31. The importance of political contact to participation is just one example of why immigrant communities are less likely to be mobilized politically. Campaigns tend to contact likely voters. Immigrant communities contain large numbers of new voters, who therefore are unlikely to be targeted for mobilization. Yet findings from recent get-out-the-vote experiments indicate that political contacts in these communities may be even more effective than for voters at large. See Ricardo Ramírez, "Getting out the Vote: The Impact of Non-partisan Voter Mobilization Efforts in Low Turnout Latino Precincts," Working Paper (Public Policy Institute of California, San Francisco, 2002); Wong, "Getting out the Vote among Asian Americans"; and Michelson, "Mobilizing the Latino Youth Vote."

32. Carol Hardy-Fanta, introduction to *Latina Politics, Latino Politics.*

33. Segura et al. had the same findings in their study of Latinos in Montebello during the 1990s. See Gary M. Segura, F. Chris García, Rodolfo O. de la Garza, and Harry Pachón, *Social Capital and the Latino Community* (Claremont, Calif.: Tomás Rivera Policy Institute, 2000), 42–52.

34. Melissa R. Michelson, "Political Trust among Chicago Latinos," *Journal of Urban Affairs* 23 (2001): 323–34, 327.

35. Tannen posits that in conversation, women look for commonality and connection whereas men attempt to establish themselves vis-à-vis the other on a hierarchical scale. It could be that these men interpreted admitting a lack of efficacy or interest in politics as something that would affect their hierarchical position in our conversation, making them less likely than women to express these feelings. See Tannen, *You Just Don't Understand.*

36. See Alejandro Portes and Rubén G. Rumbaut, *Immigrant America: A Portrait,* 2d ed. (Berkeley: University of California Press, 1996), chap. 4; and Louis DeSipio, *Counting on the Latino Vote: Latinos as a New Electorate* (Charlottesville: University Press of Virginia, 1996), 121.

37. We will see a more direct discussion of their feelings of political attack in the discussion of naturalization.

38. David L. Leal, "Political Participation by Latino Non-Citizens in the United States," *British Journal of Political Science* 32 (2002): 353–70, 369.

39. Cass Sunstein, introduction to *Feminism and Political Theory.*

40. Immigration scholars use the term 1.5 to describe the experience of being foreign born (and thus subject to the immigration and naturalization processes)

but having spent the bulk of one's life and schooling in the United States. For a more detailed definition of this category, see Rubén G. Rumbaut and Kenji Ima, "Determinants of Educational Attainment among Indochinese Refugees and Other Immigrant Students" (paper presented at the annual meeting of the American Sociological Association, Atlanta, Ga., 1988).

41. Mark Hugo López, "Electoral Engagement among Latino Youth," Fact Sheet (Center for Information and Research on Civic Learning and Engagement, Washington, D.C., 2003), 12.

42. Ibid.

43. Scott Keeter, Cliff Zukin, Molly Andolina, and Krista Jenkins, "The Civic and Political Health of the Nation: A Generational Portrait," Working Paper (Center for Information and Research on Civic Learning and Engagement, Washington, D.C., 2002).

44. *La raza* is a term commonly used to refer to the Mexican American community in the United States.

45. In this section, Gilbert is referring to the large-scale freeway construction that took place in East Los Angeles during the 1960s that subdivided the community.

46. The Brown Berets were the Chicano equivalent of the Black Panthers. They wore tan and brown military-style uniforms and attempted to provide the same sort of civilian protection from police, child breakfast programs, and Maoist teaching as the Black Panthers, but they were never as organized or as effective.

47. Adrian D. Pantoja and Gary M. Segura, "Does Ethnicity Matter? Descriptive Representation in Legislatures and Political Alienation among Latinos," *Social Science Quarterly* 84 (2003): 441–60.

48. Tannen, *You Just Don't Understand.*

49. Michelson, "Political Trust among Chicago Latinos."

50. GAIN is a California state welfare program that requires that recipients attend school for a certain number of hours every week in order to receive their welfare benefits. In both Montebello and East Los Angeles, the participants tended to be young unwed mothers.

51. Knoke, "Networks of Political Action," 1042.

52. During World War II, Mexican Americans won more Congressional Medals of Honor than any other group (17 total) and constituted a large percentage of the casualties. Julie Leininger Pycior, *LBJ and Mexican Americans: The Paradox of Power* (Austin: University of Texas Press, 1998), 53.

53. Portes and Rumbaut, *Immigrant America*, 115.

54. Louis DeSipio, "The Engine of Latino Growth: Latin American Immigration and Settlement in the United States," in F. Chris García, ed., *Pursuing Power: Latinos and the Political System* (Notre Dame: University of Notre Dame Press, 1997), 331–37.

55. According to the March 1997 Current Population Survey, 85.4 percent of Mexican immigrants in the United States are not naturalized.

56. DeSipio, *Counting on the Latino Vote,* chap. 5.

57. DeSipio, "The Engine of Latino Growth." See also David S. North, "The Long Grey Welcome: A Study of the American Naturalization Program," *International Migration Review* 21 (1987): 311–26.

58. DeSipio, "The Engine of Latino Growth." It is important to note that the U.S. Citizenship and Immigration Service has only existed since March 2003. We do not yet know if it will process applications more efficiently than its predecessor, the INS. But the record thus far (including the lack of movement on the backlog of applications) makes it reasonable to assume that the new agency will have many of the same bureaucratic problems as its predecessor.

59. While it is true that children under the age of fourteen can be granted U.S. citizenship automatically when their parents naturalize, none of these 1.5-generation respondents had had that happen. As a result, they all needed to decide about their citizenship status.

60. The INS received more than 850,000 citizenship applications in fiscal year 1998 and at the end of that year was estimated to have an application backlog of 2 million applications. During the 106th Congress, $171 million was appropriated to the INS to help the agency process applications in those cities with the largest backlogs, one of which is Los Angeles. But the changes in application review that were implemented after September 11, 2001, along with the reorganization of the INS into the USCIS, expanded the problem. At the end of fiscal year 2003 the backlog was estimated to be 3.4 million cases. The average waiting time then was thirty-five months—almost three years.

61. Harry P. Pachon, "Naturalization: Determinants and Process in the Hispanic Community," *International Migration Review* 21 (1987): 299–310.

62. See Portes and Rumbaut, *Immigrant America.*

63. Other evidence of this transnational trend among immigrants can be seen in a series of articles run by the *New York Times* about the experiences of Latin American, Asian, and African immigrants in New York City. See Deborah Sontag and Celia W. Dugger, "The New Immigrant Tide: A Shuttle between Worlds," *New York Times,* 19 July 1998, A1, A27–28; Deborah Sontag, "A Mexican Town That Transcends All Borders," *New York Times,* 21 July 1998, A1, A16–A17; and Editorial, "The New Immigrant Experience," *New York Times,* 22 July 1998, A22.

64. Pete Wilson was governor of California from 1990 to 1998. During his second reelection campaign, he was one of the sponsors of the "Save Our State" (SOS) campaign, which sponsored Proposition 187, the 1994 ballot measure that denied services to undocumented immigrants. He also sued the federal government to recoup the costs to the state to educate, house, and give medical care to

undocumented immigrants. Many Latinos saw these measures as targeting the Latino community in particular.

65. See previous discussion of Tannen, *You Just Don't Understand*. These findings echo those of Hardy-Fanta in *Latina Politics, Latino Politics* and the theoretical arguments made by Sunstein in the introduction to *Feminism and Political Theory* and by Iris Marion Young in *Justice and the Politics of Difference* (Princeton: Princeton University Press, 1990).

66. Sunstein, introduction to *Feminism and Political Theory*.

67. James P. Smith and Barry Edmonston, eds., *The New Americans: Economic, Demographic and Fiscal Effects of Immigration* (Washington, D.C.: National Academy Press, 1997), 378–82.

68. Noncitizens have municipal voting rights in five cities in Maryland: Takoma Park, Barnesville, Martin's Additions, Somerset, and Chevy Chase. Noncitizens can vote in school board elections in the city of Chicago. Noncitizen parents can vote for and serve on community and school boards under New York State education law so long as they have not been convicted of a felony or voting fraud. As of 1992 there were 56,000 noncitizens registered as parent voters in New York. Virginia Harper-Ho, "Noncitizen Voting Rights: The History, the Law and Current Prospects for Change," *Law and Inequality* 18 (2000): 271–322; and Ronald Hayduk, "Noncitizen Voting Rights: Shifts in Immigrant Political Status during the Progressive Era," paper presented at the annual meeting of the American Political Science Association, Boston, Mass., August 2002. There are no municipalities in Los Angeles County that allow permanent residents to vote in any election.

69. See Sunstein, ed., *Feminism and Political Theory*; and Schlozman et al., "Gender and Citizen Participation," 268–72.

70. Naples finds a similar process among low-income African American and Puerto Rican women in New York and Philadelphia. The difference is that I find these attitudes with regard to both electoral and nonelectoral politics. Nancy A. Naples, "'Just What Needed to Be Done': The Political Practice of Women Community Workers in Low-Income Neighborhoods," *Gender and Society* 5 (1991): 478–94.

71. See Hardy-Fanta, *Latina Politics, Latino Politics*, chap. 1.

72. Marschall, "Does the Shoe Fit?" 231.

73. Ibid., 239.

74. Since self-reporting of voting information is notoriously inflated, these numbers should be taken with a grain of salt. Again, what is more important is the degree to which they reflect underlying attitudes and issues in the community that vary generationally.

75. This may be compared to the 63.5 percent of African Americans who were

registered to vote in 1996 and the 67.7 percent of Anglos. U.S. Bureau of the Census, *Current Population Report,* Oct. 1997.

76. Since my interviews at Garfield occurred before the November 1996 election, those who were registered could only have voted in the primary.

77. This is despite the fact that California has been found to have five out of the six "best practices" listed by a recent study in terms of its registration and voting laws. In their national study, Wolfinger and colleagues found that state registration and voting laws have an especially strong negative effect on Latino turnout. While this study shows the importance of another aspect of the social context—the legal rules surrounding access to the vote—they find that California is doing relatively well in this regard. See Raymond E. Wolfinger, Benjamin Highton, and Megan Mullin, "How Postregistration Laws Affect the Turnout of Registrants," unpublished manuscript, Berkeley, Calif., 2003.

78. Little work has been done on Latino political knowledge. One of the few is Adrian Pantoja, "The Dynamics of Political Knowledge" (Ph.D. dissertation, Claremont Graduate University, 2001). Pantoja explores the relationship between group consciousness and political sophistication. He develops a dynamic theory of political knowledge and argues that Latinos have multiple levels of knowledge, and that those levels may vary over time and circumstance.

79. Michelson, "Political Trust among Chicago Latinos."

80. Proposition 227 ended bilingual education in California. There were also important county school bond measures on the same primary ballot. Both issues stimulated Latino turnout.

81. Ricardo Ramírez, "The Changing California Voter: A Longitudinal Analysis of Latino Political Mobilization and Participation" (paper presented at the annual meeting of the American Political Science Association, San Francisco, Sept. 2001).

82. See Cohen and Dawson, "Neighborhood Poverty and African American Politics"; and Marschall, "Does the Shoe Fit?"

83. See Pardo, *Mexican American Women Activists.*

CHAPTER 5. COMMUNITY PROBLEMS,
COLLECTIVE SOLUTIONS

Epigraph: Frederick Douglass, "An Address on West India Emancipation," in John W. Blassingame, ed., *The Frederick Douglass Papers,* series 1, *Speeches, Debates, and Interviews, 1855–63* (New Haven: Yale University Press, 1979).

1. Robert D. Wrinkle, Joseph Stewart Jr., J. L. Polinard, Kenneth J. Meier, and John R. Arvizu, "Ethnicity and Nonelectoral Participation," *Hispanic Journal of Behavioral Sciences* 18 (1996): 142–53, 150.

2. Ibid.

3. Henry E. Brady, Sidney Verba, and Key Lehman Schlozman, "Beyond SES: A Resource Model of Political Participation," *American Political Science Review* 89 (1995): 271–94.

4. Ibid., 273.

5. Cass Sunstein, "Notes on Feminist Political Thought," in Cass Sunstein, ed., *Feminism and Political Theory* (Chicago: University of Chicago Press), 1–11, 8–9.

6. Ibid., 3–4.

7. The concept of political efficacy was first developed by Campell, Gurin, and Miller in their study using 1952 survey data. Since then, the concept has been generally accepted by political scientists as relating to political participation patterns. See Angus Campell, Gerald Gurin, and Warren E. Miller, *The Voter Decides* (Evanston, Ill.: Row, Peterson, 1954).

8. Sidney Verba, Kay Lehman Schlozman, Henry Brady, and Norman Nie, "Race, Ethnicity and Political Resources: Participation in the United States," *British Journal of Politics* 23 (1993): 453–97.

9. Wrinkle et al., "Ethnicity and Nonelectoral Participation."

10. The walkouts were supposed to be a modern restaging of the 1968 Blow Outs in Los Angeles, which many mark as the beginning of the Chicano Movement in California. The students left school at that time to protest the substandard education they felt they were receiving in their classrooms.

11. Amy Pyle and Beth Shuster, "10,000 Students Protest Prop. 187 Immigration: Walkouts around Los Angeles Are Largest Yet Showing Campus Opposition to Initiative. The Teen-Agers Are Mostly Peaceful, with Only 12 Arrests Reported," *Los Angeles Times*, 3 Nov. 1994.

12. Ibid.

13. Admittedly, it is likely that some proportion of the students were motivated by the opportunity to leave school, regardless of how they felt about Proposition 187.

14. Wrinkle et al., "Nonelectoral Participation," 148.

15. See Carol Hardy-Fanta, *Latina Politics, Latino Politics: Gender, Culture, and Political Participation in Boston* (Philadelphia: Temple University Press, 1993), chaps. 2–4.

16. This is similar to what Mary Pardo found motivated Latina women in both East Los Angeles and Montebello to be politically active. See Mary Pardo, *Mexican American Women Activists: Identity and Resistance in Two Los Angeles Communities* (Philadelphia: Temple University Press, 1998), esp. chaps. 5 and 6.

17. See Wrinkle et al., "Nonelectoral Participation"; Steven J. Rosenstone and John Mark Hansen, *Mobilization, Participation and Democracy in America* (New York: Macmillan, 1993); and Michael Dawson, *Behind the Mule: Race and Class in African-American Politics* (Princeton: Princeton University Press, 1994), 131–33;

and Jan Leighley, *Strength in Numbers? The Political Mobilization of Ethnic and Racial Minorities* (Princeton: Princeton University Press, 2001).

18. One such institution is the Mothers of East Los Angeles. This group does undertake the kind of mobilization mentioned here, but these women's experiences indicate that more of this kind of mobilization is necessary in these areas. For a more in-depth discussion of the activities of this group, see Mary Pardo, "Mexican American Women Grassroots Community Activists: 'Mothers of East Los Angeles,'" in F. Chris García, ed., *Pursuing Power: Latinos and the Political System* (Notre Dame: University of Notre Dame Press, 1997), 151–68; and Pardo, *Mexican American Women Activists*, chap. 3.

19. This is similar to what Hardy-Fanta found in *Latina Politics, Latino Politics* and the theoretical arguments made by Cass Sunstein in the introduction to *Feminism and Political Theory* and by Iris Marion Young in *Justice and the Politics of Difference* (Princeton: Princeton University Press, 1990).

20. See Alma García, "The Development of Chicana Feminist Discourse: 1970–1980," *Gender and Society* 3 (1989): 217–38.

21. For examples to the contrary, see Pardo, *Mexican American Women Activists*; and Pierrette Hondagneu-Sotelo, *Gendered Transitions: Mexican Experiences of Immigration* (Berkeley: University of California Press, 1994), 197–98.

22. Hondagneu-Sotelo, *Gendered Transitions*, 198.

23. Sidney Verba, Kay Lehman Schlozman, and Henry Brady, *Voice and Equality: Civic Voluntarism in American Politics* (Cambridge, Mass.: Harvard University Press, 1995).

24. These were the findings in Hardy-Fanta and Pardo's studies of Latina participation. But they both looked at activist women, so it is not clear whether their findings would apply to all Latinas. See Hardy-Fanta, *Latina Politics, Latino Politics*; and Pardo, *Mexican American Women Activists*.

25. For an in-depth analysis of the media representations of Latinos during the 187 campaign, see Otto Santa Ana, *Brown Tide Rising: Metaphors of Latinos in Contemporary American Public Discourse* (Austin: University of Texas Press, 2002).

26. This echoes Marschall's findings among both Latinos and African Americans. Melissa J. Marschall, "Does the Shoe Fit? Testing Models of Participation for African American and Latino Involvement in Local Politics," *Urban Affairs Review* 37 (2001): 227–48.

27. Aída Hurtado, Patricia Gurin, and Timothy Peng, "Social Identities: A Framework for Studying the Adaptations of Immigrants and Ethnics: The Adaptations of Mexicans in the United States," *Social Problems* 41 (1994): 129–51.

28. It could also be that the Montebello respondents, because of their socioeconomic success, have a greater belief in society's "legitimating myths." Jim Sidanius argues that societies create legitimating myths in order to justify inequality and minimize group conflict. Studies have found that members of stig-

matized groups that accept legitimating myths, rather than group prejudice, to explain experiences of stigma are more likely to have psychological problems and low self-esteem. See Jim Sidanius, "The Psychology of Group Conflict and the Dynamics of Oppression: A Social Dominance Perspective," in Shanto Iyengar and William G. McGuire, eds., *Explorations in Political Psychology* (Durham, N.C.: Duke University Press, 1993), 183–219; and Jennifer Crocker, Brenda Major, and Claude Steele, "Social Stigma," in Daniel T. Gilbert, Susan T. Fiske, and Gardner Lindzey, eds., *The Handbook of Social Psychology*, 4th ed. (New York: McGraw-Hill, 1998), 504–53, 532.

29. Hardy-Fanta, *Latina Politics, Latino Politics*, chap. 1.

30. While Chris is recommending contacting an elected official, he is not aware of the actual position that official holds. Gloria Molina is a Los Angeles County supervisor, not a member of Congress. Again we are seeing the lack of political information and knowledge in these areas.

31. Marschall, "Does the Shoe Fit?"

32. Jan E. Leighley and Arnold Vedlitz, "Race, Ethnicity, and Political Participation: Competing Models and Contrasting Explanations," *Journal of Politics* 61 (1999): 1092–1114, 1102.

33. Dalton Conley, *Honky* (Berkeley: University of California Press, 2000).

34. *Cholo* is a derogatory word used to describe a Chicano gang member and sometimes to describe any urban Chicano youth.

35. During the time of these interviews, as a result of the downsizing of the defense sector after the cold war, southern California was experiencing its worst economic downturn since the Great Depression. This situation probably made the respondents' perceptions of the region's economic outlook more pessimistic. According to the 2000 census, even after the economic boom of the late 1990s, levels of Latino unemployment and poverty in Los Angeles remained higher than that of Euro-Americans and African Americans. Latinos make up about 45 percent of the population of Los Angeles Couny but comprise more than 60 percent of those living in poverty. See Weingart Center, *Poverty in Los Angeles* (Los Angeles: Institute for the Study of Homelessness and Poverty, 2003), 2.

36. Kevin F. McCarthy and Georges Vernez, *Immigration in a Changing Economy: California's Experience* (Santa Monica, Calif.: RAND Corporation, 1997), 79–90.

37. Ibid.

38. Pew Hispanic Center/Kaiser Family Foundation, "National Survey of Latinos: Education, Summary, and Chartpack" (Washington, D.C.: Pew Hispanic Center, 2004), 3.

39. Ibid., 37.

40. For an overview of these cultural arguments, and other reasons that have been given to explain low Latino educational attainment, see Neil Fligstein and

Roberto M. Fernández, "Hispanics and Education," in Pastora San Juan Cafferty and William C. McCready, eds., *Hispanics in the United States: A New Social Agenda* (New Brunswick, N.J.: Transaction Publishers, 1994), 113–45.

41. See Georges Vernez and Allan Abrahamse, *How Immigrants Fare in U.S. Education* (Santa Monica, Calif.: RAND Corporation, 1996).

42. Martha Menchaca, *The Mexican Outsiders: A Community History of Marginalization and Discrimination in California* (Austin: University of Texas Press, 1995), chap. 8.

43. For an overview of findings from that survey, see Rodney E. Hero and Anne G. Campbell, "Understanding Latino Political Participation: Exploring the Evidence from the Latino National Political Survey," *Hispanic Journal of Behavioral Sciences*, 18 (1996): 129–41; and Wrinkle et al., "Ethnicity and Nonelectoral Participation."

CONCLUSION

Epigraph: *University of California Regents v. Bakke*, 438 US 265 (1978).

1. Wendy Brown, *States of Injury: Power and Freedom in Late Modernity* (Princeton: Princeton University Press, 1995), 27–28.

2. Alejandro Portes, "Social Capital: Its Origins and Applications in Modern Sociology," *Annual Review of Sociology* 24 (1998): 1–24, 17.

3. Ibid.

4. Jane Mansbridge and Katherine Tate, "Race Trumps Gender: Black Opinion on the Thomas Nomination," *PS: Political Science and Politics* 25 (1992): 488–92; Claudine Gay and Katherine Tate, "Doubly Bound: The Impact of Gender and Race on the Politics of Black Women," *Political Psychology* 19 (1998): 169–84.

5. Rogers Smith argues that political scientists have done a poor job of studying racial hierarchy and inequality as a fundamentally political product. See Rogers M. Smith, "The Puzzling Place of Race in American Political Science," *PS: Political Science and Politics* 37 (2004): 41–45.

6. Kimberlé Crenshaw, "Mapping the Margins: Intersectionality, Identity, Politics and Violence against Women of Color." *Stanford Law Review* 43 (1991): 1241–99; Patricia Hill Collins, *Feminist Thought: Knowledge, Consciousness and the Politics of Empowerment*, 2d ed. (New York: Routledge, 2000).

7. bell hooks, *Feminist Theory: From Margin to Center*, 2d ed. (Boston: South End Press, 2000).

8. Michael Dawson, *Behind the Mule: Race and Class in African-American Politics* (Princeton: Princeton University Press, 1994).

9. Cathy J. Cohen, *The Boundaries of Blackness* (Chicago: University of Chicago Press, 1999).

10. My thanks to Molly Patterson for collecting and analyzing these different approaches to measuring social identity. None of these works addresses the empirical problem of measuring the intersection (and effects) of multiple identities, but all employ significantly better measures of race than what is commonly employed in political behavior studies, namely, the dummy variable. For a review of this literature, see Deborrah S. Frable, "Gender, Racial, Ethnic, Sexual, and Class Identities," *Annual Review of Psychology* 48 (1997): 139–62.

11. Steven Greene, "The Social-Psychological Measurement of Partisanship," *Political Behavior* 24 (2002):171–97.

12. Jean Phinney, "Stages of Ethnic Identity in Minority Group Adolescents," *Journal of Early Adolescence* 9 (1989): 34–49.

13. Kathleen A. Ethier and Kay Deaux, "Negotiating Social Identity When Contexts Change: Maintaining Identification and Responding to Threat," *Journal of Personality and Social Psychology* 67 (1994): 243–51.

14. Riia Luhtanen and J. Crocker. "A Collective Self-Esteem Scale: Self-Evaluation of One's Social Identity," *Personality and Social Psychology Bulletin* 18 (1992): 302–18.

15. David Knoke, "Networks of Political Action: Toward Theory Construction," *Social Forces* 68 (1990): 1041–63.

16. Cathy J. Cohen and Michael C. Dawson, "Neighborhood Poverty and African American Politics," *American Political Science Review* 87 (1993): 286–302, 287.

17. Jan E. Leighley, *Strength in Numbers? The Political Mobilziation of Racial and Ethnic Minorities* (Princeton: Princeton University Press, 2001).

18. Rodney Hero, *Faces of Inequality: Social Diversity in American Politics* (New York: Oxford University Press, 2000).

19. Rodney E. Hero, "Social Capital and Racial Inequality in America," *Perspectives on Politics* 1 (2003): 113–22.

20. For a review of political socialization as a field, see Yali Peng, "Intellectual Fads in Political Science: The Cases of Political Socialization and Community Power Studies, " *PS: Political Science and Politics* 27 (1994): 100–109. Some examples of political socialization studies are Fred I. Greenstein, *Children and Politics* (New Haven: Yale University Press, 1965); David Easton and Jack Dennis, *Children in the Political System: The Origins of Political Legitimacy* (New York: McGraw-Hill, 1969); M. Kent Jennings and Richard G. Niemi, "The Transmission of Political Values from Parent to Child," *American Political Science Review* 62 (1968): 169–84; M. Kent Jennings and Richard G. Niemi, *The Political Character of Adolescence: The Influences of Family and School* (Princeton: Princeton University Press, 1974); Bruce A. Campbell, "A Theoretical Approach to Peer Influence in Adolescent Socialization," *American Journal of Political Science* 24 (1980): 324–44.

21. For critiques of the socialization literature, see Roberta S. Sigel, "New

Directions for Political Socialization Research," *Perspectives on Political Science* 24 (1995): 17–23; Shawn W. Rosenberg, "Sociology, Psychology, and the Study of Political Behavior: The Case of the Research on Political Socialization," *Journal of Politics* 47 (1985): 715–31; and Richard M. Merelman, "The Adolescence of Political Socialization," *Sociology of Education* 45 (1972): 134–66.

22. Wendy K. Tam Cho, "Naturalization, Socialization, Participation: Immigrants and (Non-)Voting," *Journal of Politics* 61 (1999): 1140–55.

23. Ibid., 1142.

24. Ibid., 1140.

25. Ibid., 1144.

26. James G. Gimpel, J. Celeste Lay, and Jason E. Schuknecht, *Cultivating Democracy: Civic Environments and Political Socialization in America* (Washington, D.C.: Brookings Institution, 2003), 6.

27. Some examples are Eleanor E. Maccoby, Richard E. Matthews, and Anton S. Morton, "Youth and Political Change," *Public Opinion Quarterly* 18 (1954): 23–39; Jennings and Niemi, "The Transmission of Political Values from Parent to Child"; and M. Kent Jennings, Laura Stoker, and Jake Bowers, "Politics across Generations: Family Transmission Reexamined," Working Paper (Institute for Governmental Studies, Berkeley, Calif., 2001).

28. Results from the first and second waves of the Children of Immigrants Study (CILS) can be found in Rubén G. Rumbaut and Alejandro Portes, eds., *Ethnicities: Children of Immigrants in America* (Berkeley: University of California Press, 2001); and Alejandro Portes and Rubén G. Rumbaut, eds., *Legacies: The Story of the Immigrant Second Generation* (Berkeley: University of California Press, 2001).

29. Two important exceptions to this claim are Leighley, *Strength in Numbers?* and Steven Rosenstone and John Mark Hansen, *Mobilization, Participation and Democracy in America* (New York: Macmillan, 1993).

30. For his most recent formulation, see Robert A. Dahl, *On Democracy* (New Haven: Yale University Press, 1998).

31. Anthony Downs, *An Economic Theory of Democracy* (New York: Harper, 1957); and Elmer E. Schattschneider, *Party Government* (New York: Holt, Rinehart and Winston, 1942).

32. Paul Frymer, *Uneasy Alliances: Race and Party Competition in America* (Princeton: Princeton University Press, 1999). Frymer's arguments are very similar to sociological theories of coalitional bias, which posit that dominant groups, because of social stigma, prefer to build coalitions with some groups rather than others. For a discussion of how this theory relates specifically to the Latino experience, see Rodney Hero, *Latinos and the U.S. Political System: Two-Tiered Pluralism* (Philadelphia: Temple University Press, 1992); and Mario Barrera, *Race and Class in the Southwest: A Theory of Racial Inequality* (Notre Dame: University of Notre Dame Press, 1979).

33. See Alan Gerber and Donald P. Green, "The Effects of Canvassing, Telephone Calls, and Direct Mail on Voter Turnout: A Field Experiment," *American Political Science Review* 94 (2000): 653–63; and Alan Gerber and Donald P. Green, "Do Phone Calls Increase Voter Turnout? A Field Experiment," *Public Opinion Quarterly* 65 (2001): 75–85.

34. For findings among Latinos, see Melissa Michelson, "Mobilizing the Latino Youth Vote," Working Paper 10 (Center for Information and Research on Civic Learning and Engagement, Washington, D.C., 2003); and Ricardo Ramírez, "Getting out the Vote: The Impact of Non-partisan Voter Mobilization Efforts in Low Turnout Latino Precincts," Working Paper (Public Policy Institute of California, San Francisco, 2002). For findings among Asian Americans, see Janelle Wong, "Getting out the Vote among Asian Americans: A Field Experiment" (paper presented at the annual meeting of the American Political Science Association, Philadelphia, Pa., Sept. 2003).

35. Bruce G. Link and Jo C. Phelan, "Conceptualizing Stigma," *Annual Review of Sociology* 27 (2001): 363–85.

36. Ibid., 381.

37. Ibid.

38. Rubén G. Rumbaut, "The Crucible Within: Ethnic Identity, Self-Esteem, and Segmented Assimilation among Children of Immigrants," *International Migration Review* 28 (1994): 748–94, 756. Using a separate data set, Zhou and Bankston find similar results. Min Zhou and Carl L. Bankston III, "Social Capital and the Adaptation of the Second Generation: The Case of Vietnamese Youth in New Orleans," *International Migration Review* 28 (1994): 821–45.

39. A *serenata* is a serenade. It is a tradition in Mexico to serenade loved ones on special occasions, like birthdays or anniversaries. These serenades often take place in the (very) early morning hours. A number of the respondents mentioned that it was not possible to do this in other areas because non-Latino neighbors are likely to call the police. Interestingly, that East Los Angeles is unincorporated Los Angeles County land and therefore not subject to the strict zoning and other laws in force in most of southern California is in part why this practice can be maintained.

40. This difference, of course, could be less about content and more about the teacher and his or her teaching styles and abilities. A look at the differential effects of multicultural curricula could be an interesting direction for future study.

41. Gimpel et al., *Cultivating Democracy*, 14–16.

42. Richard G. Niemi and Jane Junn, *Civic Education: What Makes Students Learn?* (New Haven: Yale University Press, 1998).

43. Michael McDevitt, Spiro Kiousis, Xu Wu, Mary Losch, and Travis Ripley, "The Civic Bonding of School and Family: How Kids Voting Students Enliven the

Domestic Sphere," Working Paper (Center for Information and Research on Civic Learning and Engagement, Washington, D.C., 2003).

44. Ibid., 2.

45. Cynthia Gibson and Peter Levine, eds., *The Civic Mission of Schools: A Report from the Carnegie Corporation of New York and CIRCLE, the Center for Information and Research on Civic Learning and Engagement* (New York: Carnegie Corporation, 2003), 6.

46. Jonathon F. Zaff, Oksana Malanchuk, Erik Michelson, and Jacquelynne Eccles, "Socializing Youth for Citizenship," Working Paper (Center for Information and Research on Civic Learning and Engagement, Washington, D.C., 2003), 1.

47. Ibid., 2.

48. Gimpel et al., *Cultivating Democracy*, chap. 6.

49. See Scott Keeter, Cliff Zukin, Molly Andolina, and Krista Jenkins, "The Civic and Political Health of the Nation: A Generational Portrait," Working Paper (Center for Information and Research on Civic Learning and Engagement, Washington, D.C., 2002); Mark Hugo López, "Volunteering among Young People," Fact Sheet (Center for Information and Research on Civic Learning and Engagement, Washington, D.C., 2003); and Peter Levine and Mark Hugo López, "Youth Voter Turnout Has Declined, by Any Measure," Fact Sheet (Center for Information and Research on Civic Learning and Engagement, Washington, D.C., 2002).

50. Here I am assuming that there is a consensus among Americans that we want full inclusion in political participation. U.S. states' unwillingness to adopt same-day registration laws, despite proof of its positive effects on turnout, and our unwillingness to make election day a national holiday suggest that this is not necessarily the goal of our electoral institutions. Our strong history of political exclusion of women and people of color also calls this assumption into question. So it is possible that a first step toward this approach to civic engagement would need to be the development of a national consensus regarding the need for full participation.

51. For an overview of Alinsky's philosophy, see Saul David Alinsky, *Rules for Radicals: A Practical Primer for Realistic Radicals* (New York: Vintage Books, 1972).

52. Benjamin Márquez, *Constructing Identities in Mexican American Political Organizations: Choosing Issues, Taking Sides* (Austin: University of Texas Press, 2003).

53. A more in-depth discussion of the Mothers of East Los Angeles is presented in chap. 1. See also Mary Pardo, *Mexican American Women Activists: Identity and Resistance in two Los Angeles Communities* (Philadelphia: Temple University Press, 1998).

54. Downs, *An Economic Theory of Democracy;* and Schattschneider, *Party Government.*

55. At the congressional level, only forty to fifty seats nationally are considered competitive during any given election cycle. The number of competitive races at the state level is not much greater.

56. Frymer, *Uneasy Alliances.*

57. John Locke, *Two Treatises of Government,* ed. Peter Laslett, 3d ed. (Cambridge: Cambridge University Press, 1988).

58. Results from the 2003 Current Population Survey show the Gini index of income inequality rising fairly consistently from 1967 to 2002. See Carmen DeNavas-Walt, Robert Cleveland, and Bruce H. Webster, *Income in the United States* (Washington, D.C.: U.S. Government Printing Office, 2003), 25-26.

59. Sidney Verba, Kay Lehman Schlozman, Henry Brady, and Norman H. Nie, "Race, Ethnicity and Political Resources: Participation in the United States," *British Journal of Political Science* 23 (1993): 453-97, 495. See also Sidney Verba, Kay Lehman Schlozman, and Henry Brady, introduction to *Voice and Equality: Civic Voluntarism in American Politics* (Cambridge, Mass.: Harvard University Press, 1995).

60. My findings are consistent with those of Weigl and Reyes, who, in a comparative study of Anglo and Latino attitudes toward politics and public life, find that Anglos and Latinos relate to civic life differently. They find that, unlike Anglos, Latinos need to identify with their primary group first before they can reach out and address political issues in the society at large. Robert C. Weigl and Jesús M. Reyes, "Latino and Anglo Political Portraits: Lessons from Intercultural Field Research," *International Journal of Intercultural Relations* 25 (2001): 235-59.

61. A few examples of authors who make this contention are Arthur M. Schlesinger Jr., *The Disuniting of America: Reflections on a Multicultural Society* (New York: Norton, 1992); Peter Brimelow, *Alien Nation: Common Sense about America's Immigration Disaster* (New York: Random House, 1995); Thomas Sowell, *A Conflict of Visions: Ideological Origins of Political Struggles* (New York: Basic Books, 2002); Brent A. Nelson, *America Balkanized: Immigration's Challenge to Government* (Monterey, Va.: American Immigration Control Foundation, 1994); Nicolaus Mills, ed., *Arguing Immigration: The Debate over the Changing Face of America* (New York: Simon and Schuster, 1994); Dirk Chase Eldredge, *Crowded Land of Liberty: Solving America's Immigration Crisis* (Bridgehampton, N.Y.: Bridge Works Press, 2001).

62. Iris Marion Young, "Structure, Difference and Hispanic/Latino Claims of Justice," in Jorge J. E. Gracia and Pablo De Greiff, eds., *Hispanic/Latinos in the United States: Ethnicity, Race and Rights* (New York: Routledge, 2000), 147-65, 149.

63. Ibid.

64. Ibid., 150.

65. Jane Junn, "Assimilating or Coloring Participation? Gender, Race and Democratic Political Participation," in Cathy J. Cohen, Kathleen B. Jones, and

Joan C. Tronto, eds., *Women Transforming Politics: An Alternative Reader* (New York: New York University Press, 1997), 387–97, 388.

66. Ibid.

67. George Lipsitz argues that this kind of tacit acceptance and lack of criticism of the status quo is a form of white supremacy. See George Lipsitz, *The Possessive Investment in Whiteness: How White People Profit from Identity Politics* (Philadelphia: Temple University Press, 1998).

Bibliography

Acuña, Rodolfo. *Anything But Mexican: Chicanos in Contemporary Los Angeles.*
New York: Verso Press, 1997.
———. *Occupied America: A History of Chicanos.* 3d ed. New York:
HarperCollins, 1988.
Alba, Richard D., and John R. Logan. "Minority Proximity to Whites in Suburbs:
An Individual-Level Analysis of Segregation." *American Journal of Sociology* 98
(1993): 1388–1427.
Alba, Richard D., John R. Logan, and Brian J. Stults. "The Changing Neigh-
borhood Contexts of the Immigrant Metropolis." *Social Forces* 79 (2000):
587–621.
Alba, Richard, John Logan, Wenquan Zhange, and Brian J. Stults. "Strangers
Next Door: Immigrant Groups and Suburbs in Los Angeles and New York."
In *A Nation Divided: Diversity, Inequality and Community in American Society,*
edited by Phyllis Moen, Donna Dempster-McClain, and Henry A. Walker.
Ithaca: Cornell University Press, 1999.
Alinsky, Saul David. *Rules for Radicals: A Practical Primer for Realistic Radicals.*
New York: Vintage Books, 1972.
Allen, James P., and Eugene Turner. *The Ethnic Quilt: Population Diversity in*

Southern California. Northridge: Center for Geographical Studies, California State University, Northridge, 1997.

Almaguer, Tomás. *Racial Fault Lines: The Historical Origins of White Supremacy in California*. Berkeley: University of California Press, 1994.

Alvarez, Fred. "Rebuilding the Economy: Businesses Adapting to a New Climate. Labor: Workers Displaced by the Devastation of the Past Four Years Are Shifting Gears, Striking Out on Their Own or Transferring Old Job Skills to New Professions." *Los Angeles Times*, 22 May 1994.

Alvarez, Fred, and Maia Davis. "1,500 Students Leave Schools Over Prop. 187." *Los Angeles Times* [Ventura West Edition], 29 October 1994.

Alvarez, R. Michael, and Lisa García Bedolla. "The Revolution against Affirmative Action in California: Politics, Economics and Proposition 209." *State Politics and Policy Quarterly* 4 (2004): 1–17.

Bailey, Eric, and Dan Morain. "Anti-Immigration Bills Flood Legislature; Rights: Republicans See the Measures as a Way to Help the State Cut Costs. Critics See the Move as Political Opportunism and, in Some Cases, Racism." *Los Angeles Times*, 3 May 1993.

Balderrama, Francisco E., and Raymond Rodríguez. *Decade of Betrayal: Mexican Rpatriation in the 1930s*. Albuquerque: University of New Mexico Press, 1995.

Banaji, Mahzarin R., and Nilanjana Dasgupta. "The Consciousness of Social Beliefs: A Program of Research on Stereotyping and Prejudice." In *Metacognition: Cognitive and Social Dimensions*, edited by Vincent Y. Yzerbyt, Guy Lories, and Benoit Dardenne. London: Sage, 1998.

Barrera, Mario. *Race and Class in the Southwest: A Theory of Racial Inequality*. Notre Dame: University of Notre Dame Press, 1979.

Bernal, Martha E., and George P. Knight, eds. *Ethnic Identity: Formation and Transmission among Hispanics and Other Minorities*. Albany: State University of New York Press, 1993.

Bourdieu, Pierre. "The Forms of Capital." In *Handbook of Theory and Research for the Sociology of Education*, edited by J. G. Richardson. New York: Greenwood Press, 1985.

Brady, Henry E., Sidney Verba, and Key Lehman Schlozman. "Beyond SES: A Resource Model of Political Participation." *American Political Science Review* 89 (1995): 271–94.

Brewer, Marilynn B., and Rupert J. Brown. "Intergroup Relations." In *The Handbook of Social Psychology*, edited by Daniel T. Gilbert, Susan T. Fiske, and Gardner Lindzey. New York: McGraw-Hill, 1998.

Brimelow, Peter. *Alien Nation: Common Sense about America's Immigration Disaster*. New York: HarperCollins, 1996.

Brown, Wendy. *States of Injury: Power and Freedom in Late Modernity*. Princeton: Princeton University Press, 1995.

Brownstein, Ronald, and Richard Simon. "Hospitality Turns into Hostility: California Has a Long History of Welcoming Newcomers for Their Cheap Labor—Until Times Turn Rough. The Current Backlash Is also Fueled by the Scope and Nature of the Immigration." *Los Angeles Times*, 14 November 1993.

Burns, Nancy, Kay Lehman Schlozman, and Sidney Verba. *The Private Roots of Public Action: Gender, Equality and Political Participation.* Cambridge, Mass.: Harvard University Press, 2001.

Calvo, María Antonia, and Steven Rosenstone. "Hispanic Political Participation." Southwest Voter Institute, San Antonio, Tex., 1989.

Camarillo, Albert. *Chicanos in a Changing Society: From Mexican Pueblos to American Barrios in Santa Barbara and Southern California, 1848–1930.* 6th ed. Cambridge, Mass.: Harvard University Press, 1996.

Campbell, Angus, Phillip E. Converse, Warren E. Miller, and Donald E. Stokes. *The American Voter.* New York: John Wiley and Sons, 1960.

Campell, Angus, Gerald Gurin, and Warren E. Miller. *The Voter Decides.* Evanston, Ill.: Row, Peterson, 1954.

Campbell, Bruce A. "A Theoretical Approach to Peer Influence in Adolescent Socialization." *American Journal of Political Science* 24 (1980): 324–44.

Carby, Hazel V. "Policing Black Woman's Body in an Urban Context." In *Women Transforming Politics: An Alternative Reader,* edited by Cathy J. Cohen, Kathleen Jones, and Joan C. Tronto. New York: New York University Press, 1997.

Carrillo, Luis A. "Perspectives on the 'Tagger Shooting': How to Kill a Latino Kid and Walk Free; The Treatment Given the Killer of an Unarmed 18-Year-Old Tagger Proves that the Real Affirmative Action Is for White Males." *Los Angeles Times,* 27 November 1995.

Chávez, John R. *Eastside Landmark: A History of the East Los Angeles Community Union, 1968–1993.* Stanford: Stanford University Press, 1998.

Chávez, Leo R. *Covering Immigration: Popular Images and the Politics of the Nation.* Berkeley: University of California Press, 2001.

Chávez, Linda. *Out of the Barrio: Toward a New Politics of Hispanic Assimilation.* New York: Basic Books, 1991.

Children Now. "A Different World: Children's Perceptions of Race and Class in Media." www.childrennow.org/media/mc98/DiffWorld.html, 1998.

Cho, Wendy K. Tam. "Naturalization, Socialization, Participation: Immigrants and (Non)-Voting." *Journal of Politics* 61 (1999): 1140–55.

Cohen, Cathy J. *The Boundaries of Blackness: AIDS and the Breakdown of Black Politics.* Chicago: University of Chicago Press, 1999.

Cohen, Cathy J., and Michael C. Dawson. "Neighborhood Poverty and African American Politics." *American Political Science Review* 87 (1993): 286–302.

Coleman, James S. "Social Capital in the Creation of Human Capital." *American Journal of Sociology* 94 (1988): S95–S120.

Conley, Dalton. *Honky.* Berkeley: University of California Press, 2000.

Conway, M. Margaret. *Political Participation in the United States.* 2d ed. Washington, D.C.: Congressional Quarterly Press, 1991.

Crenshaw, Kimberlé. "Mapping the Margins: Intersectionality, Identity, Politics and Violence against Women of Color." *Stanford Law Review* 43 (1991): 1241–99.

Crenshaw, Kimberlé, Kendall Thomas, Neil Gotanda, and Gary Peller, eds. *Critical Race Theory: The Key Writings That Formed the Movement.* New York: New Press, 1995.

Crocker, Jennifer, Brenda Major, and Claude Steele. "Social Stigma." In *Handbook of Social Psychology,* 4th ed., edited by Daniel T. Gilbert, Susan T. Fiske, and Gardner Lindzey. New York: McGraw-Hill, 1998.

Cruz, José E. *Identity and Power: Puerto Rican Politics and the Challenge of Ethnicity.* Philadelphia: Temple University Press, 1998.

Dahl, Robert A. *On Democracy.* New Haven: Yale University Press, 1998.

Davis, Mike. *City of Quartz: Excavating the Future in Los Angeles.* New York: Verso Press, 1990.

———. "The Social Origins of the Referendum." *NACLA Report on the Americas* 29 (1995): 24–28.

Dawson, Michael C. *Behind the Mule: Race and Class in African-American Politics.* Princeton: Princeton University Press, 1994.

———. *Black Visions: The Roots of Contemporary African-American Political Ideologies.* Chicago: University of Chicago Press, 2001.

de la Garza, Rodolfo, and Adela Flores. "The Impact of Mexican Immigrants on the Political Behavior of Chicanos: A Clarification of Issues and Some Hypotheses for Future Research." In *Mexican Immigrants and Mexican Americans: An Evolving Relation,* edited by Harley L. Browning and Rodolfo de la Garza. Austin: University of Texas Press, 1986.

DeNavas-Walt, Carmen, Robert Cleveland, and Bruce H. Webster. *Income in the United States.* Washington, D.C.: U.S. Government Printing Office, 2003.

DeSipio, Louis. *Counting on the Latino Vote: Latinos as a New Electorate.* Charlottesville: University Press of Virginia, 1996.

———. "The Engine of Latino Growth: Latin American Immigration and Settlement in the United States." In *Pursuing Power: Latinos and the Political System,* edited by F. Chris García. Notre Dame: University of Notre Dame Press, 1997.

Deutsch, Sarah. *No Separate Refuge: Culture, Class and Gender on the Anglo-Hispanic Frontier in the American Southwest, 1880–1940.* New York: Oxford University Press, 1987.

Deverell, William. *Whitewashed Adobe: The Rise of Los Angeles and the Remaking of Its Mexican Past.* Berkeley: University of California Press, 2004.

Dorinson, Joseph. "The Educational Alliance: An Institutional Study in

Americanization and Acculturation." In *Immigration and Ethnicity: American Society — "Melting Pot" or "Salad Bowl?"* edited by Michael D'Innocenzo and Josef P. Sirefman. Westport, Conn.: Greenwood Press, 1992.

Downs, Anthony. *An Economic Theory of Democracy.* New York: Harper, 1957.

Easton, David, and Jack Dennis. *Children in the Political System: The Origins of Political Legitimacy.* New York: McGraw-Hill, 1969.

Edwards, John. "Language in Group and Individual Identity." In *Social Psychology of Identity and Self Concept,* edited by Glynis M. Breakwell. London: Surrey University Press, 1992.

Eldredge, Dirk Chase. *Crowded Land of Liberty: Solving America's Immigration Crisis.* Bridgehampton, N.Y.: Bridge Works Press, 2001.

Emirbayer, Mustafa. "Manifesto for a Relational Sociology." *American Journal of Sociology* 103 (1997): 281–317.

Emirbayer, Mustafa, and Jeff Goodwin. "Network Analysis, Culture and the Problem of Agency." *American Journal of Sociology* 99 (1994): 1411–54.

Escalante, Virginia. "El Pueblo de Simons." *Los Angeles Times,* 23 September 1982.

Espinosa, Suzanne, and Benjamin Pimentel. "Anger at Immigration Overflow." *San Francisco Chronicle,* 27 August 1993.

Espiritu, Yen Le. *Home Bound: Filipino American Lives across Cultures, Communities, and Countries.* Berkeley: University of California Press, 2003.

Ethier, Kathleen A., and Kay Deaux. "Negotiating Social Identity When Contexts Change: Maintaining Identification and Responding to Threat." *Journal of Personality and Social Psychology* 67 (1994): 243–51.

Fishman, Joshua A. *Language and Ethnicity in Minority Sociolinguistic Perspective.* Philadelphia: Multilingual Matters, 1989.

———. "Macrosociolinguistics and the Sociology of Language in the Early Eighties." *Annual Review of Sociology* 11 (1985): 113–27.

Fligstein, Neil, and Roberto M. Fernández. "Hispanics and Education." In *Hispanics in the United States: A New Social Agenda,* edited by Pastora San Juan Cafferty and William C. McCready. New Brunswick, N.J.: Transaction Publishers, 1994.

Flores, William V., and Rina Benmayor, eds. *Latino Cultural Citizenship: Claiming Identity, Space, and Rights.* Boston: Beacon Press, 1997.

Fogelson, Robert M. *The Fragmented Metropolis: Los Angeles 1850–1930.* Cambridge, Mass.: Harvard University Press, 1967.

Frable, Deborrah S. "Gender, Racial, Ethnic, Sexual and Class Identities." *Annual Review of Psychology* 48 (1997): 139–62.

Fraga, Luis Ricardo, and Ricardo Ramírez. "Unquestioned Influence: Latinos and the 2000 Election in California." In *Muted Voices: Latinos and the 2000 Elections,* edited by Rodolfo de la Garza and Louis DeSipio. New York: Rowman and Littlefield, 2004.

Frymer, Paul. *Uneasy Alliances: Race and Party Competition in America.* Princeton: Princeton University Press, 1999.

Gándara, Patricia. "Learning English in California: Guideposts for the Nation." In *Latinos: Remaking America,* edited by Marcelo M. Suárez-Orozco and Mariela M. Páez. Berkeley: University of California Press, 2002.

García, Alma. "The Development of Chicana Feminist Discourse: 1970–1980." *Gender and Society* 3 (1989): 217–38.

García, F. Chris. *Pursuing Power: Latinos and the Political System.* Notre Dame: Notre Dame University Press, 1997.

García, F. Chris, and Rodolfo de la Garza. *The Chicano Political Experience: Three Perspectives.* Notre Dame: University of Notre Dame Press, 1977.

García, F. Chris, Angelo Falcón, and Rodolfo de la Garza. "Ethnicity and Politics: Evidence from the Latino National Political Survey." *Hispanic Journal of Behavioral Sciences* 18 (1996): 91–103.

García, John A. "Political Participation: Resources and Involvement among Latinos and the American Political System." In *Pursuing Power: Latinos and the Political System,* edited by F. Chris García. Notre Dame: University of Notre Dame Press, 1997.

García, Juan Ramón. *Operation Wetback: The Mass Deportation of Mexican Undocumented Workers in 1954.* Westport, Conn.: Greenwood Press, 1980.

García, María Cristina. *Havana USA: Cuban Exiles and Cuban Americans in South Florida, 1959–1994.* Berkeley: University of California Press, 1996.

García, Mario T. *Mexican Americans: Leadership, Ideology and Identity, 1930–1960.* New Haven: Yale University Press, 1989.

———, ed. *Rubén Salazar, Border Correspondent: Selected Writings, 1955–1970.* Berkeley: University of California Press, 1995.

García, Matt. *A World of Its Own: Race, Labor and Citrus in the Making of Greater Los Angeles.* Chapel Hill: University of North Carolina Press, 2002.

García, Ofelia, José Luis Morín, and Klaudia M. Rivera. "How Threatened Is the Spanish of New York Puerto Ricans? Language Shift with Vaivén." In *Can Threatened Languages Be Saved? Reversing Language Shift, Revisited: A 21st Century Perspective,* edited by Joshua Fishman. Buffalo, N.Y.: Multilingual Matters, 2001.

García Bedolla, Lisa. "The Identity Paradox: Latino Language, Politics and Selective Dissociation." *Latino Studies* 1 (2003): 264–83.

Gay, Claudine, and Katherine Tate. "Doubly Bound: The Impact of Gender and Race on the Politics of Black Women." *Political Psychology* 19 (1998): 169–84.

Gerber, Alan, and Donald P. Green. "Do Phone Calls Increase Voter Turnout? A Field Experiment." *Public Opinion Quarterly* 65 (2001): 75–85.

———. "The Effects of Canvassing, Telephone Calls, and Direct Mail on Voter

Turnout: A Field Experiment." *American Political Science Review* 94 (2000): 653–63.

Gibson, Cynthia, and Peter Levine, eds. *The Civic Mission of Schools: A Report from the Carnegie Corporation of New York and CIRCLE, the Center for Information and Research on Civic Learning and Engagement.* New York: Carnegie Corporation, 2003.

Gilliam, Frank, Iyengar Shanto, Adam Simon, and Oliver Wright. "Crime in Black and White: The Violent, Scary World of Local News." *Harvard International Journal of Press/Politics* 1 (1996): 6–23.

Gilligan, Carol. *In a Different Voice: Psychological Theory and Women's Development.* Cambridge, Mass.: Harvard University Press, 1982.

Gimpel, James G., J. Celeste Lay, and Jason E. Schuknecht. *Cultivating Democracy: Civic Environments and Political Socialization in America.* Washington, D.C.: Brookings Institution, 2003.

Gómez Quiñones, Juan. *Chicano Politics: Reality and Promise, 1940–1990.* Albuquerque: University of New Mexico Press, 1990.

González, Gilbert. *Chicano Education in the Era of Segregation.* Philadelphia: Balch Institute Press, 1990.

———. *Labor and Community: Mexican Citrus Worker Villages in a Southern California County, 1900–1950.* Urbana: University of Illinois Press, 1994.

Gordon, Judith R. *Organizational Behavior: A Diagnostic Approach.* 5th ed. Saddle River, N.J.: Prentice Hall, 1996.

Gordon, Milton. *Assimilation in American Life.* New York: Oxford University Press, 1964.

Gracia, Jorge J. E., and Pablo De Greiff, eds. *Hispanics/Latinos in the United States: Ethnicity, Race, and Rights.* New York: Routledge, 2000.

Greene, Steven. "The Social-Psychological Measurement of Partisanship." *Political Behavior* 24 (2002): 171–97.

Greenstein, Fred I. *Chidren and Politics.* New Haven: Yale University Press, 1965.

Griswold del Castillo, Richard. *The Los Angeles Barrio, 1850–1890.* Berkeley: University of California Press, 1979.

Gutiérrez, David G. *Walls and Mirrors: Mexican Americans, Mexican Immigrants, and the Politics of Ethnicity.* Berkeley: University of California Press, 1995.

Haas, Lisbeth. *Conquests and Historical Identities in California, 1769–1936.* Berkeley: University of California Press, 1995.

Haney-López, Ian F. *White by Law: The Legal Construction of Race.* New York: New York University Press, 1996.

Hardy-Fanta, Carol. *Latina Politics, Latino Politics: Gender, Culture and Political Participation in Boston.* Philadelphia: Temple University Press, 1993.

Harper, Kathryn. "Immigrant Generation, Assimilation and Adolescent Psychological Well-Being." *Social Forces* 79 (2001): 969–1004.

Harper, Richard Conant. *The Course of the Melting Pot Idea to 1910.* New York: Arno Press, 1980.

Harper-Ho, Virginia. "Noncitizen Voting Rights: The History, the Law and Current Prospects for Change." *Law and Inequality* 18 (2000): 271–322.

Hayduk, Ronald. "Noncitizen Voting Rights: Shifts in Immigrant Political Status during the Progressive Era." Paper presented at the annual meeting of the American Political Science Association, Boston, Mass., August 2002.

Hernández, Efraín. "Masters Will Clean Trash, Not Graffiti: Judge Changes Punishment for Gun Violations due to Concerns for the Safety of a Man Who Killed a Tagger." *Los Angeles Times,* 28 December 1995.

Hero, Rodney. *Faces of Inequality: Social Diversity in American Politics.* New York: Oxford University Press, 2000.

———. *Latinos and the U.S. Political System: Two-Tiered Pluralism.* Philadelphia: Temple University Press, 1992.

———. "Social Capital and Racial Inequality in America." *Perspectives on Politics* 1 (2003): 113–22.

Hero, Rodney E., and Anne G. Campbell. "Understanding Latino Political Participation: Exploring the Evidence from the Latino National Political Survey." *Hispanic Journal of Behavioral Sciences* 18 (1996): 129–41.

Hill Collins, Patricia. *Black Feminist Thought: Knowledge, Consciousness and the Politics of Empowerment,* 2d ed. New York: Routledge, 2000.

Hochschild, Jennifer. *Facing Up to the American Dream: Race, Class, and the Soul of the Nation.* Princeton: Princeton University Press, 1995.

Hoffman, Abraham. *Unwanted Mexican Americans in the Great Depression: Repatriation Pressures, 1929–1939.* Tucson: University of Arizona Press, 1974.

Hogg, M. A., and J. C. Turner. "Intergroup Behaviour, Self Stereotyping and the Salience of Social Categories." *British Journal of Social Psychology* 26 (1987): 325–40.

Hondagneu-Sotelo, Pierrette. *Gendered Transitions: Mexican Experiences of Immigration.* Berkeley: University of California Press, 1994.

hooks, bell. *Feminist Theory: From Margin to Center.* Boston: South End Press, 1984.

Howard, Judith A. "Social Psychology of Identities." *Annual Review of Sociology* 26 (2000): 367–93.

Hritzuk, Natasha, and David K. Park. "The Question of Latino Participation: From SES to a Social Structural Explanation." *Social Science Quarterly* 81 (2000): 151–66.

Hurtado, Aída, and Carlos H. Arce. "Mexicans, Chicanos, Mexican Americans, or Pochos . . . ¿Qué somos? The Impact of Language and Nativity on Ethnic Labeling." *Aztlán* 17 (1987): 103–30.

Hurtado, Aída, Patricia Gurin, and Timothy Peng. "Social Identities: A Framework for Studying the Adaptations of Immigrants and Ethnics: The Adaptations of Mexicans in the United States." *Social Problems* 41 (1994): 129–51.

Jackson, James S., Patricia Gurin, and Shirley J. Hatchett. *The 1984 Black Election Study.* Ann Arbor, Mich.: Interuniversity Consortium for Political and Social Research, 1989.

Jennings, James, and Monte Rivera. *Puerto Rican Politics in Urban America.* Westport, Conn.: Greenwood Press, 1984.

Jennings, M. Kent, and Richard G. Niemi. *The Political Character of Adolescence: The Influences of Family and School.* Princeton: Princeton University Press, 1974.

———. "The Transmission of Political Values from Parent to Child." *American Political Science Review* 62 (1968): 169–84.

Jennings, M. Kent, Laura Stoker, and Jake Bowers. "Politics across Generations: Family Transmission Reexamined." Working Paper. Institute for Governmental Studies, Berkeley, Calif., 2001.

Jones-Correa, Michael. *Between Two Nations: the Political Predicament of Latinos in New York City.* Ithaca: Cornell University Press, 1998.

Junn, Jane. "Assimilating or Coloring Participation? Gender, Race and Democratic Political Participation." In *Women Transforming Politics: An Alternative Reader,* edited by Cathy J. Cohen, Kathleen B. Jones, and Joan C. Tronto. New York: New York University Press, 1997.

Keeter, Scott, Cliff Zukin, Molly Andolina, and Krista Jenkins. "The Civic and Political Health of the Nation: A Generational Portrait." Working Paper. Center for Information and Research on Civic Learning and Engagement, Washington, D.C., 2002.

Kershner, Vlae. "A Hot Issue for the '90s: California Leads in Immigration—and Backlash." *San Francisco Chronicle,* 21 June 1993.

Knoke, David. "Networks of Political Action: Toward Theory Construction." *Social Forces* 68 (1990): 1041–63.

Kousser, J. Morgan. *Colorblind Injustice: Minority Voting Rights and the Undoing of the Second Reconstruction.* Chapel Hill: University of North Carolina Press, 1999.

Krauss, Robert M., and Chi-Yue Chiu. "Language and Social Behavior." In *The Handbook of Social Psychology,* 4th ed., edited by Daniel T. Gilbert, Susan T. Fiske, and Gardner Lindzey. New York: McGraw-Hill, 1998.

Lake, Ronald La Due, and Robert Huckfeldt. "Social Capital, Social Networks and Political Participation." *Political Psychology* 19 (1998): 567–84.

Latina Feminist Group. *Telling to Live: Latina Feminist Testimonies.* Durham, N.C.: Duke University Press, 2001.

Leal, David L. "Political Participation by Latino Non-Citizens in the United States." *British Journal of Political Science* 32 (2002): 353–70.

Leighley, Jan E. *Strength in Numbers? The Political Mobilization of Racial and Ethnic Minorities.* Princeton: Princeton University Press, 2001.

Leighley, Jan E., and Arnold Vedlitz. "Race, Ethnicity and Political Participation: Competing Models and Contrasting Explanations." *Journal of Politics* 61 (1999): 1092–1114.

Levine, Peter, and Mark Hugo López. "Youth Voter Turnout Has Declined, by Any Measure." Fact Sheet. Center for Information and Research on Civic Learning and Engagement, Washington, D.C., 2002.

Link, Bruce G., and Jo C. Phelan. "Conceptualizing Stigma." *Annual Review of Sociology* 27 (2001): 363–85.

Lipsitz, George. *The Possessive Investment in Whiteness: How White People Profit from Identity Politics.* Philadelphia: Temple University Press, 1998.

Locke, John. *Two Treatises of Government.* 3d ed. Edited by Peter Laslett. Cambridge: Cambridge University Press, 1988.

Logan, John R., Brian J. Stults, and Reynolds Farley. "Segregation of Minorities in the Metropolis: Two Decades of Change." *Demography* 41 (2004): 1–22.

López, Mark Hugo. "Electoral Engagement among Latino Youth." Fact Sheet. Center for Information and Research on Civic Learning and Engagement, Washington, D.C., 2003.

———. "Volunteering among Young People." Fact Sheet. Center for Information and Research on Civic Learning and Engagement, Washington, D.C., 2003.

Lorde, Audre. *Sister/Outsider: Essays and Speeches.* Freedom, Calif.: Crossing Press, 1984.

Lubenow, Gerald C., and Bruce Cain, eds. *Governing California: Politics, Government and Public Policy in the Golden State.* Berkeley: Institute for Governmental Studies, 1997.

Luhtanen, Riia K., and Jennifer Crocker. "A Collective Self-Esteem Scale: Self-Evaluation of One's Social Identity." *Personality and Social Psychology Bulletin* 18 (1992): 302–318.

Maccoby, Eleanor E., Richard E. Matthews, and Anton S. Morton. "Youth and Political Change." *Public Opinion Quarterly* 18 (1954): 23–39.

Macedo, Donaldo, Bessie Dendrinos, and Panayota Gounari. *The Hegemony of English.* Boulder, Colo.: Paradigm Publishers, 2003.

MacKinnon, Catharine. *Feminism Unmodified: Discourses on Life and Law.* Cambridge, Mass.: Harvard University Press, 1987.

Mansbridge, Jane, and Katherine Tate. "Race Trumps Gender: Black Opinion on the Thomas Nomination." *PS: Political Science and Politics* 25 (1992): 488–92.

Markman, Jon D. "Prop 187's Quiet Student Revolution Activism," *Los Angeles Times,* 6 November 1994.

Márquez, Benjamin. *Constructing Identities in Mexican American Political Organizations: Choosing Issues, Taking Sides.* Austin: University of Texas Press, 2003.

Marschall, Melissa J. "Does the Shoe Fit? Testing Models of Participation for African American and Latino Involvement in Local Politics." *Urban Affairs Review* 37 (2001): 227–48.

Marsden, Peter. "Core Discussion Networks of Americans." *American Sociological Review* 52 (1987): 122–31.

Martin, Mart. *The Almanac of Women and Minorities in American Politics.* Boulder, Colo.: Westview Press, 1999.

Martínez, Gebe. "The Times Poll; As Orange County Neighborhoods Change, Tensions Build. Ethnic Makeup of Many Communities Is Shifting. Many Fear the Change is Not Always for the Better." *Los Angeles Times,* 26 October 1993.

Martínez, Gebe, and Patrick J. McDonnell. "Proposition 187 Backers Counting on Message, Not Strategy." *Los Angeles Times,* 30 October 1994.

Massey, Douglas S., and Nancy A. Denton. *American Apartheid: Segregation and the Making of the Underclass.* Cambridge, Mass.: Harvard University Press, 1993.

———. "Trends in the Residential Segregation of Blacks, Hispanics and Asians, 1970–80." *American Sociological Review* 52 (1987): 802–25.

Matute-Bianchi, María Eugenia. "Ethnic Identities and Patterns of School Success and Failure among Mexican Descent and Japanese-American Students in a California High School: An Ethnographic Analysis." *American Journal of Education* 95 (1986): 233–55.

Mayer, Robert. *Los Angeles: A Chronological and Documentary History, 1542–1976.* Dobbs Ferry, N.Y.: Oceana Publications, 1978.

Mazón, Mauricio. *The Zoot Suit Riots: The Psychology of Symbolic Annihilation.* Austin: University of Texas Press, 1984.

McCarthy, Kevin F., and Georges Vernez. *Immigration in a Changing Economy: California's Experience.* Santa Monica, Calif.: RAND Corporation, 1997.

McClung, William Alexander. *Landscapes of Desire: Anglo Mythologies of Los Angeles.* Berkeley: University of California Press, 2000.

McDevitt, Michael, Spiro Kiousis, Xu Wu, Mary Losch, and Travis Ripley. "The Civic Bonding of School and Family: How Kids Voting Students Enliven the Domestic Sphere." Working Paper. Center for Information and Research on Civic Learning and Engagement, Washington, D.C., 2003.

McLellan, Dennis. "Stirring up Activist Passion in Today's Youth." *Los Angeles Times,* 4 November 1994.

McPherson, Miller, Lynn Smith-Lovin, and James M. Cook. "Birds of a Feather: Homophily in Social Networks." *Annual Review of Sociology* 27 (2001): 415–44.

Menchaca, Martha. *The Mexican Outsiders: A Community History of Marginaliza-tion and Discrimination in California*. Austin: University of Texas Press, 1995.
————. *Recovering History, Constructing Race: The Indian, Black, and White Roots of Mexican Americans*. Austin: University of Texas Press, 2002.
Merelman, Richard M. "The Adolescence of Political Socialization." *Sociology of Education* 45 (1972): 134–66.
Meyer, David S. "Political Opportunity and Nested Institutions." *Social Movement Studies* 2 (2003): 17–35.
Michelson, Melissa. "Mobilizing the Latino Youth Vote." Working Paper 10. Center for Information and Research on Civic Learning and Engagement, Washington, D.C., 2003.
————. "Political Trust among Chicago Latinos." *Journal of Urban Affairs* 23 (2001): 323–34.
Milroy, Lesley. "Language and Group Identity." *Journal of Multilingual and Mul-ticultural Development* 3 (1982): 207–16.
Mills, Nicolaus, ed. *Arguing Immigration: The Debate over the Changing Face of America*. New York: Simon and Schuster, 1994.
Mohoff, George W., and Jack P. Valov. *A Stroll through Russiantown*. Los Angeles, Calif.: G. W. Mohoff and P. Valov, 1996.
Montebello Chamber of Commerce. "A History of the City of Montebello." Pamphlet. Montebello, Calif., 1985.
Montebello News, 4 September 1936.
Monroy, Douglas. *Thrown among Strangers: The Making of Mexican Culture in Frontier America*. Berkeley: University of California Press, 1993.
Montoya, Lisa J. "Gender and Citizenship in Latino Political Participation." In *Latinos: Remaking America*, edited by Marcelo Suárez-Orozco and Mariela M. Páez. Berkeley: University of California Press, 2002.
Morales, Alejandro. *The Brick People*. Houston: Arte Público Press, 1992.
Morales, Ed. *Living in Spanglish: The Search for Latino Identity in America*. New York: St. Martin's Press, 2002.
Morales, Rebecca, and Paul M. Ong. "The Illusion of Progress: Latinos in Los Angeles." In *Latinos in a Changing U.S. Economy*, edited by Rebecca Morales and Frank Bonilla. Newbury Park, Calif.: Sage, 1993.
Muñoz, Carlos. *Youth, Identity, Power: The Chicano Movement*. New York: Verso Press, 1989.
Naples, Nancy A. "'Just What Needed to Be Done': The Political Practice of Women Community Workers in Low-Income Neighborhoods." *Gender and Society* 5 (1991): 478–94.
Nelson, Brent A. *America Balkanized: Immigration's Challenge to Government*. Mon-terey, Va.: American Immigration Control Foundation, 1994.
New York Times. "The New Immigrant Experience." Editorial. 22 July 1998.

Niemi, Richard G., and Jane Junn. *Civic Education: What Makes Students Learn?* New Haven: Yale University Press, 1998.

Nieto, Margarita. "Chicano History Brick by Brick." *Los Angeles Times,* 18 September 1988.

North, David S. "The Long Grey Welcome: A Study of the American Naturalization Program." *International Migration Review* 21 (1987): 311–26.

Oboler, Suzanne. *Ethnic Labels, Latino Lives: Identity and the Politics of (Re)presentation in the United States.* Minneapolis: University of Minnesota Press, 1995.

———. "It Must Be a Fake! Racial Ideolgies, Identities and the Question of Rights." In *Hispanics/Latinos in the United States: Ethnicity, Race and Rights,* edited by Jorge J. E. Gracia and Pablo De Greiff. New York: Routledge, 2000.

Ochoa, Gilda L. *Becoming Neighbors in a Mexican American Community: Power, Conflict and Solidarity.* Austin: University of Texas Press, 2004.

———. "Mexican Americans' attitudes toward and Interactions with Mexican Immigrants: A Qualitative Analysis of Conflict and Cooperation." *Social Science Quarterly* 81 (2000): 84–105.

Olsen, Marvin E. "Two Categories of Political Alienation." *Social Forces* 47 (1969): 288–99.

Olson, Mancur. *The Logic of Collective Action: Public Goods and the Theory of Groups.* 2d ed. Cambridge, Mass.: Harvard University Press, 1971.

Omi, Michael, and Howard Winant. *Racial Formation in the United States from the 1960s to the 1990s.* New York: Routledge, 1994.

O'Neill, Ann W., and Nicholas Riccardi. "Hurt Tagger Was Treated as Suspect, not Victim, Lawyer Says Crime: Police Deny Accusations that Investigation of Jan. 31 Shooting Favored the Gunman. They Cite Conflicting Stories Given by the Youth." *Los Angeles Times,* 15 March 1995.

Pachon, Harry P. "Naturalization: Determinants and Process in the Hispanic Community." *International Migration Review* 21 (1987): 299–310.

Padilla, Amado M., and David Durán. "The Psychological Dimension in Understanding Immigrant Students." In *California's Immigrant Children: Theory, Research, and Implications for Educational Policy,* edited by Rubén G. Rumbaut and Wayne A. Cornelius. San Diego: Center for U.S.-Mexican Studies, University of California, San Diego, 1995.

Padilla, Amado, and William Pérez. "Acculturation, Social Identity, and Social Cognition: A New Perspective." *Hispanic Journal of Behavioral Sciences* 25 (2003): 35–55.

Pantoja, Adrian. "The Dynamics of Political Knowledge." Ph.D. dissertation, Claremont Graduate University, 2001.

Pantoja, Adrian D., and Gary M. Segura. "Does Ethnicity Matter? Descriptive Representation in Legislatures and Political Alienation among Latinos." *Social Science Quarterly* 84 (2003): 441–60.

Pardo, Mary. *Mexican American Women Activists: Identity and Resistance in Two Los Angeles Communities.* Philadelphia: Temple University Press, 1998.

———. "Mexican American Grassroots Community Activists: 'Mothers of East Los Angeles.'" In *Pursuing Power: Latinos and the Political System,* edited by F. Chris García. Notre Dame: University of Notre Dame Press, 1997.

Peng, Yali. "Intellectual Fads in Political Science: The Cases of Political Socialization and Community Power Studies." *PS: Political Science and Politics* 27 (1994): 100–109.

Pew Hispanic Center/Kaiser Family Foundation. "National Survey of Latinos: Education, Summary, and Chartpack." Washington, D.C.: Pew Hispanic Center, 2004.

Phinney, Jean. "Stages of Ethnic Identity in Minority Group Adolescents." *Journal of Early Adolescence* 9 (1989): 34–49.

Pitt, Leonard. *Decline of the Californios: A Social History of the Spanish-Speaking Californians, 1846–1890.* 2d ed. Berkeley: University of California Press, 1994.

Pitt, Leonard, and Dale Pitt. *Los Angeles A to Z: An Encyclopedia of the City and County.* Berkeley: University of California Press, 1997.

Polletta, Francesca, and James M. Jasper. "Collective Identity and Social Movements." *Annual Review of Sociology* 27 (2001): 283–305.

Portes, Alejandro. "Social Capital: Its Origins and Applications in Modern Sociology." *Annual Review of Sociology* 24 (1998): 1–24.

———, ed. *The Economic Sociology of Immigration: Essays on Networks, Ethnicity, and Entrepreneurship.* New York: Russell Sage Foundation, 1995.

Portes, Alejandro, and Robert L. Bach. *Latin Journey: Cuban and Mexican Immigrants in the United States.* Berkeley: University of California Press, 1984.

Portes, Alejandro, and Rubén G. Rumbaut. *Immigrant America: A Portrait.* 2d ed. Berkeley: University of California Press, 1996.

———, eds. *Legacies: The Story of the Immigrant Second Generation.* Berkeley: University of California Press, 2001.

Portney, Kent E., and Jeffrey M. Berry. "Mobilizing Minority Communities: Social Capital and Participation in Urban Neighborhoods." *American Behavioral Scientist* 40 (1997): 632–44.

Putnam, Robert D. *Bowling Alone: The Collapse and Revival of American Community.* New York: Simon and Schuster, 2000.

Pycior, Julie Leininger. *LBJ and Mexican Americans: The Paradox of Power.* Austin: University of Texas Press, 1997.

Pyle, Amy, and Greg Hernández. "10,000 Students Protest Prop. 187 Immigration: Walkout in Orange and L.A. Counties Is Largest Yet." *Los Angeles Times* [Orange County Edition], 3 November 1994.

Pyle, Amy, and Beth Shuster. "10,000 Students Protest Prop. 187 Immigration: Walkouts around Los Angeles Are Largest Yet Showing Campus Opposition to Initiative. The Teen-Agers Are Mostly Peaceful, with Only 12 Arrests Reported." *Los Angeles Times,* 3 November 1994.

Ramírez, Ricardo. "The Changing California Voter: A Longitudinal Analysis of Latino Political Mobilization and Participation." Paper presented at the annual meeting of the American Political Science Association, San Francisco, Calif., September 2001.

———. "Getting Out the Vote: The Impact of Non-partisan Voter Mobilization Efforts in Low Turnout Latino Precincts." Working Paper. Public Policy Institute of California, San Francisco, 2002.

Rand, Christopher. *Los Angeles, the Ultimate City.* New York: Oxford University Press, 1967.

Rasmussen, Cecelia. "Brick Firm Cemented Lives." *Los Angeles Times,* 6 November 1995.

———. "Community Profile: Montebello." *Los Angeles Times,* 24 January 1997.

Ray, Kathryn, Mike Savage, Gindo Tampubolon, Alan Warde, Brian Longhurst, and Mark Tomlinson. "The Exclusiveness of the Political Field: Networks and Political Mobilization." *Social Movement Studies* 2 (2003): 38–60.

Riordan, Cornelius, and Josephine Ruggiero. "Producing Equal-Status Interracial Interaction: A Replication." *Social Psychology Quarterly* 43 (1980): 131–36.

Robinson, Jerry W., and James D. Preston. "Equal-Status Contact and Modification of Racial Prejudice: A Reexamination of the Contact Hypothesis." *Social Forces* 54 (1976): 911–24.

Rodríguez, David. *Latino National Political Coalitions: Struggles and Challenges.* New York: Routledge, 2002.

Rodríguez, Richard. *Hunger of Memory: The Education of Richard Rodriguez.* New York: Bantam Books, 1983.

Romero, Mary, Pierrette Hondagneu-Sotelo, and Vilma Ortiz, eds. *Challenging Fronteras: Structuring Latina and Latino Lives in the United States. An Anthology of Readings.* New York: Routledge, 1997.

Romero, Simon. "1,500 Students Leave Class to Protest against Prop. 187." *Los Angeles Times,* 15 October 1994.

Romo, Ricardo. *East Los Angeles: History of a Barrio.* Austin: University of Texas Press, 1983.

Rosenberg, Shawn W. "Sociology, Psychology, and the Study of Political Behavior: The Case of the Research on Political Socialization." *Journal of Politics* 47 (1985): 715–31.

Rosenstone, Steven J., and John Mark Hansen. *Mobilization, Participation, and Democracy in America.* New York: Macmillan, 1993.

Ruiz, Vicki L. *Out of the Shadows.* New York: Oxford University Press, 1998.

Ruiz, Vicki L., and Ellen Carol DuBois, eds. *Unequal Sisters: A Multicultural Reader in U.S. Women's History.* 2d ed. New York: Routledge, 1994.

Rumbaut, Rubén G. "The Crucible Within: Ethnic Identity, Self-Esteem, and Segmented Assimilation among Children of Immigrants." *International Migration Review* 28 (1994): 748–94.

Rumbaut, Rubén G., and Kenji Ima. "Determinants of Educational Attainment among Indochinese Refugees and Other Immigrant Students." Paper presented at the annual meeting of the American Sociological Association, Atlanta, Ga., 1988.

Rumbaut, Rubén, and Alejandro Portes, eds. *Ethnicities: Children of Immigrants in America.* Berkeley: University of California Press, 2001.

Sampson, Robert J., Jeffrey D. Morenoff, and Thomas Gannon-Rowley. "Assessing 'Neighborhood Effects': Social Processes and New Directions in Research." *Annual Review of Sociology* 28 (2002): 443–78.

Sánchez, George J. *Becoming Mexican American: Ethnicity, Culture and Identity in Chicano Los Angeles, 1900–1945.* New York: Oxford University Press, 1993.

———. "'Go after the Women:' Americanization and the Mexican Immigrant Woman, 1915–1929." In *Unequal Sisters: A Multicultural Reader in U.S. Women's History,* 2d ed., edited by Vicki L. Ruiz and Ellen Carol DuBois. New York: Routledge, 1994.

Sanders, Jimy M. "Ethnic Boundaries and Identity in Plural Societies." *Annual Review of Sociology* 28 (2002): 327–57.

Sankoff, Gillian. *The Social Life of Language.* Philadelphia: University of Pennsylvania Press, 1980.

Santa Ana, Otto. *Brown Tide Rising: Metaphors of Latinos in Contemporary American Public Discourse.* Austin: University of Texas Press, 2002.

Schattschneider, Elmer E. *Party Government.* New York: Holt, Rinehart and Winston, 1942.

Schlesinger, Arthur M., Jr. *The Disuniting of America: Reflections on a Multicultural Society.* New York: Norton, 1992.

Schlozman, Kay Lehman, Nancy Burns, Sidney Verba, and Jesse Donahue. "Gender and Citizen Participation: Is There a Different Voice?" *American Journal of Political Science* 39 (1995): 267–93.

Schmidt, Ronald, Sr. *Language Policy and Identity Politics in the United States.* Philadelphia: Temple University Press, 2000.

Sedillo-López, Antionette, ed. *Historical Themes and Identity: Mestizaje and Labels.* New York: Garland, 1995.

Seidman, Irving. *Interviewing as Qualitative Research: A Guide for Researchers in Education and the Social Sciences.* 2d ed. New York: Teachers College Press, 1998.

Segura, Gary M., F. Chris García, Rodolfo O. de la Garza, and Harry Pachón. *Social Capital and the Latino Community.* Claremont, Calif.: Tomás Rivera Policy Institute, 2000.

Shorris, Earl. *Latinos: A Biography of the People.* New York: Avon Books, 1992.

Shuster, Beth, and Chip Johnson, "Students at 2 Pacoima Schools Protest 187." *Los Angeles Times* [Valley Edition], 21 October 1994.

Sidanius, Jim. "The Psychology of Group Conflict and the Dynamics of Oppression: A Social Dominance Perspective." In *Explorations in Political Psychology,* edited by Shanto Iyengar and William G. McGuire. Durham, N.C.: Duke University Press, 1993.

Sigel, Roberta S. "New Directions for Political Socialization Research." *Perspectives on Political Science* 24 (1995): 17–23.

Sigelman, Lee, and Susan Welch. "The Contact Hypothesis Revisited: Black-White Interaction and Positive Racial Attitudes." *Social Forces* 71 (1993): 781–95.

Sigelman, Lee, Timothy Bledsoe, Susan Welch, and Michael Combs. "Making Contact? Black-White Social Interaction in an Urban Setting." *American Journal of Sociology* 101 (1996): 1306–32.

Simpson, Andrea. *The Tie That Binds: Identity and Political Attitudes in the Post–Civil Rights Generation.* New York: New York University Press, 1998.

Skerry, Peter. *Mexican Americans: The Ambivalent Minority.* Cambridge, Mass.: Harvard University Press, 1995.

Skocpol, Theda. "Unraveling from Above." *American Prospect* 25 (1996): 20–25.

Small, Mario Luis. "Culture, Cohorts, and Social Organization Theory: Understanding Local Participation in a Latino Housing Project." *American Journal of Sociology* 108 (2002): 1–54.

Smith, James P., and Barry Edmonston, eds. *The New Americans: Economic, Demographic, and Fiscal Effects of Immigration.* Washington, D.C.: National Academy Press, 1997.

Smith, Rogers M. *Civic Ideals: Conflicting Visions of Citizenship in U.S. History.* New Haven: Yale University Press, 1997.

———. "The Puzzling Place of Race in American Political Science." *PS: Political Science and Politics* 37 (2004): 41–45.

———. *Stories of Peoplehood: The Politics and Morals of Political Membership.* Cambridge: Cambridge University Press, 2003.

Sonenshein, Raphael J. *Politics in Black and White: Race and Power in Los Angeles.* Princeton: Princeton University Press, 1993.

Sontag, Deborah. "A Mexican Town That Transcends All Borders." *New York Times,* 21 July 1998.

Sontag, Deborah, and Celia W. Dugger. "The New Immigrant Tide: A Shuttle between Worlds." *New York Times,* 19 July 1998.

Sowell, Thomas. *A Conflict of Visions: Ideological Origins of Political Struggles.* New York: Basic Books, 2002.

Stepick, Alex, and Carol Dutton Stepick. "Becoming American, Constructing

Ethnicity: Immigrant Youth and Civic Engagement." *Applied Developmental Science* 6 (2002): 246–57.

Stokes, Atiya Kai. "Latino Group Consciousness and Political Participation." *American Politics Research* 31 (2003): 361–78.

Strauss, Anselm, and Juliet Corbin. *Basics of Qualitative Research: Techniques and Procedures for Developing Grounded Theory.* 2d ed. Thousand Oaks, Calif.: Sage, 1998.

Sunstein, Cass, ed. *Feminism and Political Theory.* Chicago: University of Chicago Press, 1990.

Tajfel, Henri, and J. C. Turner. "An Integrative Theory of Intergroup Conflict." In *The Social Psychology of Intergroup Relations,* edited by William G. Austin and Stephen Worchel. Monterey, Calif.: Brooks/Cole Books, 1979.

———. "The Social Identity Theory of Intergroup Behavior." In *Psychology of Intergroup Relations,* edited by Stephen Worchel and William G. Austin. Chicago: Nelson-Hall, 1986.

Takaki, Ronald. *A Different Mirror: A History of Multicultural America.* Boston: Back Bay Books, 1993.

Tannen, Deborah. *You Just Don't Understand: Women and Men in Conversation.* New York: Morrow, 1990.

———, ed. *Gender and Conversational Interaction.* New York: Oxford University Press, 1993.

Tate, Katherine. *Black Faces in the Mirror: African Americans and Their Representatives in the U.S. Congress.* Princeton: Princeton University Press, 2003.

———. *From Protest to Politics: The New Black Voters in American Elections.* Cambridge, Mass.: Harvard University Press, 1993.

Tolbert, Caroline J., and Rodney E. Hero. "Race/Ethnicity and Direct Democracy: An Analysis of California's Illegal Immigration Initiative." *Journal of Politics* 58 (1996): 806–18.

Torres, Andrés, and José E. Velázquez, eds. *The Puerto Rican Movement: Voices from the Diaspora.* Philadelphia: Temple University Press, 1998.

Torres, Rodolfo D., and George Katsiaficas, eds. *Latino Social Movements: Historical and Theoretical Perspectives: A New Political Science Reader.* New York: Routledge, 1999.

U.S. Bureau of the Census. *Current Population Survey.* Washington, D.C., March 1997.

———. *Current Population Report.* Washington, D.C., October 1997.

———. *Current Population Survey.* Washington, D.C., March 2000.

———. *Current Population Survey.* Washington, D.C., 2003.

U.S. Senate. Henry Cabot Lodge. "Speech to the Senate." 28th Cong. *Congressional Record,* vol. 177 (1896).

Unz, Ron. Roundtable presentation to the Heritage Foundation. Washington, D.C., October 1998.

Urciuoli, Bonnie. *Exposing Prejudice: Puerto Rican Experiences of Language, Race, and Class.* Boulder, Colo.: Westview Press, 1997.

Valle, Victor M., and Rodolfo D. Torres. *Latino Metropolis.* Minneapolis: University of Minnesota Press, 2000.

Verba, Sidney, and Norman H. Nie. *Participation in America: Political Democracy and Social Equality.* Chicago: University of Chicago Press, 1972.

Verba, Sidney, Norman H. Nie, and Jae-on Kim. *Participation and Political Equality: A Seven-Nation Comparison.* Cambridge: Cambridge University Press, 1978.

Verba, Sidney, Kay Lehman Schlozman, and Henry E. Brady. *Voice and Equality: Civic Voluntarism in American Politics.* Cambridge, Mass.: Harvard University Press, 1995.

Verba, Sidney, Kay Lehman Schlozman, Henry Brady, and Norman Nie. "Race, Ethnicity and Political Resources: Participation in the United States." *British Journal of Politics* 23 (1993): 453–97.

Vernez, Georges, and Allan Abrahamse. *How Immigrants Fare in U.S. Education.* Santa Monica, Calif.: RAND Corporation, 1996.

Vigil, James Diego. *A Rainbow of Gangs: Street Cultures in the Mega City.* Austin: University of Texas Press, 2002.

Waldinger, Roger, and Mehdi Bozorgmher. *Ethnic Los Angeles.* New York: Russell Sage Foundation, 1996.

Weber, David J., ed. *Foreigners in Their Native Land: Historical Roots of the Mexican Americans.* Albuquerque: University of New Mexico Press, 1973.

Weigl, Robert C., and Jesús M. Reyes. "Latino and Anglo Political Portraits: Lessons from Intercultural Field Research." *International Journal of Intercultural Relations* 25 (2001): 235–59.

Weingart Center. *Poverty in Los Angeles.* Los Angeles: Institute for the Study of Homelessness and Poverty, 2003.

Weintraub, Daniel. "State's Budget Mess: Will It Ever Clear Up?" *Los Angeles Times,* 24 October 1994.

Weiss, Robert S. *Learning from Strangers: The Art and Method of Qualitative Interview Studies.* New York: Free Press, 1994.

Welch, Susan, and Lee Sigelman. "Getting to Know You? Latino-Anglo Social Contact." *Social Science Quarterly* 81 (2000): 67–83.

Wing, Adrien Katherine, ed. *Critical Race Feminism: A Reader.* New York: New York University Press, 1997.

Wolfinger, Raymond E., Benjamin Highton, and Megan Mullin. "How Postregistration Laws Affect the Turnout of Registrants." Unpublished manuscript. Berkeley, Calif., 2003.

Wolfinger, Raymond E., and Steven J. Rosenstone. *Who Votes?* New Haven: Yale University Press, 1980.

Wong, Janelle. "Getting Out the Vote among Asian Americans: A Field Experiment." Paper presented at the annual meeting of the American Political Science Association, Philadelphia, Pa., September 2003.

Worchel, Stephen, J. Francisco Morales, Darío Páez, and Jean-Claude Deschamps. *Social Identity: International Perspectives.* London: Sage, 1998.

Wrinkle, Robert D., Joseph Stewart Jr., J. L. Polinard, Kenneth J. Meier, and John R. Arvizu. "Ethnicity and Nonelectoral Participation." *Hispanic Journal of Behavioral Sciences* 18 (1996): 142–53.

Young, Iris Marion. *Justice and the Politics of Difference.* Princeton: Princeton University Press, 1990.

———. "Structure, Difference, and Hispanic/Latino Claims of Justice." In *Hispanic/Latinos in the United States: Ethnicity, Race and Rights,* edited by Jorge J. E. Gracia and Pablo De Greiff. New York: Routledge, 2000.

Zaff, Jonathon F., Oksana Malanchuk, Erik Michelson, and Jacquelynne Eccles. "Socializing Youth for Citizenship." Working Paper. Center for Information and Research on Civic Learning and Engagement, Washington, D.C., 2003.

Zentella, Ana Celia. *Growing Up Bilingual: Puerto Rican Children in New York.* New York: Blackwell, 1997.

———. "Lexical Leveling in Four New York City Spanish Dialects: Linguistic and Social Factors." *Hispania* 73 (1990): 1094–2015.

Zhou, Min, and Carl L. Bankston III. "Social Capital and the Adaptation of the Second Generation: The Case of Vietnamese Youth in New Orleans." *International Migration Review* 28 (1994): 821–45.

Zycher, Benjamin. "Governor Wilson, Come Clean on the Tax Hike Instead of Immigrant-bashing, Let's Talk about the Catastrophe Left by His Budget 'Solution.'" *Los Angeles Times,* 22 October 1994.

Index

African American politics: linked fate and, 10; political behavior and, 17, 101, 103–4, 212n80. *See also* Cohen, Cathy; Dawson, Michael; Tate, Katherine

agency: agency oriented theoretical perspective, 3; collective identity and, 8–10; definition of, 2; mobilizing identity and, 6–7; political engagement and, 3, 106; structure and, 2–3, 12, 14. *See also* ideology

Alatorre, Richard, 50

Alien Land Law, 34

Alinsky, Saul, 50, 188

Allen, James P. (and Eugene Turner), 41

American Immigration Control Foundation, 29

Arce, Rene, 31–33. *See also* tagger shooting

Asian American politics, 13, 104. *See also* Wong, Janelle

Bankston, Carl L., 8, 11, 16

Belvedere Park, 48; Chicano Moratorium March and, 51, 213n90

Blow Outs, 240n10. *See also* Chicano Movement; Proposition 187

border crossing, 2

bounded solidarity, social networks and, 14–15

brick making. *See* Simons Brick Plant

Brimelow, Peter, 66. *See also* English monolingualism; literacy tests

Brown, Wendy, 176

Burns, Nancy, et al., 102, 137–38

California: anti-immigrant sentiment in, 21, 26, 28–30, 34, 39; budget crisis in, 27–28; citizenship rights in, 38; demographic changes in, 28, 40–41; segregation in, 41–46. *See also* Californio(s); East Los Angeles; Mexican American War; Montebello

California Civil Rights Initiative, 33. *See also* Proposition 209

Californians against Discrimination and Preferences, 33. *See also* Proposition 209

Californio(s): citizenship and, 38; definition of, 36; Democratic Party and, 39, 40; demographic change and, 40–41; 1856 election and, 39; elective office and, 39, 40–41; electoral participation and, 40–41; Know-Nothing Party and, 39; land claims and, 37–38; legal system and, 37; in Montebello, 53–54; political system and, 38; segregation of, 41–44; social status of, 39–40. *See also* Mexican Americans

Calvo, María Antonia, 17

Camarillo, Albert, 36

Carmargo, Heriberto, 31. *See also* Proposition 187

Chávez, César, 50

Chicano Moratorium, 51

Chicano Movement, 51, 113, 212–13n90, 240n10

Chicano Studies, group attachment and, 11, 185

Chinese Exclusion Act, 34

Cho, Wendy Tam, 180–81

Cinco de Mayo, 48

Citizen Participation Study, 18

Citizen's Committee on Immigration Policy, 29

civic education, 186–88. *See also* political engagement; political socialization

Coffey, Ruth, 30. *See also* Proposition 187

Cohen, Cathy, 83, 103–4, 178, 179–80

collective identity: definition of, 7, 206n30; electoral participation and, 104, 123–35, 175; immigrant adaptation and, 4–5, 8, 11–12, 16; intersection of race, gender, and class, 7, 52, 100–103, 126, 146–48; intragroup conflict and, 89–94; language and, 61–64, 76–82; Latino self-identification and, 78–79; linked fate and, 9–10; measurement of, 17, 176–79; multicultural curricula and, 185; negative consequences of, 11–12; nonelectoral participation and, 139; organizations and, 188; perceptions of stereotypes and, 82–94; political engagement and, 8–10, 16–18, 22–25, 175–76, 248n60; relational aspects and, 3–4, 7; segregation and, 45–46, 48–49, 173; social context and, 3–6, 103–4, 128–29, 143, 175; Spanish-language media and, 124; stigma and, 4–6, 8–9, 24, 104. *See also* group attachment; group worthiness; linked fate; mobi-lizing identity; political mobilization; stigma

Collins, Patricia Hill, 7

Community Political Organization (CPO), 49

community problems, 154–60. *See also* non-electoral participation

Community Service Organization (CSO), 49–50

community work: definition of, 139; gender and, 146–47. *See also* non-electoral participation

Conley, Dalton, 156

Conroy, Mickey, 29, 33

contextual capital, 12–18; definition of, 12; East Los Angeles, 26; measures of, 17; Montebello, 26, 53, 55–59; political effects of, 12; political institutions as, 13; social networks as, 13–16

Corbin, Juliet, 20

Coronel, Antonio, 39

Cortez, Eddie, 31. *See also* Proposition 187

counternarrative, group attachment and, 11, 185, 208n48

Crenshaw, Kimberlé, 7

Crocker, Jennifer, 62, 179

Dahl, Robert, 182

Dawson, Michael, 10, 100, 103–4, 177–78, 179–80. *See also* African American politics; linked fate

Deaux, Kay, 179

de la Guerra, Pablo, 38

demobilizing identity, 12

DeSipio, Louis, 17, 118

Deverell, William, 35, 36, 41, 43, 56, 57–58

discrimination: intracommunity relations and, 93; perceptions of, 85–88. *See also* stereotypes; stigma

Domínguez, Manuel, 38, 40

Downs, Anthony, 182

East Los Angeles: demographics of, 19, 213–14n96; gerrymandering in, 47–48, 52; history of, 46–52; political influence and, 47–48; political organizing in, 48–52; segregation and, 43–44, 48; social networks in, 67. *See also* Garza case; mutualistas

East Los Angeles Community Union (TELACU), 51

Either, Kathleen, 179
electoral participation: area differences and, 127–29; Californios and, 39–40; collective identity and, 16–17, 23, 102, 104, 127–28, 134–35, 146–47, 176–79; East Los Angeles, 134; first generation and, 123–26; generational differences and, 124, 127, 129–30; gender and, 22, 102–3, 108–9, 110, 113, 124–26, 144, 170; intragroup conflict and, 94–99; marginal groups and, 190; Montebello, 134; naturalization and, 119–23; political mobilization and, 127–28, 133–35; political socialization and, 107; registration rules and, 239n77; representation and, 23; second generation and, 127; social context and, 103–4, 110–11, 113–15, 128–29, 179–80; social networks and, 15, 135; socioeconomic status and, 11, 101–2; studies of, 101–3; third-plus generation and, 127–28
El Monte Boys, 53–54
English monolingualism, 65. See also language
Erickson, Ryan, 32. See also Proposition 187; tagger shooting
Espiritu, Yen, 3
ethnic enclave. See immigrant adaptation
Ezell, Harold, 30. See also Proposition 187

Federation for American Immigration Reform (FAIR), 29
Ferguson, Gil (State Assemblyman), 29
first generation: attitudes toward naturalization and, 119–23; community solutions and, 161–64; electoral participation and, 123–26; language and, 67–77; nonelectoral participation and, 161–64; perceptions of community problems and, 156–57, 159; perceptions of discrimination and, 68–70, 85–88; perceptions of stereotypes and, 84; political interest and, 107–10; racial identification and, 79
Fogelson, Robert M., 42
Four Winds Student Movement, 32. See also Proposition 187; tagger shooting
Frymer, Paul, 182, 189

gangs, community problems as, 159–60
Garcetti, Gil, 32. See also Proposition 187; tagger shooting

Garza case, 47–48
gender. See collective identity; community work; electoral participation; intersectionality; nonelectoral participation; political mobilization; political protest; political trust; power
Gerber, Alan, 182–83
gerrymandering: in Los Angeles, 40–41; in East Los Angeles, 48, 50
GI Bill, Mexican American politics and, 49–50
Gilliam, Frank, et al, 84
Gimpel, James, 181, 185–86, 187
Gordon, Milton, 78
Greaser law, 37
Green, Donald, 182–83
Greene, Steven, 179
Griswold del Castillo, Richard, 43, 45
grounded theory, 20. See also Corbin, Juliet; Strauss, Anselm
group attachment: fostering, 183–85; electoral participation and, 125, 127–29, 131–35; nonelectoral participation and, 141, 143, 146–50; political efficacy and, 162–70; political engagement and, 3, 175–76, 183, 190, 248n60; stigma and, 152. See also collective identity; group worthiness; linked fate; mobilizing identity
group worthiness: electoral participation and, 135, 162–68; political engagement and, 3, 9–10, 12, 25, 135, 141, 166, 174, 183. See also agency; collective identity; group attachment; linked fate; mobilizing identity; stigma
Gurin, Patricia, 148
Gutiérrez, David G., 40–41, 45, 72

hacendados, 37–38, 45
Hardy-Fanta, Carol, 17, 23, 105, 126, 141, 148
Henderson, Gary, 32. See also Proposition 187; tagger shooting
Hero, Rodney, 180
Hillo, David, 31–33. See also Proposition 187; tagger shooting
Hondagneu-Sotelo, Pierrette, 144
hooks, bell, 177
Howard, Judith, 4
Hritzuk, Natasha, 15

Huckfeldt, Robert, 15
Hurtado, Aída, 148

identity, definition of, 4. *See also* collective identity; mobilizing identity
ideology: definition of, 6; Latinos and, 8. *See also* agency; Dawson, Michael; mobilizing identity
immigrant adaptation, 2; ethnic enclaves and, 67; social networks and, 67; socio-economic status and, 11–12, 160; U.S. immigration policy and, 66–67, 205n9. *See also* internal migration
Immigration and Naturalization Services (INS), 30, 31, 44, 118–19. *See also* U.S. Citizenship and Immigration Service
internal migration, 1
intersectionality, 100, 103, 176–77; definition of, 7; electoral participation and, 126, 135; measurement of, 176–79; nonelectoral participation and, 145–48
intracommunity conflict: immigrant and native born, 70–73, 80–82, 90–92; language and, 89–94; political effects of, 94–99. *See also* language; stereotypes; stigma

job availability, as community problem, 159–60
Johnson, J. Neely, 39. *See also* Know-Nothing Party
Junn, Jane, 186, 191

Keeter, Scott, 111
Kids Voting program, 186
Knoke, David, 15, 116. *See also* social networks
Know-Nothing Party, 39

Lacey, Robert, 30. *See also* Proposition 187
Lake, Ronald, 15
language: American national identity and, 64–66; collective identity and, 61–64, 72–73, 76–82; discrimination and, 68–70; first generation and, 67–77; intracommunity conflict and, 70–73, 80–82, 90–92; Latino studies and, 61; parent/child relations and, 74–76; Proposition 227, 33–34; racial identification and, 78–79; second generation and, 74–76, 79; social networks and, 67; stigma and, 22, 62–64, 66, 73, 75, 82–83;

U.S. immigration policy and, 37, 65–66. *See also* collective identity; intracommunity conflict; stigma
Latino National Political Survey (LNPS), 17–18, 21, 118, 173
Latino(s), definition of, 3
Lay, Celeste, 181, 185–86
League of United Latin American Citizens (LULAC), 49
Leal, David, 109
legitimating myths, 63. *See also* stigma
Leighley, Jan, 101, 104, 155–56, 180
Link, Bruce G., 184
linked fate: definition of, 10, 207n41; measurement of, 177–178; political engagement and, 10, 101. *See also* African American politics; Dawson, Michael; Tate, Katherine
literacy tests, U.S. immigration policy and, 65–66
Locke, John, 190
Lodge, Henry Cabot, 65–66. *See also* English monolingualism; literacy tests
López, Henry, 50
Los Angeles, violence in: in nineteenth century, 36; in twentieth century, 32–33, 44. *See also* tagger shooting
Los Angeles County Board of Supervisors, 47
Los Angeles Police Department (LAPD), deportation campaigns and, 43–44, 51, 222n112
Luhtanen, Riia, 179

manifest destiny, Mexican American War and, 35
Markman, Jon, 18–19
Márquez, Benjamin, 188
Marschall, Melissa, 15, 104, 128, 154
Masters, William, II, 31–33. *See also* Proposition 187; tagger shooting
Matute-Bianchi, María Eugenia, 8
McCarthy, Kevin, 160
McDevitt, Michael, et al., 186
McLellan, Dennis, 18
Menchaca, Martha, 14, 72, 88, 171
Mexican American Political Association (MAPA), 50–51
Mexican Americans: deportation of, 43–44; Los Angeles Police Department and, 43–44; political organizing of, 46–52; racial identification and, 45–46; residential seg-

regation and, 40–43, 45–46. *See also* Californio(s); Chicano Movement

Mexican American War, 35, 53

Michelson, Melissa, 104

mobilizing identity: definition of, 6; electoral participation and, 103, 127, 129, 135; nonelectoral participation and, 148–49. *See also* agency; collective identity; identity

Molina, Gloria, 48, 140

Montebello: community organizations in, 59; demographics of, 19, 58, 213–14n96; history of, 52–59; middle-class identity in, 148; Pioneer Day celebration, 53; residential segregation in, 55–57; social networks in, 67; violence in, 53. *See also* El Monte Boys; Simons Brick Plant

Mothers of East Los Angeles, 25; history of, 51–52; mobilization and, 188, 241n18

multicultural history, group attachment and, 11, 185

Muñoz, Irma, 31. *See also* Proposition 187

mutualistas (mutual aid societies), 48–49

National Election Survey (NES)/Michigan, 179

National Survey of Latinos, 161

Native Americans, 37, 221n76

naturalization: attitudes towards, 119–23; collective identity and, 125; gender and, 119, 121–22; rates of, 118. *See also* immigrant adaptation

Nelson, Alan, 30. *See also* Proposition 187

Niemi, Richard, 186

nonelectoral participation: collective identity and, 23, 143, 145–46, 148, 166–67, 170; community work as, 145–54; context, identity, and, 143, 166–67, 170; definition of, 137; gender and, 23, 139, 141–46, 170, 174; minority groups and, 137–38; protest as, 139–45; social context and, 23, 138–39, 143, 145–46, 148, 166–67, 170; socioeconomic status and, 145. *See also* collective identity; contextual capital; mobilizing identity; political behavior; political efficacy; political engagement; political mobilization; psychological capital; social capital; social context; social networks

Ochoa, Gilda, 72

Olson, Mancur, 6

1.5 generation, definition of, 211n76, 235–36n40

Pantoja, Adrian D., 113

Pardo, Mary, 52

Park, David, 15

Peng, Timothy, 148

Pew Hispanic Center/Kaiser Family Foundation, 161

Phelan, Jo C., 184

Phinney, Jean, 179

Pico, Pío, 40

Pitt, Leonard, 36–37

political behavior, studies of, 5, 16–18, 19, 21, 101–5, 176–80. *See also* electoral participation; nonelectoral participation; political engagement; political mobilization

political efficacy: collective identity and, 9, 123–24, 129, 133, 143, 174; definition of, 208n50, 240n7; East Los Angeles, 166–68; electoral participation and, 101, 114, 123–24, 132–33; Montebello, 153–54, 166–70; nonelectoral participation and, 138–39, 149–54; psychological capital and, 12; social context and, 9, 123–24, 129, 133, 143, 174; stigma and, 8–10, 148. *See also* political interest; political trust

political engagement, 1–2, 175; collective identity and, 3–12, 16–17, 23, 102, 104, 127–28, 134–35, 143, 145–48, 166–67, 170, 176–79; definition of, 203n1; social context and, 12–18, 103–4, 110–11, 113–15, 128–29, 135, 143, 145–48, 166–67, 170, 179–80; social networks and, 15–16, 186. *See also* collective identity; electoral participation; nonelectoral participation; political behavior

political information: electoral participation and, 129–31, 133; Montebello, 153. *See also* political engagement; political mobilization; social networks

political interest: first generation and, 107–10; gender and, 106–10, 113–15; native born and, 106–7, 110–13, 115–17; social context and, 113–14; social networks and, 105, 115–17. *See also* electoral participation; nonelectoral participation; political efficacy; political engagement; political mobilization; social networks political mobilization: collective identity and, 188; electoral participation and, 133–35; gender and, 136, 143–46; group attachment and, 129, 146–47; immigrant communities and, 188–89; political parties and, 182, 189; Proposition 187 and, 127–28, 144; social context and, 12–18, 103–4, 134–35, 140, 143, 182–83, 189; stigma and, 182. *See also* collective identity; mobilizing identity; social context; social networks

political participation. *See* electoral participation; nonelectoral participation; political behavior; political engagement; political mobilization

political parties, political mobilization and, 182, 189. *See also* political mobilization

political protest, gender and, 140–42. *See also* nonelectoral participation

political resources, 6; gender and, 102; social movements and, 6. *See also* contextual capital; electoral participation; nonelectoral participation; political behavior; psychological capital; socioeconomic status

political socialization: community and, 11; electoral participation and, 19, 106–7; family and, 10, 181, 186; immigrant adaptation and, 2; political mobilization and, 182–83; schools and, 11, 186–88; social networks and, 116–17, 181–82; studies of, 10–11, 180–81

political trust: gender and, 131–32, 144; nativity and, 107. *See also* political efficacy; political interest

politics of difference, 190–91. *See also* Young, Iris

Portes, Alejandro, 118, 176

power: electoral participation and, 106, 113, 132; gender and, 144; language and, 83, 91–93; Latinos and, 4–5; nonelectoral participation and, 138–39; political context and, 21; stigma and, 4–5, 24, 107. *See also* stigma

Prince, Ron S., 30. *See also* Proposition 187

Proposition 187, 18, 29–30, 115; anti-immigrant effects of, 82–83; images of Latinos and, 30, 93; political mobilization and, 127–28; politics behind, 27–31; proponents of, 30–31; protests of, 18, 113, 139–42, 144, 146; respondents'

attitudes toward, 94–99; violence and, 31–32. *See also* tagger shooting; Wilson, Pete

Proposition 209, 33, 115; area voting on, 98; protests of, 140; race and voting on, 33, 219n46

Proposition 227, 33–34, 134; area voting on, 98

psychological capital, 6–12; collective identity as, 7–8; definition of, 6; political engagement and, 16; political efficacy and, 12. *See also* agency; collective identity; mobilizing identity

Putnam, Robert, 12–13, 17. *See also* social capital

racial group, definition of, 3–4. *See also* collective identity; group attachment

racial identity. *See* collective identity; group attachment; group worthiness; racial group, definition of

Ramírez, Ricardo, 134

restrictive covenants: East Los Angeles, 48; Los Angeles, 43; Montebello, 56, 57

Rosenstone, Steven, 17

Ross, Fred, 50. *See also* Community Service Organization (CSO)

Roybal, Edward, 50

Ruiz, Vicki, 1

Rumbaut, Rubén, 8, 118

Salazar, Rubén, 51, 224n149

sample, 20–21, 213n96, 214–15n97, 215n100

Sanders, Jimy, 24

Santa Ana, Otto, 34, 93

Save Our State, 29–30. *See also* Proposition 187

Schattschneider, E. E., 182

Schlesinger, Arthur, 64–65

Schuknecht, Jason, 181, 185–86

second generation, 16; community solutions and, 164–67; definition of, 211n76; electoral participation and, 127–29; language and, 74–76; nonelectoral participation and, 140; perceptions of community problems and, 157–59; perceptions of discrimination and, 85–88; perceptions of stereotypes and, 84–86; racial identification and, 79

segregation: Californios and, 41–43; collective identity and, 43–46, 170–73; community activity and, 171–73; discrimination and, 88; East Los Angeles and, 47–48; Montebello and, 55–57; positive results of, 45–46, 48–49, 173; social networks and, 14, 67

Segura, Gary, 113

selective dissociation, 89, 94

Simons Brick Plant: Americanization and, 58; history of, 54–55, 57; labor relations in, 55–56; significance of, 57–59. See also Montebello

16th of September, 11, 48

Skerry, Peter, 24

Sleepy Lagoon, 44

Sleepy Lagoon Defense Committee, 44

social capital: human capital and, 207n36; immigrant adaptation and, 7–8; increasing, 188–89; marginal groups and, 13; measures of, 12–13; political engagement and, 12–13; racial homogeneity and, 180. See also contextual capital; psychological capital; Putnam, Robert; social context; social networks

social context: electoral participation and, 103–4, 110–11, 113–15, 128–29, 179–80; measurement of, 17; nonelectoral participation and, 138–39; political engagement and, 12–18, 103–4, 110–11, 113–15, 128–29, 135, 143, 145–48, 166–67, 170, 179–80; political interest and, 113–14; political mobilization and, 12–18, 103–4, 134–35, 140, 143, 182–83, 189. See also contextual capital; political mobilization; social capital; social networks

social group. See racial group, definition of

social identity, definition of, 207n34. See also collective identity

social networks: collective memory and, 16; contextual capital and, 13–16; electoral participation and, 15, 135; gender and, 125–26; immigrant adaptation and, 66–67; naturalization and, 125–26; political engagement and, 13–14; political interest/discussion and, 105, 111–12, 115–17; political socialization and, 116–17, 181–82; racial composition of, 14–15, 173. See also contextual capital; political mobilization; social capital; social context

socioeconomic status: collective identity and, 11; community work and, 145; electoral participation and, 5–6, 19, 101–2; measures of, 155–56; nonelectoral participation and, 139; political efficacy and, 133, 208n50

Sonora Town, 42

Spanish-language media: during the nineteenth century, 46; political mobilization and, 124. See also collective identity; language; political mobilization

Spencer, Glenn, 31. See also Proposition 187

stereotypes: discrimination and, 93–94; media and, 92–93; perceptions of, 85–88. See also discrimination; stigma

stigma: collective identity and, 4–6, 8–9, 24, 104; counternarratives and, 11, 208n48; definition of, 4–5, 62; discrimination and, 68–70; group attachment and, 152; immigrant adaptation and, 5; intracommunity conflict and, 22, 70–73, 89–93; language and, 22, 62–64, 66–77, 82–83, 104, 184–85; linked fate and, 178; measurement of, 178–79; nonelectoral participation and, 152–53, 166, 170; political efficacy and, 8–10, 138, 148; political mobilization and, 182, 189; political socialization and, 11; power and, 4–5, 24, 107; psychological effects of, 62–63, 70–73; reducing, 183–85; social networks and, 14–15. See also collective identity; power

Stop Immigration Now, 30. See also Proposition 187

Strauss, Anselm, 20

Sunday laws, 37

tagger shooting, 31–33

Tate, Katherine, 101. See also African American politics

third-plus generation, 16; community solutions and, 167–70; definition of, 211n76; electoral participation and, 129–33; language and, 89–91; nonelectoral participation and, 167–70; perceptions of community problems and, 158–59; perceptions of discrimination and, 85–88; perceptions of stereotypes and, 84–86; racial identification and, 79

Torres, Rodolfo, 92
Trent, James, 19

United Neighborhood Organization, 51
Unz, Ron, 33–34. *See also* Proposition 209
U.S. Citizenship and Immigration Service,
    118–19, 237n58. *See also* Immigration and
    Naturalization Service (INS)
U.S.-Mexico Border Project of the American
    Friends Service Committee, 31. *See also*
    Proposition 187

Valle, Victor, 92
Vásquez, Tiburcio, 53–54
Vedlitz, Arnold, 101, 155–56
Verba, Sidney, et al., 18, 101, 138
Vernez, Georges, 150
Vigil, Diego, 103

Voice of Citizens Together, 31. *See also* Propo-
    sition 187
voting. *See* electoral participation

whiteness, legal definition of (in nineteenth-
    century California), 38
Wilson, Pete, 27–28, 29, 30, 120, 237–38n64
Wolfinger, Ray, 17
Wong, Janelle, 104. *See also* Asian American
    politics
Wrinkle, Robert, et al, 137, 141

Young, Iris, 3, 190–91

Zaff, Jonathon F., et al, 187
Zentella, Ana Celia, 64
Zhou, Min, 8, 11, 16
Zoot Suit Riots, 44

Text:	10/14 Palatino
Display:	Univers Condensed Light
	and Bauer Bodoni
Compositor:	BookMatters, Berkeley
Printer and binder:	Maple-Vail Manufacturing Group